CONVOY WILL SCATTER

Other books by Bernard Edwards

Masters Next to God
They Sank the Red Dragon
The Fighting Tramps
The Grey Widow Maker
Blood and Bushido
SOS – Men Against the Sea
Salvo!
Attack and Sink *
Dönitz and the Wolf Packs
Return of the Coffin Ships
Beware Raiders! *
The Road to Russia *
The Quiet Heroes *
The Twilight of the U-Boats *
Beware the Grey Widow Maker
Death in the Doldrums *
Japan's Blitzkrieg *
War of the U-Boats *
Royal Navy Versus the Slave Traders *
The Cruel Sea Retold *
War Under the Red Ensign 1914-1918 *
Wolf Packs Gather *

* *in print with Pen & Sword Books Ltd*

CONVOY WILL SCATTER

*The Full Story of Jervis Bay
and Convoy HX84*

BERNARD EDWARDS

Pen & Sword
MARITIME

First published in Great Britain in 2013 by
PEN & SWORD MARITIME
an imprint of
Pen & Sword Books Ltd
47 Church Street
Barnsley
South Yorkshire
S70 2AS

ISBN 978 1 78159 376 9

A CIP catalogue record for this book is
available from the British Library

Typeset in Ehrhardt by Chic Graphics

Printed and bound in England by
CPI Group (UK) Ltd, Croydon, CR0 4YY

Pen & Sword Books Ltd incorporates the imprints of
Pen & Sword Aviation, Pen & Sword Family History, Pen & Sword Maritime,
Pen & Sword Military, Pen & Sword Discovery, Wharncliffe Local History,
Wharncliffe True Crime, Wharncliffe Transport, Pen & Sword Select,
Pen & Sword Military Classics, Leo Cooper, Remember When,
The Praetorian Press, Seaforth Publishing and Frontline Publishing

For a complete list of Pen & Sword titles please contact
PEN & SWORD BOOKS LIMITED
47 Church Street, Barnsley, South Yorkshire, S70 2AS England
E-mail: enquiries@pen-and-sword.co.uk
Website: www.pen-and-sword.co.uk

Contents

This book is for Captain Hugh Pettigrew and the men of the *Beaverford*, who died unacknowledged in their attempt to save Convoy HX 84.

'We have fought such a fight for a day and a night
As may never be fought again!'
Alfred, Lord Tennyson, on Sir Richard Grenville

Author's Note

The story of the *Fighting Jervis Bay* is so entrenched in British contemporary history that I hesitate to take issue with it. But this I must do.

That HMS *Jervis Bay*, outgunned and outclassed, fought a valiant fight on that November night in 1940 cannot be disputed. It was fitting that the bravery of Captain Edward Fogarty Fegen and those who fought with him was recognised without delay. That being so, I question why there was no official recognition of the role played in the action by the merchant ships *Beaverford* and *Stureholm*.

My research shows that within twenty-two minutes *Jervis Bay* was out of the fight, lying smashed and burning, most of her crew dead. The defence of the convoy was then taken up by the *Beaverford*, and a number of eyewitness accounts show that she held the *Admiral Scheer* at bay for some five hours, allowing thirty-three ships to escape. Inevitably, she paid the ultimate price for her defiance, going down under the heavy guns of the German pocket battleship in a blaze of glory. She left no survivors.

In a just world Captain Hugh Pettigrew and his crew of seventy-two would have received the highest awards in recognition of their gallant fight, which went far beyond the call of duty. What they actually received was a VNC (Voyage Not Completed) against their names, and their pay stopped the moment the *Beaverford* slipped below the waves.

Likewise, Captain Sven Olander and the men of the Swedish ship *Stureholm* deserved the thanks of a grateful nation for the horrendous risks they took to rescue those few who survived the *Jervis Bay*. Theirs was a totally selfless act, again beyond the call of any duty, yet it was ignored, except by those they saved.

More than seventy years have passed since the guns fell silent, but it is still not too late to set the record straight for the men of the *Beaverford* and the *Stureholm*.

Foreword

It was winter 1940, and night was closing in on the thirty-seven deep-loaded merchantmen as they made their slow way eastwards across the North Atlantic. Sailing in nine orderly columns abreast, the ships were under the protection of an ageing ex-passenger liner mounting an array of equally ageing guns. His Majesty's armed merchant cruiser *Jervis Bay* was all the Navy could spare at the time, but in these deep waters beyond the range of the U-boats she would do – or so it seemed. Then, over the horizon came the German pocket battleship *Admiral Scheer* with a bone in her teeth, her 11-inch turrets hunting eagerly from side to side, uncertain which of this breathtaking array of sitting ducks to sink first.

For Kapitän-zur-See Theodor Krancke, commanding the *Scheer*, this was the fulfilment of a dream. This was the day when he would prove that the big-gun surface raider, not the U-boat, was the answer to Britain's domination of the high seas.

In true Nelsonian style, HMS *Jervis Bay* hoisted her battle ensigns, lifted her skirts, and charged at the enemy, her 6-inch guns spitting defiance. It was a brave gesture typical of the Royal Navy, but futile all the same. Twenty-two minutes later, the armed merchant cruiser lay smashed and out of control, on fire from end to end, and sinking.

The scene was now set for a massacre of catastrophic proportions. Then, from out of the smoke and confusion emerged the ship and the man who would save the day for HX 84. Captain Hugh Pettigrew, commanding the British cargo liner *Beaverford*, cautious and calculating, prepared to cross swords with the mighty *Admiral Scheer*, knowing full well that he and his crew faced certain death.

Chapter 1

RAIDER AT LARGE

The Second World War was little more than twenty-four hours old when, on the afternoon of 3 September 1939, ten Blenheims of RAF Bomber Command took off from Wattisham and headed east over the North Sea. Units of the German High Seas Fleet had been reported anchored off Wilhelmshaven and the bombers were under orders to hit them hard before they reached the open sea.

Soon after crossing the coast near Great Yarmouth, the Blenheims ran into the worst possible weather; 10 tenths cloud right down on the sea and extending upwards to 17,000 feet. The only option open to the relatively inexperienced pilots was to fly at low level beneath the cloud. It was an inauspicious start to Bomber Command's first raid of the war.

Skimming the wave-tops at 50 feet and navigating by dead reckoning, the North Sea crossing was a nerve-wracking experience the bomber pilots would long remember. When, after an hour flying blind, the cloud suddenly lifted to 500 feet, they were astonished to find they were crossing the German coast right on target.

A slight alteration of course brought the Blenheims over the naval anchorage at Wilhelmshaven, where the pocket battleship *Admiral Scheer* and other warships were anchored in shallow water, protected only on the landward side by a balloon barrage. Flight Lieutenant Kenneth Doran, leading the attack, wrote in his report:

We decided to make our attack slightly across the fore and aft line of the ship, and make our getaway by a sharp turn to port to avoid the balloon barrage, which was about 500 feet, and made our attack in a shallow dive. As we approached, we saw the matelots' washing hanging out around the stern and the crew idly standing about on deck. It seemed as though we had caught them literally, with their pants down.

> *However, when they realized that our intention was hostile they started running like mad, and as aircraft No.1 came over at mast-head height and dropped its bombs bang amidships, their A.A. got into action, and this together with shore-based A.A. kept us pretty busy carrying out evasive measures. The bombs from the second aircraft undershot by about ten yards and exploded in shallow water directly under the ship. No.3 found he could not get over within the 11 seconds and dropped his bombs on another target.*

The attack on the *Admiral Scheer*, the first British air operation of the war, was pressed home with admirable courage and daring, but it was all in vain. The German ship was hit by three 500lb bombs, but escaped serious damage, the bombs, fitted with 11-second delay fuses, merely bouncing overboard from her armoured deck and exploding harmlessly alongside. Four of the attacking Blenheims were shot down by *Scheer*'s anti-aircraft fire.

While the Blenheims were attacking the *Scheer* at Wilhelmshaven, fourteen Wellingtons were homing in on Brunsbüttel at the southern end of the Kiel Canal, where two of Hitler's battleships were reported tied up. Again, bad weather and heavy anti-aircraft fire thwarted the attack, and only one possible hit on a capital ship was claimed. This was at the cost of two more aircraft shot down.

This initial attempt to inflict serious damage on the German fleet before it had put to sea proved to be not only over ambitious, but disastrous, for the RAF. Seven of the twenty-nine aircraft taking part in the two raids were lost, along with their crews. It was a bad start to the war for Bomber Command.

The only positive result to come out of these early operations was to demonstrate the courage and determination of the RAF bomber crews. With very little in the way of navigational aids, they had crossed the North Sea in the most adverse weather, found their targets, and attacked them in the face of fierce anti-aircraft fire. That they had failed to inflict significant damage on the German ships was in large part due to the fact that the small semi-armour-piercing bombs they were using were totally inadequate against the 40mm-thick deck armour of their targets.

It was later learned that the ships in Brunsbüttel were left completely unscathed by the raid, and any bombs that hit the *Admiral Scheer* caused only a few bent stanchions and ventilators on deck. The only serious damage inflicted seems to have been purely accidental. One of the Blenheims attacking Wilhelmshaven flew too low and crashed on the forecastle head of the cruiser *Emden*, killing twelve of her crew and injuring a number of others. The *Emden* was fully operational again within a fortnight, but meanwhile German newspapers made great propaganda with the story, accusing the British pilot of deliberately crashing into the cruiser.

The opportunistic raid on Wilhelmshaven may have resulted in no more than a few dents in the deck of the *Admiral Scheer*, but it did reveal something of the calibre of the opposition the Royal Navy would face in this new war.

The 12,000-ton *Scheer*, named after Admiral Reinhard Scheer, hero of the Battle of Jutland in 1916, was a *Deutschland*-class heavy cruiser, a ship of revolutionary design. When her keel was laid down at the Reichsmarine yard in Wilhelmshaven in the summer of 1931, Germany was already plotting to avenge her humiliation of 1918.

The Treaty of Versailles, signed in 1919, severely limited the size of the German Navy. In rebuilding her fleet she was allowed only six heavy cruisers of no more than 10,000 tons, six light cruisers of up to 6,000 tons, twelve destroyers of no more than 800 tons, and twelve torpedo boats. Battleships and submarines, the latter which came so close to tipping the balance of power at sea in the 1914–1918 conflict, were forbidden.

Hitler could not bring back the old Navy, which lay bottom-up in Scapa Flow, but he was determined to build a fast, mobile fleet, within or without the Treaty limitations. Although it would be inferior in numbers, it would be capable of challenging the Royal Navy.

Under the terms of the Washington Naval Agreement of 1922, Britain, France, Italy, Japan and the United States of America had magnanimously agreed to limit the size of their big ships to 35,000 tons displacement, with guns of 16-inch calibre. Germany, on the other hand, was to be limited to ships of 10,000 tons with 11-inch guns. The thinking behind this was that the future German Navy would be just strong enough to defend her inshore waters, but would never again be able to challenge the Allied navies.

The German Admirals, accepting the lessons of the Great War, had already decided that the mainstay of the new *Kriegsmarine* would be the U-boat. A number of these silent underwater killers were in fact already being built at secret locations across Germany and Poland. As to the surface fleet, the country's finest marine architects were brought together and ordered to come up with something new. The result of their consultations was the *Deutschland*-class *Panzerschiffe* (armoured ship) a 12,100-ton cruiser, with 'guns of large enough calibre to out-gun almost any enemy cruiser fast enough to catch it, while being fast enough to outrun almost any enemy powerful enough to sink it'. To conform to the requirements of Versailles, the three *Deutschland*-class ships, *Deutschland*, *Admiral Graf Spee* and *Admiral Scheer* were officially declared to be 10,000 tons displacement.

Powered by eight MAN diesels giving them a speed of 28.5 knots and a range of nearly 9,000 miles; each *Deutschland*-class mounted six 11-inch, eight 5.9-inch and six 4-inch guns, plus eight 21-inch torpedo tubes. In addition, they carried an Arado 196 floatplane; a two-seater maritime reconnaissance aircraft with a maximum speed of 196 mph, and a range of 670 miles. When required, the Arado could carry two 110lb bombs under its wings, but its primary role would be as a spotter plane. The new heavy cruisers were formidable men-of-war, and soon became known in British naval circles as 'pocket battleships'. However, the primary role of these ships was not to challenge the big ships of the Royal Navy, but to harass merchant shipping. Given strategically placed supply ships, the *Deutschland*-class had the capability to remain at sea almost indefinitely. They were ideal commerce raiders.

Laid down in 1931 and commissioned in November 1934, the *Admiral Scheer* spent the next twelve months working up in the Baltic and North Atlantic. She first saw action in the summer of 1936 when, under the command of Kapitän-zur-See Wilhelm Marschall, she was deployed to Spain to evacuate German civilians caught up in the civil war raging there. Although she was ostensibly neutral, over the following two years the *Scheer* threw her weight behind General Franco, ferrying in arms for the Nationalists and occasionally using her big guns to support their operations. Whilst in Spanish waters, in May 1937, accompanied by two destroyers, she bombarded the undefended city of Almeria causing considerable damage, killing twenty civilians and injuring another fifty. This almost led to an all-out conflict between Republican Spain and Germany.

When total war came to Europe in 1939, the *Admiral Graf Spee* was the first of the pocket battleships into action. Cruising the South Atlantic, in the first three months of the war she captured and sank nine

British merchant ships, creating near panic in those waters. Before she was finally cornered in the River Plate, three battleships, two battle cruisers, four aircraft carriers and sixteen cruisers had been involved in the hunt for her. The *Graf Spee*'s career as a raider may have been short, but she had proved to be a worrying thorn in the side of the Royal Navy.

Following the attack by British bombers at Wilhelmshaven in September 1939, although she suffered only minor damage, the *Scheer* was taken out of service for a major refit, during the course of which her silhouette was considerably altered and she was given a clipper bow. After many delays caused by lack of suitable materials, she eventually emerged into the North Sea in the summer of 1940 ready to step into the shoes of her late sister the *Graf Spee*. Furthermore, in addition to her spotter plane, she was equipped with the new 'all-seeing' eye of radar, and promised to be even more effective.

As a result of the scuttling of the Kaiser's Navy in 1919, and the restrictions imposed on the German military by the Allies after the First World War, British warships far outnumbered the Germans in 1939. But it must be remembered that whereas many of the British ships were built before Jutland, the ships of Hitler's *Kriegsmarine* were all comparatively new, and equipped with the finest technology of the day.

British scientists, who mistakenly believed they were leading the field in radar, were then experimenting with radar on the shorter wavelengths, which it was claimed gave quicker and more accurate reception. Unlike the German *Würzburg*, which was large and cumbersome, and could not be fitted in anything smaller than a destroyer; the British apparatus was small and handy, suitable for use in small ships and aircraft. However, it would be the spring of 1941 before the first British radar went to sea. Meanwhile, the *Scheer* and her marauding sisters, using the cumbersome but effective *Würzburg* Apparatus, enjoyed the huge advantage of being able to see in the dark and through fog.

The *Scheer*'s first wartime deployment was to Norway, but while in Norwegian waters she experienced serious problems with her main engine and returned to Germany for repairs. Finally, on 23 October 1940, she sailed from the Baltic port of Gotenhafen (Gdynia) to fulfil her role as a commerce raider, waging war against British merchant shipping in the Atlantic. In command was Kapitän-zur-See Theodor Krancke.

Forty-seven-year-old Theodor Krancke was a product of Germany's old Imperial Navy, which he had entered as a cadet straight from school. During the First World War he was an officer in Vice Admiral Franz Ritter's 9th Torpedo Boat Flotilla, seeing action at the Battle of Jutland. In the inter-war years he held various appointments ashore and afloat, rising to the rank of Kapitän-zur-See. On the outbreak of war in 1939, he was Chief of Staff to the Commander of the North Sea Defence Area. He was given command of the *Admiral Scheer* a month later, but at the beginning of 1940 came ashore to assist in the planning of the invasion of Denmark and Norway. He returned to command the *Scheer* again in June 1940.

Although Krancke was acting under orders from the German Naval High Command, he was given complete freedom to choose his own sphere of operations, providing of course, he created maximum havoc amongst the British merchant shipping. He was, however, warned to avoid action at all costs with superior enemy warships. The *Scheer* would be operating far from home, out of reach of German repair yards, and any significant damage she suffered might have serious consequences. At all costs she was to avoid the necessity of seeking refuge in a neutral port like her sister *Graf Spee*.

The *Scheer* emerged from the Kiel Canal on the morning of 26 October, and accompanied by destroyers, with fighter aircraft overhead, entered the North Sea. The weather was unusually fine, with clear skies, calm seas and excellent visibility, all of which left the German ship dangerously exposed to enemy eyes. A flotilla of fast E-boats took over as close escort, and she hurried north to an isolated fjord near Stavanger, where she remained hidden during the remaining daylight hours. When darkness fell the *Scheer* left her hiding place and carried on to the north. Her E-boat escort left her as soon as she was well clear of the coast.

In those late autumn days of 1940 Britain faced the might of Hitler's powerful war machine alone. France had thrown in the towel in the early summer, leaving the British Expeditionary Force to fight a bitter rearguard action to the coast. There, with their backs to the Channel, British troops held the German Panzers until a brilliantly executed evacuation led by the Royal Navy snatched them from the beaches of Dunkirk. The fighting men were saved, but much of their equipment, tanks, guns, planes, was left behind. It would take many months for Britain's hard-pressed factories to replace these. Meanwhile, the remnants of a tired and demoralised army stood to with rifle and bayonet, ready to repel the invasion that seemed sure to follow. And as they did, the odds against them worsened day by day. Italy, hitherto undecided, saw an opportunity for glory, and enthusiastically joined Hitler's Axis. At the same time, the Soviet Union made a pact with Berlin, promising to supply Germany with food and raw materials should the British sea blockade take effect.

Almost overnight Great Britain had gone from being the dominant power in Europe to small island nation threatened by extinction. Churchill looked across the sea to America, but what the American people saw was Britain on her knees, and they had no time for losers. They covered their ears and looked the other way.

The tide is said to have turned in that hot summer of 1940, when the gallant pilots of RAF Fighter Command, some of them no more than schoolboys, took on the might of the *Luftwaffe* and fought it to a standstill. Only then, with this first great battle for Britain decided, did the threat of invasion that had been hanging over the country since Dunkirk finally go away.

But the agony was not yet finished. In September, as the leaves turned to gold and the nights began to draw in, Goering sent his bombers against the civilian population, deliberately raining down bombs on the crowded residential areas of Britain's cities. On 27 October, as the *Admiral Scheer* left the land astern and sailed out to begin her career as a commerce raider, London was reeling from its fiftieth night raid in succession by Goering's bombers. Fire swept through the streets and once again the gutters ran with the blood of the innocents.

Kapitän Krancke had a choice of two routes into the Atlantic, both of which were heavily patrolled by guard ships of the Royal Navy. By far the shortest route lay due west, between the Faroes and Iceland, but in the exceptionally clear weather then prevailing Krancke considered it would be suicidal to attempt a breakout to the west. The alternative route lay through the Denmark Strait, the 200-mile-wide stretch of water separating Iceland and Greenland. This would involve steaming an extra 500 miles, but it was more to Krancke's liking. The *Scheer*'s meteorological officer was forecasting a deep depression moving into the Strait with the promise of the cover of foul weather; rough seas, rain or hail, even fog. There was only one way to go. Course was set north-west for the icy waters of the Arctic Circle.

The next dawn found the *Scheer* to the north of Iceland, and heading west into the rapidly deteriorating weather forecast by her met. officer. The barometer went into a steep decline, dark clouds gathered, and the wind, north-westerly with an icy edge to it, began to keen in the rigging. As the cloud base lowered it brought with it showers of hail and snow that curtailed the visibility and made life hell for the lookouts and those working on the open deck. For the man on the bridge, Kapitän Theodor Krancke, it was heaven-sent.

By evening the *Scheer* was burying her sharp bows in the advancing rollers and frothing green seas were sweeping her decks. Krancke, anxious to transit the Denmark Strait during the hours of darkness, pressed on at 20 knots. There was a price to be paid for this. Forcing her way through the mountainous seas, the *Scheer* rolled and plunged like a demented mare. Things began to break loose on deck, and two men sent out to secure some ammunition were swept overboard. Darkness had fallen, but Krancke reversed course to look for the missing men with searchlights. It was a vain hope, for no one could have lived for more than a few minutes in this angry maelstrom of icy water. After half an hour Krancke accepted the hopelessness of the search, and resumed course. With not a shot yet fired he had lost two men to his old enemy the sea.

By midnight, as the depression moved in from the west, the wind reached hurricane force, and the advancing seas were so steep that Krancke was forced to reduce speed to avoid serious damage to his ship.

The *Scheer* entered the northern end of the Denmark Strait just before dawn on Wednesday 30 October and altered onto a south-westerly course. This put the wind and sea right astern, and Krancke found himself riding a mad roller coaster down the Strait, with his ship rolling and pitching crazily, and constantly in danger of being pooped by the immense seas piling up astern. The log book recorded the *Scheer* rolling up to 37 degrees at times, and even with the battleship's sophisticated hydraulic steering gear the helmsman was fighting a constant battle to hold her on course. Had she broached to she would have been in danger of rolling right over.

There was no sleep for anyone on board that day, no hot food or drinks, only the incessant rolling and pitching. However, Krancke was able to console himself that the weather was so atrocious, the visibility so poor, that there was little likelihood of being spotted by enemy patrols.

The German raider finally emerged from the chaos of the Denmark Strait early in the morning of 1 November, with the weather slowly moderating as she moved south. The clouds were still brushing the wave-tops and flurries of rain and snow marred the visibility; but the force had gone out of the storm, and it was safe for damage parties to venture out on deck. They found devastation everywhere, but nothing that could not be put right, with the exception of one of the cutters, which had been reduced to matchwood.

During the night, with the *Scheer* on a southerly course, Krancke received an intelligence report from Berlin informing him that the fast convoy of twenty-nine ships designated HX 84 had sailed eastbound from Halifax, Nova Scotia on the 28th. The convoy's estimated speed was given as 9 knots, but strength and composition of the escort force was unknown. Krancke, sensing a soft target, increased to full speed.

Chapter 2

THE CONVOY

While damage control parties cleared up the mess on the *Scheer*'s upper decks Theodor Krancke silently blessed the storm that had enabled him to slip through the Denmark Strait unseen by patrolling British warships. Meanwhile, Convoy HX 84 was off Cape Race, the southernmost point of Newfoundland, and also emerging into the open waters of the Atlantic.

The convoy, which overnight had been joined by nine ships from Bermuda, now consisted of thirty-eight deep loaded merchantmen sailing in nine columns abreast. They were the usual cosmopolitan mix, twenty-five British, four Norwegian, four Swedish, two Belgian, two Polish and one Greek. They ranged in size from the 16,698-ton liner *Rangitiki,* loaded with 10,000 tons of cheese, butter, meat and timber, to the tiny Polish steamer *Puck* staggering under a cargo of steel billets topped off with timber. In all, these ships, ten of them oil tankers, were carrying 126,500 tons of petroleum products, 42,000 tons of steel, 20,000 tons of general, including chemicals, refrigerated meat and explosives, 30,000 tons of sawn timber and pit props, 1,200 tons of wool, and twelve fighter aircraft. More than 200,000 tons of vital cargo was afloat and heading eastwards to replenish the shops and factories of war-torn Britain.

Leading this great armada, at the head of the centre column, was the convoy commodore's ship *Cornish City*. At just under 5,000 tons gross, she was one of the smaller ships in the convoy, a smart well-found ship, and a credit to her owners Reardon Smith Line, known worldwide as 'Smiths of Cardiff'.

Commanded by Captain John O'Neil the 14-knot *Cornish City,* barely two years old, was a fitting base for the convoy commodore Rear Admiral H.B. Maltby. Brought out of retirement with the specific purpose of leading convoys, Maltby now carried the rank of Commodore, RNR. Tall, slender, outwardly aristocratic, he was a typical regular Navy man; but plain spoken, a trait which immediately established a bond with the merchant seamen he was sailing with. He enjoyed a mutual trust with Captain O'Neil on the understanding that while he and his signals staff controlled the convoy, O'Neil at all times remained in command of his own ship.

On the *Cornish City*'s starboard quarter was one of the eleven tankers contributing to HX 84's importance. She was Eagle Oil's *San Demetrio*, a motor vessel under the command of Captain George Waite. Bound for Avonmouth from Galveston, Texas, the *San Demetrio* was carrying 12,000 tons of high octane aviation spirit, and to describe her as a floating bomb primed to go off at the slightest interruption to her progress would be an understatement. But to her British crew, hardened to the dangers of the North Atlantic crossing, this was just another routine ocean passage. It was just as well they were unaware that they and their ship were destined to add yet another glorious page to the annals of the history of Britain's Merchant Navy.

Close on the *San Demetrio*'s quarter was another ship about to make her mark. The 10,042-ton *Beaverford*, owned by Canadian Pacific Steamships of Liverpool, was one of a class of five cargo liners built in 1927-28 for the transatlantic service. They were coal-fired ships, twin-screw with four water-tube boilers fed by mechanical stokers, a very new innovation at the time. Their nominal service speed was 14 knots, but they had considerable power in reserve. Part of their cargo space was insulated for the carriage of meat and fruit, and they were each equipped with twenty-seven derricks. In 1928 the 'Beaver boats' ranked among the finest cargo liners afloat. Pre-war, they ran a regular scheduled service between the St Lawrence River and London, one ship leaving Montreal every Friday morning. In this way they formed a vital extension of the Canadian Pacific Railway, which linked Canada's west coast with the Atlantic. Not surprisingly, on the outbreak of the Second World War all five of these unusually fast and versatile ships were requisitioned by the Admiralty for the carriage of stores.

The *Beaverford*, under the command of 60-year-old Captain Hugh Pettigrew, and with a British crew of seventy-one, was on this occasion carrying a diverse mix of cargo. Deep in her lower holds were stacked billets of aluminium and copper, giving her an excess of stability, and on top of these she carried bags of maize. Her refrigerated compartments were crammed with meats and cheese, while in her tween decks drums of hazardous chemicals were stowed side by side with a large consignment of the munitions of war, cases of shells, bullets and grenades. Not content with filling her holds, the Admiralty, temporary owner/managers of the *Beaverford*, had piled her open decks with Canadian timber and several cased aircraft, all chained down and covered by tarpaulins. Not one cubic inch of space that could conceivably carry cargo on this ship had been wasted.

Although the *Beaverford* was under Admiralty control, she was still essentially a merchant ship, flying the Red Ensign, and with the exception of two DEMS gunners, crewed entirely by merchant seamen. Yet, in addition to the usual 4-inch aft, she mounted a 3-inch gun on her forecastle head. This gave her the potential to launch an attack on an enemy ship, which was not allowable under the Geneva Convention. The terms of the Convention, which Britain was following to the letter at the time, allowed merchant ships to carry guns for defence only, i.e. mounted aft and to be used when attempting to escape. Guns mounted forward of the bridge were strictly forbidden, and in the eyes of the German High Command, at least, any ship so equipped could be classed as a man-of-war. Why the *Beaverford* carried a 3-inch gun forward, and what hand the Admiralty had in this is not clear. But that this ship was special was soon to be revealed.

In complete contrast to the *Beaverford*, stationed on her port side was Ellerman & Papayanni Line's *Castilian*, twenty-one years old and struggling to maintain the convoy speed of 9 knots. She was a small ship, just over 3,000 tons gross, and in the tranquil days between the wars had been a regular Mediterranean trader. Carrying general cargo outwards, fruit, vegetables and barrels of wine home, she had rarely been out of sight of land, and never more than a month or six weeks away from home. The war had put a stop to the *Castilian*'s easy voyaging, and in October 1940 she found herself in the North Atlantic with a cargo of steel and timber. As was so often the case in these troubled days, she also carried a highly volatile consignment of explosives stowed in temporary magazines in her tween decks.

Like all other British ships in the convoy, the *Castilian* mounted a 4-inch anti-submarine gun on her poop deck. The gun was a relic of the 1914-18 war, and its crew, led by Third Officer J.R. Cooper, lacked training and gunnery experience. The Admiralty's idea of equipping merchant seamen to defend their own ships was to send them on a three-day gunnery course. This often consisted only of a few lectures on the dos and don'ts of gunnery, followed by a practice shoot with a twelve-bore shotgun disguised as a machine-gun. At the end of the third day, those who had not quit the course for the local pub or the imminent sailing of their ship, were issued with a certificate stating that they were fully competent in the maintenance and firing of any gun from a 4-inch to a Lewis .303. This was all very impressive on paper, but in reality the guns on most merchant ships were in the hands of rank amateurs.

It was to be hoped that HX 84's merchant gunners would be quick to learn their trade, as the Admiralty's plans for the defence of the convoy on passage were already in disarray.

At this stage of the war, although he had acquired new bases in the Bay of Biscay, Admiral Dönitz was still not prepared to risk his U-boats beyond 20 degrees West. This being so, on the ocean crossing, the Admiralty was content to leave the defence of a convoy to a single armed merchant cruiser, and sometimes not even that. Extra cover was provided in Canadian waters by destroyers of the Royal Canadian Navy, and a rendezvous was arranged with ships of Western Approaches Command when in or near 20 degrees West, where the U-boats were expected to strike. Ideally, all North Atlantic convoys, which were then the only thing that stood between Britain and defeat, should have been heavily escorted throughout every mile of the crossing. This was, of course, out of the question. The awful debacle of Dunkirk and the need to keep ships on station against invasion from across the Channel had left the Royal Navy grievously short of convoy escorts. The only solution was to use armed merchant cruisers.

The armed merchant cruiser owes its origins to the East Indiamen of the seventeenth century. Homeward bound ships laden with the treasures of the East had become prey to roving pirates and ships of the rival Dutch, Portuguese and French companies. The Royal Navy was too stretched to offer protection, leading to the Company's ships being heavily armed and prepared to fight their way home. It was a compromise that worked well.

The idea was revived again on the outbreak of the First World War. The Royal Navy, busy with big fleet actions, turned to commandeering passenger liners to escort convoys, chase German blockade runners and, when the opportunity occurred, harass enemy shipping in far waters.

One of the first recruits of the Great War was the Cunard passenger liner *Carmania*, requisitioned by the Navy in September 1914 and armed with eight 4.7-inch guns. The *Carmania*'s intended role was as a convoy escort, but soon after being commissioned she was sent to the South Atlantic to deal with the German commerce raider *Cap Trafalgar* – also an armed ex-passenger liner – which was threatening British shipping rounding Cape Horn.

The two makeshift warships met near the uninhabited island of Trinidade, off the coast of Brazil, and in the ensuing battle fought each other to a standstill. The *Carmania* was hit seventy-nine times, her bridge was destroyed, and she was holed below the waterline. The *Cap Trafalgar* was similarly heavily hit, and it is said that at one stage of the action the two ships closed to within a few hundred yards of each other, their rails lined with men firing machine guns. It was a scene reminiscent of Nelson's day.

The fires on board the *Carmania* were running out of control and it appeared she would have to withdraw; then the *Cap Trafalgar*, also holed below the waterline, suddenly rolled over and sank.

The Battle of Trinidade ended in victory for neither side, but it did show that a large passenger liner, suitably armed, could put up a credible fight. Faced with a shortage of convoy escorts in 1939, the Royal Navy did not hesitate to turn to the largely unoccupied passenger liners again. Suitable ships were selected and requisitioned for war service. Their decks were strengthened to take 6-inch guns, and manned by a mixture of Royal Navy and Merchant Navy personnel – often many of the liner's original crew volunteered to stay with her – they were sent to sea flying the White Ensign. The experiment was doomed from the start. The Admiralty seemed to be still fighting Jutland, unaware that the world had moved on. The U-boat had gained pre-eminence, and German surface ships, fast and heavily armed, were roaming the oceans.

The requisitioned liners, standing high out of the water, were easy targets for enemy guns. They were too slow to engage in a running fight, and their thin, unarmoured hulls were easily pierced. Set to catch enemy blockade-runners, they enjoyed a moderate success; but when matched against U-boats or larger units of the *Kriegsmarine*, they all too often ended up on the bottom of the ocean.

By the summer of 1940, the Admiralty had commissioned forty-six armed merchant cruisers, but their armament was sadly lacking. Six-inch guns, many of which had seen action at the Battle of Jutland, were mounted on open decks with only thin shields to protect their crews. These guns were past their pensionable date, and misfires and jammed mechanisms were common. Again the AMCs proved to be adequate when patrolling the Denmark Strait and northern waters to intercept German blockade-runners, but when used in desperation to protect North Atlantic convoys, they were literally out of their depth. Word was soon going the rounds that the letters AMC stood for *Admiralty Made Coffins*.

In the case of Convoy HX 84, the armed merchant cruiser *Jervis Bay* was to be the mainstay of its defence, but it was also envisaged that some of the Royal Navy's newly acquired Town-class destroyers would be in attendance for the crossing. It just so happened that while HX 84 was assembling in Halifax, eight of these destroyers were in port undergoing modification before hoisting the White Ensign.

In June 1940, after only nine months of war, Britain's navy was in a parlous state.

When Italy entered the war on Germany's side later in the month, the situation worsened. Mussolini brought with him a powerful surface fleet and over 100 submarines to supplement Admiral Raeder's *Kriegsmarine*. In desperation, Winston Churchill wrote to President Roosevelt:

> *The Italian outrage makes it necessary for us to cope with a much larger number of submarines, which may come out into the Atlantic and perhaps be based in Spanish ports. To this the only counter is destroyers. Nothing is so important as for us to have the thirty or forty old destroyers you have already had commissioned. We can fit them very rapidly with our Asdics, and they will bridge the gap of six months before our wartime new construction comes into play.*

The American destroyers – the final figure agreed on was fifty destroyers in exchange for a 99-year lease on British bases in the West Indies – were of 1917 vintage and totally unsuited for modern anti-submarine warfare. Their outdated guns had to be replaced, Asdics and depth charge projectors fitted, and dozens of major modifications made before these four-funnelled antiques were ready to go to war with the Royal Navy. The work was slow, and when the time came for HX 84 to sail from Halifax, not one of the new destroyers was ready to sail with the convoy. When the

Canadian destroyers *Columbia* and *St Francis* dipped their ensigns off Cape Race and turned for home, the defence of this large and valuable convoy was left entirely in the hands of the armed merchant cruiser HMS *Jervis Bay*. It was three days later before the newly commissioned 'four-stackers' HMS *Churchill*, *Lewes*, *Lincoln* and *Ludlow* sailed from Halifax. After refuelling at St John's on 3 November, they set off across the Atlantic hoping to catch up with HX 84. They failed to do so.

The *Jervis Bay*'s steaming station was in the middle of the convoy, surrounded by the merchant ships, and to any discerning onlooker this would have appeared to be the safest place for her. Built in the Vickers-Armstrong yard at Barrow-in-Furness, the armed merchant cruiser was unmistakeably an ageing passenger liner dressed in wartime grey. With her tall funnel, tall masts, and slab-sided hull, to a U-boat commander peering through his attack periscope she must have had that barn door look about her. Impossible to miss, even on a dark night.

Owned by the Aberdeen & Commonwealth Line, whose offices were in Leadenhall Street in London's East End, the *Jervis Bay* was 14,164 tons gross, 549 feet in length overall, and had a beam of 68 feet. Her twin screws, powered by steam turbines developing 9,000 shaft horsepower, gave her a service speed of 15 knots. She had spent her days before the war ferrying immigrants to Australia, returning with meat and produce in her refrigerated holds. It was a respectable trade, if somewhat repetitive and lacking in prestige.

In the summer of 1939, when the threat of war in Europe was imminent, the Admiralty put a sudden end to the *Jervis Bay*'s leisurely voyaging, requisitioning her for service as an armed merchant cruiser. She was given a coat of Admiralty grey overall, her holds were filled with 24,000 empty 45-gallon drums, and seven ancient 5.9-inch guns were mounted on her open decks. They may have been all that could be spared in those desperate days, but the *Jervis Bay*'s guns were not just old, they were relics of a bygone age. One was date stamped 1895, another 1899, and most would have seen service at Jutland. It was optimistically claimed that these guns had an effective range of 10,000 yards, but the rifling of their barrels was so worn that any shell surviving that distance would be likely to be well off target. As an afterthought, two 3-inch HA/LA guns were fitted for defence against aircraft, again of ancient vintage. All guns were fired over open sights, and there was no effective fire control.

The *Jervis Bay* was under the command of 48-year-old Acting Captain Edward Stephen Fogarty Fegen, a regular Navy officer with a distinguished record of service. Coincidentally, as a midshipman in the First World War, Fegen had served under HX 84's commodore, Rear Admiral Malby, while between the wars, he had been based in several shore training establishments, including the Royal Australian Navy's college at Jervis Bay, in New South Wales, where he was in command. On the outbreak of the Second World War he was serving as Executive Officer in the cruiser HMS *Emerald*.

Fegen, a quiet, unassuming Irishman born in County Tipperary, was the son of Rear Admiral Frederick Fogarty Fegen, who had distinguished himself in the struggle to end the African slave trade, and was himself the son of a naval captain. Edward Fogarty Fegen was a bachelor and a devout Roman Catholic, a patient and fair man, traits that endeared him to all those he commanded.

Predictably, Fegen entered the Royal Navy at an early age, soon proving himself as a first class seaman and a man of exceptional courage. In March 1918, while a lieutenant in command of the destroyer HMS *Garland*, he went to the rescue of the American naphtha tanker *O.B. Jennings*, on fire in the Channel after a collision with a British ship. The tanker and the sea around her were enveloped in flames, yet Fegen took his ship into the heart of the inferno, put her alongside the *O.B. Jennings*, and rescued all twenty-six men on board. This act of mercy earned him the Silver Sea Gallantry Medal.

Whilst commanding the cruiser *Suffolk* on the China Station in 1931, Fegen took the cruiser's boats through heavy seas 30 miles inshore to rescue the crew of the Dutch steamer *Hedwig*, which had run aground on the Patras Reef in the South China Sea. This was a rescue of unprecedented bravery and daring, and in recognition of his outstanding leadership Fegen received an Admiralty commendation and a Dutch medal for saving life at sea.

In the early days of the Second World War, when a merchant ship was requisitioned by the Royal Navy – then only recently aroused from its peacetime slumber and desperately short of trained men – it was customary for some of the ship's merchant crew to be given the option of staying with her. Officers who volunteered to stay were given appropriate ranks in the Royal Naval Reserve, while petty officers and ratings signed what is known as the T-124 Agreement. Under the terms of this agreement, they retained their ranks and rate of pay, but in effect became temporary members of the Royal Navy Volunteer Reserve, and were subject to naval discipline.

In the case of the *Jervis Bay*, Captain Fogarty Fegen's first lieutenant, Lieutenant Commander Keith Morrison, RNR, had recently been First Officer with the Orient Line, while thirty-five of the AMC's forty-three officers were merchant seamen who had manned the liner before requisition. On the bridge, Chief Officer George Roe became Lieutenant Commander Roe, RNR, and likewise Second Officer Walter Hill became Lieutenant Hill, RNR. Third Officer Norman Wood changed uniforms, and re-emerged as Temporary Lieutenant, RNR, as did Fourth Officer Harold Moss, who was also given the rank of Temporary Lieutenant, RNR. In the engine-room, Chief Engineer James Chappell remained in charge as Temporary Commander (E), while the majority of his engineer officers also took temporary commissions in the Reserve.

Of the *Jervis Bay*'s 212 petty officers and ratings, ninety-seven were drawn from her original crew, signed on under the T-124 Agreement. On completion of her conversion to an armed merchant cruiser, the liner went to sea flying the White Ensign with a total complement of 255, of which no less than 133 were merchant seamen. The latter were all experienced in the day-to-day running of a merchant ship, but relatively ignorant of the arts of war. They were stiffened by a core of specialist petty officers and ratings from the regular navy and the volunteer reserve.

In effect, His Majesty's Ship *Jervis Bay* was no more than a stripped down merchantman, mounting a few old guns, and crewed substantially by merchant seamen. It is on record that three out of four manning those guns were T-124 men. But whatever they lacked in experience, the auxiliary's crew made up for with the enthusiasm to carry the war to the enemy. Not that the *Jervis Bay* had had a very successful war to date. Shortly after being commissioned she sank a destroyer, but unfortunately not one of the enemy's. In October 1939, while coming to her berth in Rosyth, she rammed HMS *Sabre*, ripping open her hull so that she sank to deck level. The destroyer was raised again, but she did not return to active service until the summer of 1940.

Undoubtedly, the greatest threat to HX 84 lay in Admiral Dönitz's U-boats, but even with the newly acquired bases on the Biscay coast of

France, the Type VIICs, which formed the bulk of the operational boats, were loath to venture beyond 20 degrees West. That left 1,500 miles of deep ocean, where the only perceived danger to the slow-moving merchant ships might come from an enemy surface raider, and at the time that possibility was judged to be very remote. In which case, it seemed feasible that an armed merchant cruiser would provide adequate cover for the ocean crossing.

To the east of 20 degrees West lay another far more dangerous world, where the U-boats held sway. This was the province of Western Approaches Command, where the fast, battle-hardened destroyers, sloops and corvettes took over, leaving the AMC to return westwards. This was not an ideal solution, but under the circumstances then prevailing, it seemed a fair compromise. But it did not always work out, as instanced by the *Jervis Bay*'s previous ocean crossing.

Convoy HX 72 sailed from Halifax in early September 1940, and consisted of forty-two merchantmen carrying some 300,000 tons of cargo. The ocean crossing was completed without incident, and at sunset on the 20th HMS *Jervis Bay* was detached to return across the Atlantic at full speed to meet HX 84, which was then assembling in Halifax. The local escort was not due to join HX 72 until the afternoon of the 21st, leaving the convoy unprotected for twenty-four hours. The weather at the time was unusually benign, with excellent visibility and occasional rain squalls offering temporary cover for an attacker. Perfect U-boat weather, in other words.

Unknown to the now unprotected ships, shortly after the *Jervis Bay* left them to their own resources Günther Prien in U-47 had sighted the convoy and was silently following in its wake. In answer to Prien's call other boats came homing in on U-47.

Otto Kretschmer in U-99 was first to arrive. He attacked that night, penetrating the convoy on the surface, as was his usual practice, sinking three ships one after the other. The Glasgow-registered tanker *Invershannon*, carrying a full load of oil, caught fire and sank within minutes. Her fellow Scot, the 3,668-ton *Baron Blythswood* was next. With her holds full of iron ore, she went down in 40 seconds: there were no survivors. It was turning out to be a bad night for the Scots, for Kretschmer's next target was Andrew Weir's *Elmbank*. A torpedo crippled her, but her cargo of timber kept her afloat until next morning, when Kretschmer and Prien sank her with gunfire.

U-99, having used up all her torpedoes, left for Lorient; while Prien was joined by five other boats, U-65, U-38, U-43, U-32 and U-100. Fortunately, HX 72's local escort force also arrived during the day. Led by the sloop *Lowestoft*, the destroyer *Shikari* and the corvettes *Calendula*, *Heartsease* and *La Malouine*, they attempted to throw a defensive ring around the convoy, but were outnumbered and outmanoeuvred by the U-boats. In the night that followed Joachim Schepke in U-100 alone sent seven loaded merchantmen to the bottom, while others were damaged. The convoy scattered in confusion.

As the result of being inadequately protected in dangerous waters, HX 72 lost eleven ships totalling 72,727 tons gross, to say nothing of the precious cargoes that went down with them. A new era, with the U-boats hunting in packs, had arrived.

Tuesday, 5 November 1940 dawned fine and clear over Convoy HX 84, then in mid-Atlantic. The sky was overcast, the wind light easterly, and with the exception of the long, rolling swell, the sea was relatively calm. Uncharacteristically for the time of the year, the North Atlantic was again showing a kindly face. Some of the older hands in the ships, used to the North Atlantic in its worst moods, muttered darkly that payment would be exacted for the fair winds. However, HX 84 had by now reached the halfway mark in the crossing. Unless anything untoward happened, in another forty-eight hours the convoy would be under the protection of Western Approaches Command.

Rear Admiral Maltby and Captain O'Neil were sharing the starboard wing of the *Cornish City*'s bridge, enjoying the clean, crisp morning air. Both men looked drawn and tired, for although the passage from Halifax had been so far without serious incident, the strain of holding together thirty-eight unpredictable merchantmen was beginning to tell. Two ships were already missing from the ranks. One of these, the Polish steamer *Morska Wola*, unable to maintain convoy speed, had been left behind three days earlier. Ironically, this straggler subsequently crawled across the Atlantic alone, unprotected and unmolested, to deliver her cargo in Manchester, a little late, but intact. Later, on the 2nd, the British tanker *San Demetrio*, plagued by engine troubles, had also dropped out, but she rejoined just before dawn, much to Maltby's relief. He could not afford to lose a ship loaded with 11,200 tons of gasoline.

As the sky lightened further and the shadowy outlines of the ships around him became more distinct, Commodore Maltby surveyed his flock with some satisfaction. The rest of them were all there, steaming purposefully and in good order, nine columns abreast, with 3 cables between columns and 2 cables, bow to stern, between ships. It was a tight formation that allowed for no mistakes, and it was fortunate that the weather was so kind.

On the *Cornish City*'s port quarter, steaming between Columns 4 and 5, the escorting AMC *Jervis Bay* looked impressive enough. She was twice the size of most of the other ships, a smart ship, the large White Ensign at her stern snapping in the breeze; but to Maltby, a regular Navy officer for much of his life, she was a poor substitute for a brace of fast destroyers capable of putting a ring of steel around the convoy at the first sign of an enemy. The high-sided ex-passenger liner with her superannuated guns could offer little in the way of defence against U-boats, and as to the, admittedly unlikely, event of meeting with a German surface raider...the Commodore gave an involuntary shudder.

Just before 10 o'clock, an uneasy stir swept through the convoy when the masts and funnels of a ship were sighted on the horizon astern. It was soon evident that the stranger was overtaking the convoy at speed. Certainly she was too fast for an ordinary merchant ship. Engine-rooms were warned, guns were manned.

A tense half hour passed, at the end of which the overtaking ship was identified as a fast cargo ship, probably a British fruit carrier. This was confirmed when the *Jervis Bay* challenged her by lamp. She was one of Elders & Fyffes, the 5389-ton *Mopan*, bound Liverpool from Kingston, Jamaica with a full cargo of bananas. She was invited to join the convoy, but politely declined. By noon, the *Mopan* was hull down on the horizon ahead, steaming at a speed that aroused a great deal of envy amongst the struggling 9-knotters of HX 84.

Chapter 3

THE LONE RUNNER

For those who sailed in British merchant ships in the 1930s, officers and men alike, life was far removed from the glamorous image so often portrayed in popular fiction. The British shipowner being notoriously parsimonious, conditions on board the average merchantman were far from ideal. Accommodation was sparse and cramped, almost an afterthought, as though the shipowner was reluctant to sacrifice any space that was not freight-earning. The ratings, sailors, firemen and stewards lived right forward in the bows of the ship, sleeping in two-tiered bunks that rose and fell like high-speed lifts with every swell that passed under the bow. Sleep was impossible in bad weather. Deck officers lived amidships, under the bridge, in cabins just big enough to swing the proverbial cat. Engineers spent their off-watch time in similar cabins perched on top of the steam-filled engine-room. Only captains and chief engineers enjoyed the luxury of their own bathrooms; the rest took their place in a queue in the alleyway.

Wages and conditions of work for officers and ratings were usually the minimum allowed by law. A first mate holding a foreign-going Master's certificate earned about £23 a month, and ordinary seaman just £6. For this they were expected to work ten hours a day, seven days a week, and at any other time when the safety of the ship or her cargo so required. There was no paid leave at the end of a voyage, which might last anything up to two years.

The food was usually appalling. Few ships carried refrigerators, and the staple fare was salt beef, salt port, potatoes, half rotten after a couple of weeks at sea, haricot beans, rice and oatmeal. In port, this diet was supplemented by a limited amount of fresh meat and vegetables, 'when procurable at reasonable cost', which was not too often.

In many ships, in the depth of winter, men hovered on the brink of hypothermia, their suffering only sometimes eased by a cranky, inefficient steam heating system. In port, after cargo working hours, both heating and electric lighting were turned off in the interest of fuel economy, leaving those remaining on board huddled around smoking oil lamps in overcoats and mufflers. Little wonder that, in Britain alone, there were more than 150 charities devoted to the welfare of merchant seamen.

War came along in 1939, for the second time in a generation, and to the hardship of everyday life was added the awful, mind–numbing experience of sailing in convoy. Herded together like sheep, hemmed in on all sides, and ordered to creep across the wide oceans at a snail's pace, life was one continuing close-quarter situation. Most Masters would have preferred to sail alone, relying on the vastness of the ocean to hide them from the enemy. There were some exceptions to the rule. A minority of faster ships, those capable of speeds in excess of 14 knots, were allowed to sail independently. One such was Elders & Fyffes' *Mopan*.

Built in 1929 at Cammell Laird's shipyard on the Mersey, the 5,389-ton *Mopan* was a refrigerated fruit-carrier, a banana boat to be precise. She had fine lines, comfortable accommodation, and with a service speed of 15 knots, she was twice as fast as the average merchant ship of the day. Sailing unescorted, she invariably covered the 4,000-mile passage from Jamaica to Liverpool in ten to eleven days, giving just enough time for her cargo of green bananas to ripen. Her regular itinerary was two weeks at sea on the outward passage, a week in Jamaica, where the lights burned bright and the rum flowed free, then ten days home. The *Mopan* was a good ship to sail in. Consequently, there was never any problem in finding a crew for her, the same men coming back voyage after voyage. However, as 1940 drew to a close with seven of Elders & Fyffes' lone runners having already been sunk on voyage, there were signs that this free and easy sailing was about to end.

It might seem strange that a country involved in a total war should still be using ships to import a luxury cargo like bananas; in fact, most of Elders' ships were engaged in carrying meat, eggs and bacon across the Atlantic. But, there again, the *Mopan* was an exception. The British Government still had an eye to the health of its citizens, and as the banana was considered to be a wonder fruit, packed full of vitamins and minerals, it was still imported on a limited basis.

The *Mopan* sailed from Liverpool in ballast in mid-October 1940, bound for Kingston, Jamaica to pick up the usual consignment of bananas. In command was 49-year-old Captain Stanley Sapsworth, and she had on board twelve passengers and a total crew of seventy, which included several naval gunners of the DEMS service.

Like all British ocean-going merchant ships of her day, the *Mopan* was 'defensively armed' with a 4-inch anti-submarine gun mounted aft. The gun, as with all those supplied to merchant ships, was ancient, rescued from an Admiralty store where it had lain draped in cobwebs since before the turn of the century. But old though the gun may have been, it was well preserved, and in the hands of the DEMS gunners, backed by crew members, was capable of giving a severe headache to any aggressive U-boat commander.

The *Mopan* had in fact already had her baptism of fire, being attacked by a U-boat in the Western Approaches within days of the outbreak of war, and before she was even armed. Chased by the U-boat, she had made a run for it, and zigzagging wildly, had evaded a barrage of sixty to seventy German shells, escaping destruction only by virtue of her superior speed.

With the Atlantic in an unusually quiet mood for the equinox, the westbound crossing was going smoothly for the *Mopan*, then, in mid-ocean, one of her passengers fell seriously ill. Being licensed for only twelve passengers, the ship was not required to carry a doctor, all medical matters being in the hands of Captain Sapsworth and his medical bible, the *Ship Captain's Medical Guide*. But this was something more than the usual minor ailments they were called upon to deal with, and Sapsworth was forced to break radio silence to ask Liverpool for advice. Little help was forthcoming, except that he was told to continue on to Kingston, using all possible speed.

Under pressure, the *Mopan*'s engines gave of their best, and she reached Kingston several days ahead of schedule. The sick man was landed into hospital, and as her cargo was not yet ready the *Mopan* faced several idle days at a lay-by berth. However, merchant ships earn no bonuses tied up at empty jetties, and her owners quickly produced a cargo which had been warehoused awaiting another ship. Early on the morning of 28 October, the *Mopan* sailed with 70,000 stems of bananas on board, bound for Garston, Liverpool. She was back on schedule.

Taking advantage of the unseasonably good weather, HX 84 was also forging ahead. On the morning of 5 November, eight days out of Halifax, the convoy was just four and a half days steaming from the safety of the North Channel. It was also within forty-eight hours of U-boat waters, and there was a noticeable air of nervousness spreading through the orderly columns of ships. Lookouts were constantly alert, sweeping the horizon with their binoculars, guns' crews loitered near their guns, and lifejackets were kept close at hand.

Aboard the twin-funnelled *Rangitiki*, leading column 6, arguably the most vulnerable ship in the convoy, Captain Barnett had co-opted some of his passengers as anti-submarine lookouts. Meanwhile, below decks in the engine-room, his engineers were working flat out to deal with a cracked piston. In the event of an attack, the *Rangitiki* would need every possible knot her twin Brown-Sulzer diesels could offer.

With all eyes intent on the surface of the sea looking for periscopes, not one of HX 84's eager lookouts thought to scan the sky above. Had they done so, it was still unlikely that they would have spotted the tiny black speck drifting in and out of the clouds some 20 miles to the north. The *Admiral Scheer*'s Arado, launched by Krancke shortly after dawn had found the British convoy and was observing its movements.

Later, it transpired that the *Scheer*'s spotter plane had in fact been seen by one keen pair of eyes in the convoy. Third Officer Bill Fellingham, of the *Trefusis*, sailing as fourth ship of Column 4, wrote in his report of a later date:

On the morning of 5th November 1940 I took my usual 8–12 bridge watch, taking morning longitude by chronometer sights by brief shots of the sun appearing through a generally overcast sky. There was a light easterly breeze and the sea was relatively calm with the normal long rolling North Atlantic swell, but the barometer was falling steadily. The TREFUSIS had a very small wheelhouse, just big enough for the helmsman, so officers kept their watch out on the open bridge. At about 1120, ship's time, I heard a faint, but unmistakeable, sound of an aeroplane from somewhere abaft the starboard beam. The sky was fully overcast, with, I would estimate, the cloud base at about 2,000 feet but there were some small breaks here and there. I picked up the binoculars and searched the cloud from where I heard the aeroplane sound coming. For a very brief moment I saw a small aeroplane passing through a break in the cloud and then it was gone. I called the Commodore ship, which was leading column 5, by Aldis lamp and reported that I had sighted a seaplane. The Commodore asked me to confirm that it was a

seaplane, which I did and, of course, also reported it to my own
Captain.

The significance of sighting a seaplane in mid-Atlantic, which could only
have come from a large warship, must have been apparent to Commodore
Maltby. Yet he appears not to have raised the alarm.

Meanwhile, the *Scheer*'s Arado, under orders to keep radio silence,
was winging its way back to report to its mother ship, then about 90
miles to the north. By noon, Krancke knew the whereabouts of HX 84,
the number of ships, their course and speed. Furthermore, the Arado
pilot reported that the convoy was unescorted, which at this stage of the
war was not unusual. This being so, Krancke now had the perfect
opportunity to create havoc amongst the helpless ships of HX 84 before
the destroyers of Western Approaches Command arrived on the scene,
probably sometime on the 6th. But to be successful the attack must be
made before darkness fell. Krancke increased to full speed.

What HX 84's lookouts did eventually see was the masts and funnel
of a ship which appeared to be overtaking the convoy on the starboard
quarter. An uneasy stir ran through the convoy, calm only returning
when the stranger was identified as a lone merchant ship, most probably
a fast fruit carrier homeward from the West Indies. There were many
envious glances and even the odd restrained cheer when the *Mopan* came
up at a fast clip and began to overtake. With the flags denoting her signal
letters at the yardarm and ensign at the stern snapping in the breeze, she
sailed past the columns of slow moving ships with almost contemptuous
ease.

The *Jervis Bay* challenged the newcomer by lamp, and satisfied with
her credentials, wished her God speed. Commodore Maltby, watching
from the bridge of the *Cornish City*, felt obliged to invite the *Mopan* to
join the convoy, but was neither surprised nor disturbed when Captain
Sapsworth politely declined the offer.

By noon the leading ships of HX 84 were dropping rapidly astern,
and Sapsworth turned his attention to the voyage ahead. Noon sights
put the *Mopan* in position 52° 29' N 33°10' W, with less than 1,000 miles
to go to the North Channel, two and a half days hard steaming. The
locks at Garston were already beckoning, but Sapsworth was not about
to throw caution to the winds. He had an eye on the barometer, which
was falling steadily, indicating that the idyllic weather they had

experienced since sailing from Jamaica was about to come to an end. For the time being, he would push on at full speed.

Following a good lunch – being passenger/cargo the *Mopan* fed well – Captain Sapsworth was in his cabin attempting to deal with the ever-increasing mountain of paperwork building up on his desk, when at 1430 the Second Officer reported from the bridge that the lookout in the crow's nest had sighted a single mast on the horizon to the north. Sapsworth was immediately suspicious. Merchant ships, almost without exception, had two masts, warships just one.

By the time Captain Sapsworth reached the wheelhouse the approaching ship was hull-up on the horizon, her tall fighting tower and gun turrets clearly visible through his binoculars. She was bow-on, the white froth at her bow showing that she was bearing down on the *Mopan* at speed.

Sapsworth had received no warning of enemy surface ships being in the area, but the Admiralty's instructions on the situation he was facing were quite clear. Without waiting to discover whether the unknown warship was friend or foe, he was to alter away and immediately transmit by W/T the RRR signal, code for 'I AM BEING ATTACKED BY AN ENEMY SURFACE WARSHIP'. This may have been very sound advice to hand out when behind a desk at the Admiralty, but Sapsworth had other considerations. If the stranger was hostile, any distress signal sent would immediately bring down a hail of shells on the *Mopan*, if she were friend, at the very least a delay for identification would follow. Taking a calculated gamble, Sapsworth decided to ignore the other ship and remain on course. He did, however, call for more speed. Like the thoroughbred she was, the *Mopan* took the bit between her teeth, and had soon worked up to a cracking 15 knots. If Sapsworth's gamble paid off two and a half days would see her in the North Channel, perhaps even docking in Garston before dark on the 7th. On the other hand…

Any doubts Sapsworth had about the identity of the stranger were dispelled when the DEMS gunlayer appeared on the bridge. He was handed a pair of binoculars and asked to give his opinion of the approaching ship. Without hesitation he replied, 'British. One of the Royal Oak class.' This coming from a time-served Navy man was enough for Sapsworth. Ordering the ensign and signal letters to be hoisted again so that the *Mopan*'s identity would be clear, he decided to press on at full speed. As a precaution, he sent his gunners aft to stand by the 4-inch, although what he expected them to do is not quite clear. The *Mopan*'s 4-inch, one of a miscellany of ancient weapons retrieved from the Admiralty's scrapyard at the outbreak of war, would be of little use against the big guns that even now might be trained on them.

Kapitän Krancke was also inclined to err on the side of caution, although as soon as his lookouts reported the *Mopan*'s smoke he had sent his men to their action stations. Following the Arado pilot's report, he had been expecting to sight the convoy, but just one single plume of smoke was puzzling. She could be one of two things, either a fast Allied merchantman sailing alone, or a British armed merchant cruiser. He must approach warily, all guns manned and lookouts alert for torpedo tracks.

As the distance between the two ships closed, it soon became obvious to Krancke that the stranger was no merchant cruiser. She was too small, and appeared to have only one gun, the usual 4-inch anti-submarine gun on the stern. Her Red Ensign was also now visible. However, her behaviour puzzled Krancke. He was aware that Admiralty orders to all Allied merchantmen sighting a warship, friend or foe, were to alter course away from the danger and transmit the RRR signal by W/T. This ship was doing neither. He decided to take action before this seemingly unsuspecting freighter woke up and began broadcasting to the world that the *Admiral Scheer* was at large.

Aboard the *Mopan*, news that a British battleship was approaching had brought men flocking to the rails bursting with curiosity. It still did not occur to any of them that they were about to meet the enemy.

Still not fully convinced that the *Mopan* was not the innocent she appeared to be, Krancke approached with extreme caution flying the flag signal 'WZ', which in the international code spells 'YOU SHOULD STOP YOUR VESSEL INSTANTLY'. This was backed up by the *Scheer*'s signal lamp flashing a warning to the British ship that she was not to use her wireless. The *Mopan* steamed blithely on, giving no indication that she had either seen or read the *Scheer*'s signals.

The blatant disregard of his signals decided the issue for Krancke. He ordered his gunnery officer to put a few shots across the arrogant Britisher's bow.

The *Scheer*'s gunners, perhaps bored by previous inactivity, opened fire with unwarranted enthusiasm, their shells landing within a few feet of the *Mopan*'s port bow. Tall geysers of water erupted and shell splinters whistled through the air to reduce her port forward lifeboat to a pile of smoking matchwood. There was a moment of panic aboard the British ship when it was realised that the stranger was not after all a friendly warship closing to wish them well on their voyage. Then the discipline of a well-run ship prevailed. Accepting the inevitable, that their ship was about to become a prize of the German Navy, men started to gather together a few essentials. Some changed into their best shore-going clothes, others were content with cigarettes, razor, toothbrush. If they were going into captivity, they might as well be prepared. The bridge of the *Mopan* went on to full alert, lifejackets were kept close at hand, and those without a specific action station edged nearer to the boat deck. In the galley, an irate cook took the slowly roasting chickens from the oven and put them to one side. Dinner would be late.

Captain Sapsworth had been about to order his radio officer to send out the RRR signal, when the unmistakeable message of the German shells stayed his hand. By now the raider would have guns trained on the *Mopan*'s wireless room, and the first tap of the Morse key would bring down a hail of shells on the bridge. Resistance was clearly out of the question, and he must now look to the safety of his crew. Sapsworth rang the engine-room telegraph to stop, and gave the order to abandon ship.

The Captain's decision to keep radio silence and, in effect, surrender to the attacker, was logical and humane, yet there were dissenting voices aboard the *Mopan*.

Assistant Steward/Gunner Urban Peters said: 'The biggest thing that bothered us was that the radio operator, James Mcintosh, said the Captain wouldn't let him send a message out because he was afraid. All he had to do was send the letter 'R'. Jimmy said he asked him two or three times. He said the Captain was panic-stricken, he was laying on his face on the bridge. He should have sacrificed the ship...We never got the abandon ship order. But there was the Skipper away in his boat with his suitcase. Somebody in our boat shouted, "Women and skippers first!" '

Others saw things in a different light. Quartermaster Gerard Riley reported that he overheard the radio operator ask Sapsworth whether he should send out a distress message, and the Captain reply, 'For God's sake. No! She'll blow us out of the water if you do.' Third Officer Hedley Jones said, 'The abandonment was conducted in a calm and orderly manner despite intermittent shelling by the *Scheer*.' He added, 'Captain Sapsworth was an efficient shipmaster. However, he was a secretive and lonely man, and assumed sometimes an overbearing attitude towards the ship's crew.'

Years later, after the war, Urban Peters withdrew his criticisms, which were most likely to have been prompted by Captain Sapsworth's perceived offhand treatment of his crew. This was wartime, and a time for taking risks, but in this instance to resist would have been a risk too far. What is certain is that had Sapsworth agreed to the RRR signal being sent, the *Mopan*'s crew would not have been given the opportunity to abandon their ship before she was obliterated by the *Admiral Scheer*'s massive broadsides. Captain Sapsworth's apparently timid response undoubtedly saved the lives of everyone on board.

The signal lamp was flashing again, the message ordering Sapsworth and his crew to take to the boats and row across to the raider to surrender themselves. Sapsworth had no other option but to comply, even though he knew he was condemning himself and his crew to a German prisoner of war camp. He ordered the remaining three lifeboats to be lowered to the water.

Theodor Krancke watched events unfolding aboard the other ship with growing impatience, regretting, perhaps, that he had not sunk the *Mopan* on sight. Sunset was only an hour away, and he had no time to spare if he was to attack the convoy before dark. From a distance it did seem that the lifeboats pulling away from the ship were deliberately going slowly with the object of thwarting his plans. It may be that Captain Sapsworth had something like that in mind, but a more likely explanation is that the British seamen were finding the heavy wooden lifeboats difficult to handle in the swell.

Krancke's patience eventually ran out, and with the three boats only just clear of the line of sight, he opened fire on the abandoned ship. At such close range it was almost impossible for the German gunners to miss, and shell after shell slammed into the *Mopan*, holing her on the waterline and laying waste to her pristine upperworks. Soon she was on fire from stem to stern and listing heavily as the sea poured into holds. And still she stubbornly refused to sink. It was almost as though the ship was colluding in the conspiracy to waste time. Eventually, Krancke brought more guns to bear, and under the hail of shot the battered British ship staggered, came upright again, and began to sink bodily.

The sun was well on its way down to the horizon when the *Mopan* finally gave up the fight and sank below the waves. She went down with her ensign still flying proudly at her stern.

Held at gunpoint on the deck of the *Admiral Scheer*, Captain Sapsworth and his men were forced to watch as the ship that had been their home went to her last resting place 2,000 fathoms deep in the cold Atlantic. Herded below decks, the British prisoners of war would not taste freedom for another four years. They were transferred to the supply ship *Nordmark* in the South Atlantic and spent five months cooped up in the hold of that ship before being put ashore in Bordeaux. After some months kicking their heels in a transit camp, they were herded into cattle trucks, and ended up in *Milag Nord*, the Merchant Navy prisoner of war camp near Bremen, where they sat out the rest of the war.

Although it will have been of little consolation to them if they had been aware, the crew of the *Mopan* had been fortunate enough to incur the kinder of two fates. Had their ship not met up with the *Admiral Scheer*, they might well have found themselves sailing blindly into a far more dangerous situation.

Some 600 miles to the east of where the *Mopan* went down, Dönitz's 'ace of aces' 'Silent Otto' Kretschmer was at sea in U-99 and causing mayhem in the convoy lanes 250 miles off the notorious Bloody Foreland. Coincidentally, Kretschmer's first victim, sunk on the night of 3 November, had been an elder sister of the *Mopan*, the 5,375-ton *Casanare*. Out of the same yard, and also owned by Elders & Fyffes, the *Casanare*, under the command of Captain John Moore, was homeward bound from the Cameroons and also sailing unescorted. Kretschmer put a torpedo into her, and was about to move off, when he saw another, much larger ship looming up out of the night.

Unknown to Kretschmer, the other ship was the armed merchant cruiser HMS *Laurentic*, an 18,000-ton two-funneller ex-White Star Line commanded by Captain E.P. Vivian, RN (RD). The *Laurentic* had been steaming north close behind the *Casanare*, and was now racing in to answer the torpedoed ship's distress call. Captain Vivian must have been aware that a U-boat was lurking somewhere in the darkness, yet he made the mistake of slowing down to take on survivors from the *Casanare*. Otto Kretschmer was not one to pass up an opportunity, and he aimed his second torpedo at the *Laurentic*'s engine-room as she approached.

The AMC did not sink, but she was hit hard, the sea pouring into her hull through the great jagged hole Kretschmer's torpedo had torn in her side, while several fires were started below decks. It cost Kretschmer two more torpedoes before the British ship broke her back and began to settle in the water.

U-99 did not escape retribution, for all this time the *Laurentic*'s forward guns were lobbing shell after shell at U-99, some of which were landing uncomfortably close. When another ship appeared on the scene, obviously in answer to the continuous stream of distress calls emanating from the two torpedoed ships, Kretschmer decided to withdraw to a safe distance, but remained on the surface.

The new arrival was another armed merchant cruiser, HMS *Patroclus*, under orders to escort the *Casanare* on the final stage of her homeward passage. The 11,000-ton *Patroclus*, commanded by Captain G.C. Wynter, RN (RD), an ex-Blue Funnel Line Far East trader, with a top speed of 15½ knots and armed with six ancient 6-inch guns was really no match for a Type VII U-boat. As he approached the sinking *Laurentic*, Captain Wynter dropped two depth charges, but as Kretschmer was still on the surface, these had no effect on U-99.

Although Wynter must have been aware that a U-boat might still be in the area, he committed the same cardinal sin that cost Captain Vivian his ship; he slowed down and prepared to pick up survivors.

Starshell fired by the stricken *Laurentic* had by now died out, and the night seemed blacker than ever. U-99 was still out there in the shadows; still on the surface and waiting for the opportunity to strike again.

The *Patroclus* had now stopped to allow the *Laurentic*'s lifeboats to come alongside and she was at her most vulnerable. Unseen and unheard, Kretschmer began his stealthy approach. When he was within 300 yards of the *Patroclus*, he fired a single torpedo, aimed at her engine-room.

The torpedo went home in the British ship's after hold and, unfortunately, directly below a loaded lifeboat from *Laurentic*, which was then being hoisted inboard. The lifeboat and all on board were blown to pieces, while the torpedo blasted a huge hole in the cruiser's hull, which disgorged a stream of empty 40-gallon drums into the sea. She was losing her emergency reserve buoyancy. A second torpedo, which hit forward, produced a similar deluge of empty drums, a sign to Kretschmer, then hiding in the darkness nearby, that he had chosen a target that would be difficult to put down.

At that point U-99 must have been spotted, for the *Patroclus'* guns opened fire, landing a salvo of shells close to the surfaced U-boat. Kretschmer wisely decided to beat a retreat. As he did so, there was a roar of aircraft engines and a huge winged apparition dropped out of the sky, guns spitting fire. A Sunderland of RAF Coastal Command had joined in the fight. A very unsilent Otto Kretschmer cleared the conning tower and took U-99 down at a rush.

Kretschmer, impatient to finish the job, stayed below for only 30 minutes before coming to the surface again. When he did, the attacking Sunderland had gone, but the two damaged AMCs were still afloat, the sea around them littered with empty drums, lifeboats and rafts.

As Kretschmer closed in on the helpless ships, a cry from one of his lookouts alerted him to a destroyer, which had appeared on the horizon. Now would have been the time for the U-boat to cut and run, but not Otto Kretschmer. He was determined to finish the work he had started. Moving in closer to the *Laurentic*, he fired a torpedo, which set in motion a train of events that all but ended in disaster for U-99.

Kretschmer's torpedo, fired from a distance of less than 250 yards, literally blew the stern off the *Laurentic*. Unfortunately, this section contained racks of depth charges that had not been defused. As they sank with the wreckage, some charges set to shallow exploded. This triggered the rest of the charges, resulting in a massive explosion, the blast from which threw U-99 on her side, almost capsizing her. When she righted herself again, a bruised and battered Otto Kretschmer had the satisfaction of seeing the remains of the *Laurentic* finally sink below the waves.

The avenging British destroyer, HMS *Achates*, was now only 6 miles off, and charging in to attack. Even so, Kretschmer, always ready to meet a challenge, estimated he still had time to finish off the other AMC. Turning to the *Patroclus*, he blew another hole in her waterline with a torpedo, then began shelling her with his deck gun. To his great surprise, the *Patroclus* hit back with one of her 3-inch guns, the only gun remaining serviceable. U-99's conning tower was hit, and her gun's crew was forced to run for cover.

Frustrated and angry, Kretschmer retaliated with two more torpedoes, which slammed into the merchant cruiser, increasing the havoc already reigning on board. But still she refused to sink. In desperation, for *Achates* was now within gun range, Kretschmer loosed off yet another torpedo. This hit the *Patroclus* squarely amidships, and finally broke the stubborn ship's back. Her stern section sank immediately, the bow drifting away into the darkness to go down two hours later.

Kretschmer was tempted to use one of his last remaining torpedoes on the approaching destroyer, but accepting that this might be a risk too far, he submerged, taking U-99 deep, leaving *Achates* to pick up the hundreds of British survivors left in the water.

It had been a good night's work for Otto Kretschmer and U-99; two armed merchant cruisers and a freighter sunk, 35,000 tons of the enemy's shipping that would sail no more. Kretschmer's grand total of sinkings had now reached 217,198 tons, an achievement which earned him the immediate award of the Oak Leaves to his Knights Cross. He would now have been justified in setting course for home, but he still had one torpedo left, and the next eastbound convoy was only just over the horizon.

Kretschmer sighted the 36-ship convoy HX 83 before dark on the 4th, and in the early hours of 5 November he used his last remaining torpedo to send the British oil tanker *Scottish Maiden* and her cargo of 9,500 tons of oil to the bottom. It was a fitting end to U-99's sixth patrol. With Admiral Dönitz's blessing, she returned to Lorient. She did not, however, leave a vacuum behind her. Seven German and two Italian U-boats continued to trawl the convoy routes.

Chapter 4

JERVIS BAY TAKES UP THE CHALLENGE

Completely unaware of the drama being enacted just over the horizon in the north, HX 84 steamed on at a sedate 9 knots. On the bridge of HMS *Jervis Bay*, keeping station inside the columns and near the leaders, Captain Edward Fogarty Fegen looked around him, amazed by the quiet serenity of the scene. It could almost have been a fleet passing in review in times of peace. For eight days since leaving Halifax they had sailed in close company, covering nearly 1,500 miles of ocean without serious incident. Granted, the weather had been unusually kind; in fact, it was Fegen's experience that the North Atlantic had rarely shown such a kindly face. There had been problems, of course, the persistent stragglers, the rompers, ships whose funnels were forever belching black smoke, and those who committed the cardinal sin of showing a light at night. But in twelve months of escorting convoys across the Atlantic Fegen had learned that the men who manned the merchant ships were a fiercely independent breed. They were also in many ways unpredictable, grudgingly allowing themselves to be dictated to by the Navy, but always ready, when the opportunity presented itself, to go their own way.

This time it was all running like clockwork. The convoy had less than a thousand miles to go to the North Channel, and just two days' steaming to the rendezvous point 400 miles west of Ireland, where the destroyers of Western Approaches Command would take over. For the first time since leaving Halifax Captain Fegen actually felt that he could afford to relax. Then, at 1545, the *Cornish City*'s signal lamp began to flash urgently.

Commodore Maltby was reporting that a lookout aboard the liner *Rangitiki*, leading ship of Column 4, had sighted smoke on the horizon, bearing 020°. Fegen did not regard the report as being particularly significant. This could well be another of the *Mopan*'s breed, a fast cargo ship sailing alone, not an unusual sight in mid-ocean. However, having come so far unmolested, he was not about to take anything for granted. Ordering the lookouts to keep a special watch on the horizon to the north and north-east, he passed the word for all guns' crews to stand to.

The smoke sighted by the *Rangitiki* was, in fact, very significant. It came from the *Mopan*, on fire and about to take her last plunge. The *Scheer*'s 4-inch guns had pumped shell after shell into her, systematically destroying everything above the waterline before blasting open her hull. When the *Mopan* finally disappeared beneath the waves, the once-smart fruit-carrier was just a blackened and burning hulk.

It became apparent that all was not well when, twenty minutes later, the British ship *Briarwood*, third ship of Column 4, commanded by Captain W.H. Lawrence, signalled *Jervis Bay* and the Commodore alerting them to an unidentified ship on the horizon. In a report written later, Captain Lawrence said:

> *The 3rd Officer who was on watch saw what appeared to be the mast and crotchet yard of a merchant ship bearing 005° from us, practically N., apparently steaming towards the Westward...Two minutes later the enemy altered course to approximately 180° and came up over the horizon sufficiently for us to see his control tower and tripod. She was bows on and the tower looked like the front side of a hexagonal. I thought it was a British warship and went below to have my tea.*

Not for the first time that afternoon the *Admiral Scheer* had been mistaken for a British battleship. But the alarm had been raised. Signal lamps flashed, flag hoists were broken out and reports were coming in thick and fast as ship after ship became aware of the menacing presence of a large warship on the horizon. Captain Lawrence was obliged to forego tea in the saloon for sandwiches on the bridge.

Satisfied that his prompt action had prevented the *Mopan* from sending out a distress signal before his guns blasted her out of the water, Theodor Krancke approached HX 84 at speed, but with caution. The radar screen was now filled with flickering targets, and Krancke climbed to the foretop to get a better view. From there he could clearly see the forest of masts and funnels on the horizon, which his powerful binoculars revealed as merchant ships of all shapes and sizes. But only merchant ships; not a warship in sight anywhere.

Krancke was aware that it was not unusual for Allied convoys to cross the Atlantic completely unescorted, safe in the knowledge that the U-boats did not venture out into the deep waters. If this was one such convoy, then it promised to be no more than just another practice shoot for the *Scheer*'s gunners. There might be some token resistance. British merchant ships were quick to let fly when danger threatened, and their guns, obsolete though they might be, could inflict serious damage. Krancke intended to stay well out of range.

Then, as the *Scheer* moved in closer, two ships, both near the head of the convoy, stood out in stark contrast to the others. They were big, high-sided ships, the larger of the two having twin tall funnels. In which case they were passenger liners, troopships perhaps? Or were they that particularly British improvisation: armed merchant cruisers? Krancke strongly suspected the latter.

All became clear when the smaller of the two liners broke away from the convoy and turned bow-on to the *Scheer*. A lamp flashed from her bridge, sending the international call sign in Morse AA...AA...AA. It was the size of the lamp that gave her away. Merchant ships almost invariably used a 6-inch Aldis lamp, but this was far bigger – 10 inches at least, and powerful. Only a warship would carry such a lamp. Krancke ordered his guns to cover the stranger.

Aboard the *Jervis Bay* speculation was equally rife. Various identifications were offered, but the consensus was that the approaching ship was a British battleship of the 'R' class. Fegen was undecided. It could be just coincidence that a British capital ship was in the area, and had decided to run an eye over the convoy. On the other hand – and this was the more probable explanation – it could be the enemy. To settle the matter, he ordered his yeoman to signal by lamp the challenge for the day, 'M-A-G' three times. If the ship was British, she would flash back the correct coded answer.

Krancke knew he was being challenged to identify his ship, but he had no idea what the answering challenge was. He had examined the British ship through his binoculars, and any doubts he had had about her identity were settled. Her guns were clearly visible, and they were manned. She was an armed merchant cruiser. In order to gain time,

Krancke told his signallers to repeat the 'M-A-G' back to his British ship, requesting that she be the first to identify herself.

This was an old ruse, and it cut no ice with the experienced Captain Fegen. He now knew he was confronting an enemy warship, and a very powerful one at that. The challenge he now faced was to fight or run. And only he could make the decision. A fight would almost certainly end in the total destruction of his ship, and in the deaths of many of his crew. Like any ship's captain, his first duty was to see to the safety of his men; on the other hand, thirty-seven merchant ships carrying cargoes vital for the survival of Britain were looking to him for protection. It took just seconds to make the choice.

Fegen hit the alarm bells, and rang for full emergency speed. It was clear to him that he was hopelessly outgunned and outranged; his puny 6-inch guns were only effective up to 6 miles, if that. If he was going to fight, he must close the range as fast as possible.

As the *Jervis Bay*, battle ensigns streaming in the wind, surged forward, the *Admiral Scheer* turned broadside on, bringing all six 11-inch guns to bear. The time was 1700, with the weak winter sun slipping below the horizon, and darkness already closing in.

The bridge of the *Jervis Bay* had by now identified the stranger by her silhouette as a German pocket battleship of the *Graf Spee* class, and when he saw the ripple of flashes run along her side, Fegen knew what would follow. Petty Officer James 'Slinger' Wood later put Fegen's fears into words:

> *It was a clear day, and we could see Jerry plainly in the distance. He was steering a course that would have brought him directly across our bow. But almost immediately he altered course, broadside to us. I knew what was coming. He wanted to get all his guns into action...*

John Barker, a young hostilities-only gunner, remembered:

> *On the day of the action I was to keep the Second Dog Watch. At about four o'clock I went down to do a bit of dhobeying. A little later the alarm bells rang. I grabbed my duffle coat – I had on my service boots, trousers and football jersey. At my action station I could see a dark smudge over the port side – the Admiral Scheer. The Battle Ensign went up on the mainmast and very soon the first salvo of 11-inch shells came over...*

The six 670lb projectiles, nearly 4,000lbs of hot steel and high explosive, came roaring across the intervening sky like a swarm of avenging hornets. This first salvo fell to starboard of the *Jervis Bay*, close enough to shower the merchant cruiser's bridge with salt spray, but causing no damage on board. The *Scheer*'s guns thundered again, and this time her shells exploded 100 yards off the *Jervis Bay*'s port side. Again no damage, but she had been bracketed, and every man jack on board, from the lowly galley boy to Captain Fegen himself knew what must happen next. Young John Barker was under no false illusions:

> *To have two turrets with three guns in each firing shells at you was pretty horrific. We had four vintage 6-inch guns forrard and three aft; they were vintage ones. I think one was dated 1894. They were open without turrets. They were no match for the Admiral Scheer…*

At 1706 Fegen sent a coded signal to the Admiralty giving his unidentified attacker's bearing, course and position; at the same time he signalled the *Cornish City*, ordering Commodore Maltby to scatter the convoy under the cover of a smoke screen. The receipt of the distress was recorded in the Admiralty's War Diary:

> *At 2006 today (London Time) Jervis Bay escorting HX 84 in mid-North Atlantic signalled that an enemy battleship was in sight and reports that the convoy was being attacked were received. Battleships Renown, Barham, Australia and Hood ordered to rendezvous. Five Town-class destroyers on passage to the UK ordered to spread out to locate Scheer and three of which were nearest the position of the attack were to close HX 84 to rescue survivors and attack raider if possible.*

Whitehall now pulled out all the stops, and late that night the battlecruisers *Hood* and *Repulse*, the anti-aircraft cruisers *Phoebe*, *Naiad* and *Bonaventure*, accompanied by the destroyers *Eskimo*, *Mashona*, *Matabele*, *Electra*, *Somali* and *Punjabi* sailed from Scapa Flow for the position given by the *Jervis Bay*.

It was a classic example of the stable door being closed with a bang after the event. At 1100 on the 6th, when the rescue force was passing through the Minches, the Admiralty ordered *Repulse*, *Bonaventure* and the destroyers *Mashona*, *Matabele* and *Electra* to head out into the

Atlantic towards the last known position of the *Admiral Scheer*. HMS *Hood*, the anti-aircraft cruisers *Phoebe* and *Naiad*, with the remaining destroyers were sent to cover the approaches to Brest and Lorient. *Bonaventure* and *Mashona* were first to reach the mid-Atlantic position of the attack, but not until 0400 on the 8th, by which time only a few pathetic pieces of debris littered the sea. The *Admiral Scheer* was by then 1,000 miles further south.

And now the airwaves were alive with cries of outrage, as the merchant ships broke radio silence to call for help. Whereas the *Jervis Bay*'s message to the Admiralty had been in code, the merchantmen were broadcasting in plain language. Their frantic calls were picked up by Mackay Radio, on New York's Long Island, and within minutes all the world knew that an Allied convoy was facing destruction in mid-Atlantic.

The *Scheer*'s third salvo covered the 12 miles separating the two warships in 20 seconds, just as long as it took the frightening roar of the six spinning projectiles to reach the ears of those aboard the *Jervis Bay*. It was then that Fegen came to terms with the impossible task he had set himself and his crew. At best, his 6-inch guns had a range of 8 miles, and he could not hope to lay a finger on the pocket battleship. But Edward Fogarty Fegen, third generation Navy, knew only that fire must be met with fire. He gave the order for his guns to open fire, even though he knew the range was too great. It was far better to make some sort of show of force, however futile. Nothing raised morale more than the sound of your own guns. And, God knows, his men needed that right now.

Third Officer J.R. Cooper of Ellerman Line's *Castilian*, third ship of Column 3 had a grandstand view of the action as he ran aft to the 4-inch gun. He saw the *Scheer*'s first salvo land right ahead of the *Jervis Bay*, the second salvo in her wake. She was neatly bracketed, and Cooper saw the third salvo hit the cruiser's bridge. Fires broke out immediately throughout the length of the ship.

Able Seaman Sam Patience, who was at the helm of the *Jervis Bay* at the time, and later in action on the forward port 3-inch gun, takes up the story:

> *The third salvo hit us. It must have been from 22 to 25,000 yards, and our range was only 10,000 yards – and that's when the guns were new.*

The newest gun we had was 1896...The shells were coming over. You could hear the whine of the shells. You didn't know where they were going to land. First of all the bridge got hit, and the radio room. The ship was on fire and salvos were coming over and blokes standing beside you were getting killed, burned alive, and all this, and heads blown off where I was standing, or P1 Gun, which was my action station. I was relieved at the wheel and went up to P1, and we were told to put the smoke floats over the side, which were big canisters like dustbins. We pulled the stoppers out and chucked them over the side. That was the smokescreen we laid to protect the convoy...

By desperate manoeuvring Fegen had reduced the range to 18,000 yards, but though the barrels of his 6-inch guns grew hot, his shells were still falling well short. The enemy's shells, on the other hand, were coming in thick and fast, like a shower of flaming meteorites. Captain Fegen was well aware that he had little chance of hitting back at his opponent at this range, but there was a faint hope that if he kept going he might be able to ram. Then, a single British shell, possibly from a gun whose rifling was less well-worn than the others, landed close to the *Scheer*, sending a shower of spray over her decks.

Krancke, consumed by the need to avoid serious damage to his ship, hesitated. He could not afford to be hit by even one shell, rogue or otherwise. For seconds only, he debated whether it might be wiser to sheer away from his persistent attacker and concentrate his fire on the merchant ships, then he dismissed the idea.

The *Scheer*'s third and fourth salvos missed their target completely, indicating that all was not well with her gun control. Years later, Chief Officer David Braid, of the *Mopan*, then prisoner on board the German ship, stated that the electrical equipment controlling her gun turrets had failed. As a result, he and some of his fellow prisoners were made to haul the turrets around using rope tackles. It seems that this highly sophisticated German fighting machine had developed an Achilles heel.

The *Jervis Bay* was now well alight, burning like a giant Olympic torch, with a dense cloud of black smoke trailing astern and adding to the murk created by her smoke floats. The ex-liner, built at the height of luxury sea travel, had broad sweeps of teakwood decks for her passengers to promenade on, and her opulent accommodation was lined throughout with polished oak panelling. None of this had been stripped out when she went to war. As dry as tinder from years in tropical waters, it now burned readily and fiercely.

Now the *Scheer*'s gunners had got the range, and their shells began to hit home. Sam Patience, still manning the port 6-inch on the forecastle, remembered the agony of the moment:

> *The shells were coming over so quickly and you thought the next one was going to get you…I recall looking up and seeing the bridge alight. I remember Captain Fegen looking down. His arm was partially shot away. The shells were coming over, you could hear the whine of them. You didn't know whether they were going to fall on you or not, and one particular Leading Seaman, I think it was Frank Russell, said to me "Get that bloody hose and try to get in the Sick Bay." A shell had hit there. And this fellow he picked up the hose by the nozzle, and I'm pulling the rest of it behind, and a shell came over and I was left with the severed hose in my hand, and he got blown up. It happened just like that…It was terrible. All I could smell was the cordite from the shell, and our cordite as well. There was no smell of death as such…*

'Slinger' Wood, manning one of the midship guns, went down under a rain of shrapnel:

> *I looked down and saw my left leg was skinned and that I had stopped a piece in my right leg…We were helpless, but we kept our guns firing as long as we could. It wasn't much use but it was something to occupy our minds…*

The *Admiral Scheer*'s shells had completely demolished the *Jervis Bay*'s bridge house, which included the chartroom and wireless room, and in the midst of this burning hell Captain Fegen had been severely wounded. Eyewitnesses said that most of his left arm had been shot away and one of his legs was shredded. He lost consciousness briefly when he crawled out of the burning wreckage, but he was soon shouting for the surgeon to tend to his wounds. Surgeon Commander T.G. Evans could do no more than stem the flow of blood from the dreadful wounds with gauze and bandages, but it was obvious to him the captain was dying.

Before he was hit, Fegen had signalled to Admiral Maltby to scatter the convoy, and rockets were still soaring into the night sky from the

Cornish City's bridge, bursting with brilliant red stars. The message to the other ships was 'Scatter and proceed with the utmost speed'.

Eight days earlier, in a smoke-filled room at naval headquarters in Halifax, Admiral Maltby had instructed the merchant ship captains in the procedure to follow in the event – and Maltby stressed that this was most unlikely – of an attack by an enemy surface raider. On the signal from the commodore ship they were to scatter to all points of the compass away from the enemy. Each ship was given a course to steer towards a pre-arranged rendezvous point, where it was hoped the convoy would be reformed when the danger was passed. This was all very well in theory, but in practice, with thirty-seven diverse and heavily laden merchantmen totally unused to manoeuvring in close proximity to one another, it was a recipe for a huge mid-ocean pile-up.

Second Officer R.L. McBrearty of the *Lancaster Castle*, bound from Three Rivers to Grangemouth with a full cargo of grain, caught the mood:

> *Scatter meant just that. You were now on your own and had to find the best way out...One ship came so close to us going in the opposite direction that we could hear them shouting to us as she slid down our starboard side...I believe she was the Rangitiki...*

Propped up in the smoking remains of the *Jervis Bay*'s bridge, Captain Fegen, grieviously wounded though he might be, was far from finished. The telemotor gear, which transmits the movements of the helm aft to the steering engine, had been completely destroyed, leaving the *Jervis Bay* virtually rudderless. For a brief while Fegen, determined to ram the *Admiral Scheer*, attempted to steer using his twin screws. This proved unsuccessful, the ship sheering wildly under the pull of the separate propellers. Fortunately, by this time a damage control party led by the *Jervis Bay*'s chief engineer, now Commander (E), James Chappell, had by this time succeeded in connecting up the emergency steering gear. This involved working in cramped conditions in the after steering flat, firstly securing the rudder which was slamming from side to side out of control, then connecting it directly to the steering engine. The ship could then be steered by a hand-wheel on the engine, using the spare magnetic compass on the after docking bridge. It was a crude method involving several men and relayed helm orders, but it was all that Fegen had left. He propped himself up on the docking bridge, preparing to carry on the fight.

Steering an erratic course, the battered and burning merchant cruiser continued at full speed, her bows continually seeking her vastly superior enemy. Her tall superstructure, which in the balmy days of peace had housed the elegant cabins of the rich, was glowing red, flames and smoke reaching for the sky. Miraculously, some of her guns were still firing, although the range was still too great for them to damage her attacker.

Krancke, furious at the delay this British apology for a fighting ship was causing him, was now desperate to end the farce. In addition to the two 11-inch turrets blasting away at the *Jervis Bay*, he now brought into the fight his 5.9s, eight more muzzles spitting hot steel at this crazy fool bearing down on him.

Nothing could survive under the massive barrage being laid down by the pocket battleship. One by one the British guns began to fall silent, blown from their mountings, their crews lying dead or dying alongside them. Soon, only one of the after guns was still firing, its crew working like automatons in a holocaust of smoke and flame. Then, after a direct hit by a German shell, that too fell silent.

And that should have been the end of the matter, and it would have been were it not for a bizarre twist of fate. Anxious to get on with the real work of the night, which was the destruction of as many of the merchant ships as possible, Krancke was about to give the order to cease fire on his obviously beaten enemy. Then, aboard the battered *Jervis Bay* the fire reached the bags of cordite lying around on the after gun platform, and the flashes of these exploding gave the impression that the gun had resumed firing.

At the same time, the AMC, her decks strewn with dead and dying, the flames leaping to her mast-tops, seemed to take a lunge at the *Scheer*. No one was giving orders anymore, and it was almost as if the ship herself had taken charge, and was driving at her tormentor, hell-bent on exacting revenge.

The sight of this latter-day fire ship bearing down on him rang alarm bells for Krancke. If the *Jervis Bay* somehow managed to ram the *Scheer*, or even land a lucky shot in a vital spot, it could mean the end of her first raiding cruise before it had really started. In desperation, he ordered every gun that could be brought to bear to open fire on the enemy ship.

And that really was the end for the *Jervis Bay*. A full salvo of 11-inch scored a direct hit on her engine-room blowing part of the main engine through the skylight. Slowly, she lost steerage way, and then lay stopped wallowing in the swell, listing heavily as the sea poured in to her hull through holes below the waterline. She was on fire from end to end, most of her crew dead. Differing eyewitness accounts put Fogarty Fegen still standing defiantly on the poop, or back in the ruins of the bridge amidships. Wherever he was, he must have been near death, for he was never seen again.

Twenty-two minutes after she took the fight to the *Admiral Scheer*, HMS *Jervis Bay* was lying dead in the water, burning furiously. Fegen's Number One, Lieutenant Commander Keith Morrison, himself twice wounded, had now taken command. Standing erect on the foredeck, flanked by his great friend Lieutenant Commander Surgeon T.G. Evans, also wounded, he gave the order to abandon ship. Neither Morrison nor Evans survived.

Ironically, the dying agonies of the *Jervis Bay* were prolonged by the very thing meant to preserve her; the hundreds of empty 45-gallon barrels packed in her holds. One by one they were ejected through the great holes in her battered hull as she slowly sank lower and lower.

Looking back over the years, it is fair to question why it took the *Admiral Scheer* so long to subdue the *Jervis Bay*. Here was a modern German capital ship, equipped with the best technology of her day, including radar, and armed with a total of twenty heavy-calibre guns, matched against an ageing ex-passenger liner mounting a handful of well out-of-date artillery. The result should have been swift and decisive. Yet the *Jervis Bay* put herself between the raider and the convoy, and held her at bay until she herself was reduced to a burning wreck manned by the dead and dying. True to the tradition of the Royal Navy, Captain Edward Fogarty Fegen and his men had faced insurmountable odds, selling their lives dearly in the process. The conduct of the *Admiral Scheer*, on the other hand, was almost timid. The only explanation for this reluctance to fight at close quarters must lie with Theodor Krancke's fear of receiving damage that could not be repaired at sea. The thought of a repetition of the *Graf Spee* incident did not bear contemplation.

This was not the first time that Hitler's big ships had shown reluctance to get to grips with one of the Royal Navy's substitute warships.

On 23 November 1939, with the Second World War not yet three months old, the armed merchant cruiser HMS *Rawalpindi*, an ex-P&O passenger liner, commanded by Captain Edward Kennedy, was patrolling between the Faroe Islands and Iceland on the lookout for German blockade-runners. The 16,697-ton *Rawalpindi*, built in 1925, had been snatched from the London-Bombay run by the Admiralty, armed with a few antique guns, and allocated to the Northern Patrol. Her role in the war was to stop and arrest the odd German or neutral merchantman attempting to run the blockade. It was cold and extremely boring work, for winter in northern waters was long and the blockade-runners were few. Then, late in the afternoon of 23 November 1939, the *Rawalpindi* came face to face with war in all its terrible reality.

It was a bitterly cold afternoon, made even more miserable by the presence of icebergs and dense fog patches. The night ahead promised to be even worse. By 1530, as the pale November sun was nearing the horizon, a lookout in the crow's nest reported a ship on the starboard bow.

Peering through his binoculars, Captain Kennedy at first thought he had flushed out another enemy blockade runner. Then, as the silhouette of the stranger became clearer, Kennedy recognised it for what it was; a German battle cruiser. He sent his men to their action stations and altered course to run away from what was obviously a vastly superior enemy. She was later identified as the 35,000-ton battle cruiser *Scharnhorst*.

Commissioned shortly before the outbreak of war, the *Scharnhorst* had a speed of 31 knots and was armed with nine 11-inch and twelve 6-inch guns. She was also equipped with every possible refinement that modern German technology could supply. On her own she was a fearsome opponent, and she was not alone. Just over the horizon, and following in her wake was her sister ship, the equally fearsome *Gneisenau*.

When Captain Kennedy realised what he was up against, he had no hesitation in declaring, 'We'll fight them both, they'll sink us – and that will be that.'

The engagement that followed was short and brutal, a fight that could have only one conclusion. Approaching to within a range of 4 miles, the German ships called on Kennedy to surrender. His answer was to open fire on the *Gneisenau* with his 6-inch guns. The British shells burst harmlessly against the battle cruiser's armoured hull.

Caught in the crossfire from eighteen 11-inch guns, the *Rawalpindi* was quickly reduced to a pitiful wreck, on fire and out of control. Fifteen minutes later, she was gone beneath the waves, taking the gallant Kennedy and all but thirty-eight of his crew of 276 with her. When a British rescue force arrived, the *Scharnhorst* and *Gneisenau* were long gone from the scene.

It was late evening before the *Jervis Bay* finally gave up the fight, rolled over, and sank, hissing and sighing into the cold depths of the Atlantic. She had sold her life dearly in the defence of her convoy, giving up only after she could take no more pounding from the *Admiral Scheer*'s big guns. It had cost the Germans no fewer than 335 shells to sink her, a third of the total carried by the pocket battleship. If the German High Command required proof of the superiority of the U-boat over the big-gun ship, the *Jervis Bay* had gone a long way towards providing it.

Chapter 5

GUNS AND GUNNERS

For more than four hundred years, from the days when the tall East Indiamen first braved the long passage to and from the East, it has been customary to arm British merchant ships in times of danger. When the First World War came along, and with it the German U-boat menace, it was recognised by international treaty, with certain provisos, that merchantmen must have the right to defend themselves when attacked. Only one heavy calibre gun was allowed, and that was to be mounted at the stern. The Mark VI 4-inch naval gun was chosen for the purpose, most probably because this was the main gun used by the Royal Navy's destroyers, and was therefore in plentiful supply.

The Mark VI 40 Calibre fired a 35lb shell and had a range of 10,000 yards. By the spring of 1917 most British ocean-going merchantmen carried one of these stern-mounted guns, and they were being used to good effect. More than half of the ships attacked by surfaced U-boats were escaping by fighting off their assailant while running away. Unfortunately, their success led to unrestricted submarine warfare, the U-boats attacking under water and torpedoing without warning. The bloodbath that followed caused international outrage, and almost cost Britain the war.

When Britain and Germany again went to war in 1939, the Mark VIs, which had been stored in major seaports, were dusted off and brought back into service. Within a year of the outbreak of war more than 3,000 British merchantmen were under arms and hitting back at the U-boats. It must be said that many of the guns they were using dated from the turn of the century, and having seen considerable action, their rifling was often worn smooth, and their range considerably reduced. The guns' crews also left much to be desired. By and large, they consisted of those of the ship's crew who had undergone a three-day gunnery course ashore, with a Royal Navy gunlayer, usually on the retired list, providing a modicum of expertise. If insufficient 'trained' gunners were available, then it was not unusual for guns to be manned by cooks, stewards, off-duty firemen, with the galley boy supplying mugs of hot char in any lull in the fighting. Surprisingly enough, there were times when the old Mark VIs, in the hands of their enthusiastic scratch crews, gave the U-boats a bloody nose. For defence against aircraft, most ships carried four or more .303-inch Hotchkiss or Lewis machine-guns, usually mounted on the bridge and boat deck. Merchant ships being commercial vessels, with masts, rigging, aerials and derricks, meant careful siting of these guns was necessary to avoid gunners causing damage to their own ships in the heat of the moment. There were many instances of galley funnels being demolished, flag halyards shot away and wireless aerials brought down. Friendly aircraft were constantly complaining of being shot at, but it was certain that any aircraft, friend or foe, approaching a British merchantman without first identifying itself was sure of a hot reception.

In the grey light of dawn on 10 October 1939, just five weeks after Hitler marched into Poland, the two West Hartlepool tramps *Heronspool* and *Stonepool* hove in their anchors and sailed from Milford Haven in company with seven other ships. Three hours later, a rendezvous was made off the Smalls with seven ships from Liverpool, and OB 17, the first westbound convoy of the war was under way. The sixteen merchant ships were escorted by two destroyers.

The 5,202-ton *Heronspool*, under the command of Captain Sydney Batson, was down to her marks with 8,000 tons of anthracite for Montreal, while the *Stonepool* carried a similar amount of 'best Welsh' steaming coal for the bunker station at St Vincent, Cape Verde Islands. The southbound *Stonepool*, slightly smaller than her sister at 4,803 tons, was commanded by Captain Albert White. The two captains were friends of long standing.

During their stay in the Bristol Channel the ships had each been fitted with a vintage 4-inch mounted on the poop. With these guns came two gunlayers from the Royal Navy, Able Seaman John Pearson to the *Heronspool*, and Able Seaman John Hayter to the *Stonepool*. Both men were pensioners recalled to the colours, and had the unenviable task of licking their merchant seamen guns' crews into shape.

OB 17 had not been many hours at sea before it became apparent that whoever set the convoy's speed at 8½ knots had been wildly over-optimistic. Already half the ships were straggling behind, and others were showing signs of dropping out. Among the stragglers were the *Heronspool* and *Stonepool*, and although the two ageing tramps were struggling valiantly against the rising westerly swell, they were falling further and further astern. When daylight came of the 12th, they found themselves alone but for each other. Finally, it was decided that they might as well part company, and the *Heronspool* continued to the west, while the *Stonepool* broke away onto a southerly course.

After a long day scanning the horizon in search of marauding U-boats, Sydney Batson was still haunting the bridge of the *Heronspool* at sunset. The long Atlantic swell was beginning to heave and roll and the barometer was falling steadily, all of which indicated to Batson's experienced eye that a blow was in the offing. His worst fears were confirmed when he was handed a message from the United States Lines' 24,000-ton liner *Manhattan*, then 800 miles to the west, reporting she was having difficulties with 'tremendous seas'.

Batson's preoccupation with the weather was cut short when a lookout sighted a ship on the port bow. Dusk was drawing in, but it was still light enough for the stranger to be identified as a large tanker apparently stopped. Close alongside her was a long, low silhouette. A submarine. Quite by chance, the *Heronspool* had surprised U-48 in the act of sinking the 14,000-ton French tanker *Emile Miguet*.

Batson was tempted to intervene, to try out his newly fitted 4-inch; then he realised that John Pearson, the DEMS gunlayer, was the only man on board familiar with the gun. His crew of enthusiastic amateur gunners had yet to fire even a practice shot. Hesitating only for a brief moment, Captain Batson decided that discretion was the better part of valour. He ordered the helm hard over to put the submarine and her prey astern, and rang for full emergency speed. He then made the mistake of using the steam whistle to call his crew to action stations. The screech of the whistle was heard by Herbert Schultze in the conning tower of U-48, and he hurriedly finished off the French tanker, then took off in pursuit of the *Heronspool*.

Having steamed at full speed for the better part of two hours, Batson dared to believe he was out of danger, and he passed word to the engine-room to ease down. The *Heronspool* ceased her wild vibrations, and settled down again to a comfortable 8 knots. However, Herbert Schultze was not a man to give up easily. He had been following stealthily in the British tramp's wake, and was soon within striking distance. At precisely 2000, as the bells signalled the change of the watch aboard the *Heronspool*, Schultze opened fire with his 88mm deck gun.

Any hope Captain Batson had of relaxing was rudely shattered by the loud crack of the gun and the tall column of water that shot skywards close on the *Heronspool*'s starboard quarter. He acted instinctively, giving a double ring on the engine-room telegraph. The ship started to vibrate again as she strained to escape from her persistent attacker.

Another twenty minutes passed without incident; then, just when Batson thought he had again evaded his pursuer, a signal lamp winked out of the darkness astern. Schultze, unsure of the *Heronspool*'s identity, and perhaps unwilling to risk sinking an innocent neutral this early in the war, was challenging by lamp.

Sydney Batson, by nature of his profession, was no stranger to making snap decisions, but this was a tough one. The choice was to surrender his ship and take to the boats, or to fight it out. No one would have condemned him for taking the easy way out; the U-boat had twice the speed of his ship on the surface and, unlike Gunlayer Pearson's raw team, her gun's crew would be trained to perfection. Then, as Batson struggled to come to terms with the situation, indecision turned to anger. Snatching up the engine-room voice pipe, he demanded more speed, then passed the order for the gun's crew to open fire.

Gathered around the 4-inch on the *Heronspool*'s poop, where they had been at action stations for more than two hours, Gunlayer Pearson and his scratch crew needed no urging on. Within seconds of receiving the order to open fire the first shell was in the breech and the U-boat was in their sights. The antique gun thundered and recoiled. Working swiftly, with only the occasional fumble, the inexperienced crew cleared the breech, swabbed out, reloaded, and fired again. No fall of shot was observed, but the U-boat was seen to dive in a hurry. The first round was to the *Heronspool*.

Hauling out to the west, Batson made another bid to escape, and steaming at absolute maximum speed, with every rivet in her rust-stained hull rattling, the heavily laden tramp zigzagged away into the night. Almost three hours passed, and with perhaps 30 miles covered, Batson was ready to believe he had escaped. Again he was cruelly disappointed.

Like Banquo's ghost, as soon as the *Heronspool* eased back to normal speed, there in the light of the stars was the long shadowy shape of U-48 creeping up astern. Without waiting for orders from the bridge, Pearson's 4-inch barked, and two more shots were seen to fall close to the surfaced submarine. With a loud rush of compressed air she disappeared underwater again in a welter of foam and spray.

A tense half an hour went by, then U-48 popped up again. This time she was on the port quarter, her gun's crew spilling out onto the casings while they were still streaming water. And so the running battle began, with U-48 surfacing from time to time to swop shells with the stubborn little British tramp that refused to surrender. Gunlayer John Pearson, who had entertained doubts as to the ability of his ragbag gun's crew, was visibly glowing with pride. His men fought with a careless precision born of countless battles in dockside pubs around the world. They stood shoulder to shoulder, as they had then; sailors, firemen, stewards, all eager to defend the good name of the *Heronspool*. Even the youngest member of her crew, 14-year-old deckboy Frank Elders, showed his contempt for the enemy by appearing on the gun platform with mugs of steaming tea during each lull in the fighting.

This was an unequal contest between a sophisticated German war machine and an ageing British merchantman armed with a second-hand gun crewed by rank amateurs. Schultze had already fired four torpedoes, all of which, unseen by those on the *Heronspool*, had missed their target. Then, shortly after midnight, U-48 landed a shell so close alongside the British ship that she rolled onto her beam ends. When she righted herself again, Sydney Batson glanced at the wheelhouse clock, and sucked at his teeth. Friday the Thirteenth had arrived.

The end came an hour later, when Herbert Schultze decided that the fight had gone on long enough. He slipped below the waves again, moved in to point blank range, and fired his fifth torpedo. This time the torpedo ran true and the *Heronspool* was rocked by a violent explosion that lifted her clean out of the water. Hatchboards, hatch beams and tarpaulins flew into the air, and the ship took a heavy list as the sea poured into her holds through the jagged hole blown in her hull by Schultze's torpedo. Cursing his luck, Captain Batson reached for the whistle lanyard to sound the abandon ship. The *Heronspool* had fought her last fight.

The horror of the night was made worse when, at the first urgent tug at the whistle lanyard, the whistle jammed wide open emitting a mournful shriek that went on and on almost turning confusion into blind panic. On the poop, Gunlayer Pearson and his crew struggled to extricate themselves from the wreckage of their gun platform, which had collapsed under them. On the boat deck, Chief Officer Clifford and his men battled to clear the boats away ready for lowering. In the wireless room, Radio Officer George Haresnape bent over his key tapping out a frantic SOS. On the bridge, angry and sad that his old ship was going, Captain Batson calmly prepared the secret code books for dumping over the side. But in spite of the increasing list, the blackness of the night, and the ear-shattering shriek of the steam whistle, discipline held. Fortunately, the sea was relatively quiet, and the *Heronspool*'s two lifeboats were launched without mishap.

A headcount taken in the boats revealed there had been no casualties of the attack, and Batson decided to lay off his sinking ship and await the help he had been assured was on the way. Came the dawn, the *Heronspool* was still afloat, but clearly beyond saving. Daylight also brought with it the American passenger liner *President Harding*, and rescue.

While the *Heronspool*'s grateful survivors were being hauled on board the *President Harding*, some 90 miles to the south-west the *Stonepool* was going through her normal morning routine. Star sights taken earlier by Chief Officer Peter Love had put her 430 miles due west of Ushant, with just under 2,000 miles to go to the Cape Verdes. Captain Albert White was well satisfied with the progress of the voyage, estimating that another two days' steaming would see them out of reach of the U-boats.

Sweeping an empty horizon with his binoculars, White was contemplating a leisurely breakfast. Then, as the early morning mist lifted, he saw what appeared to be the funnel of another ship on the bow. A homeward-bounder coming up over the horizon, he assumed; but as the shimmering haze cleared altogether the 'funnel' became the conning tower of a surfaced submarine. U-42 and Kapitänleutnant Rolf Dau, both as yet untried in war, had found their first potential victim.

The U-boat was no more than 3 miles off, and as White reached for the whistle lanyard to sound the alarm, her 88mm gun barked, and a shell screamed across the intervening water to land just ahead of the *Stonepool*'s blunt bows. It was the proverbial 'one across the bows', and the import was obvious.

Ignoring the warning shot, Albert White ordered the helm hard over and rang for more speed. By the time Gunlayer John Hayter and his crew, which included Third Officer Leonard Corney and Chief Steward John Shipman, had reached the poop, the ship was stern-on to the attacking submarine. They quickly took up their positions around the 4-inch, and within minutes were returning U-42's fire.

Over the following twenty minutes a fierce gun battle ensued, with Captain White on the bridge of the *Stonepool* using full helm to throw the ship from side to side in a mad zigzag. All the while, Hayter and his crew, who had fired only three practice rounds since their 4-inch was fitted, were confidently returning shot for shot with U-42. Below decks, in the *Stonepool's* engine-room, Chief Engineer Richard Parsons, at Captain White's urging, had screwed down the boiler safety valves and advanced the control lever hard up against the stops. The old ship responded with a will, surging forward with a froth in her bow-wave rarely seen since her trials on the Tees more than a decade earlier.

The chase might have gone on and on, but the more accurate shooting of the U-boat's 88mm soon began to take its toll. The zigzagging *Stonepool* was hit time and time again. Both her lifeboats were blown to pieces, fires raged along her decks; but still she fought on.

It seemed inevitable that the U-boat's superior firepower must prevail – then the *Stonepool's* part-time gunners found the range, and their shells began to land uncomfortably close to the enemy. In desperation, Rolf Dau attempted to put an end to the stubborn tramp with a torpedo, but this too failed. Albert White, enthusiastically directing operations from the bridge of the *Stonepool*, was not about to be caught napping. He saw the track of the approaching torpedo from afar, and easily avoided it. As the *Stonepool* slewed to comb the track of the torpedo, one of Gunlayer Hayter's shells slammed into U-42's casing, and she crash dived in a cloud of spray and smoke.

Ten minutes passed, then the submarine suddenly resurfaced. White immediately ordered his gunners to carry on firing, and it soon became apparent that the U-boat was not firing back. In fact, her deck gun was out of action, hit by the shell that had caused Dau to take cover below in a hurry. He had resurfaced to pick up his gunners, who had been left struggling in the water when he had crash-dived.

And Kapitänleutnant Dau had had enough. Not only had his big gun been smashed, but U-42's pressure hull had been holed and she was unable to submerge. He motored away into the night, leaving his intended victim still afloat.

The *Stonepool* was only just afloat. She had been repeatedly hit by U-42's shells, and was holed below the waterline. It soon became clear that she was taking on water at an alarming rate, and with her only lifeboats reduced to matchwood, White decided to reverse course and head back to the Bristol Channel, hoping to make port before his ship sank under him.

Four hours later, the destroyers *Imogen* and *Ilex*, alerted by the *Stonepool*'s frantic radio calls, caught U-42, still on the surface and attempting to make her way home at reduced speed. She was scuttled by her own crew as the destroyers approached. Later reports say that twenty-six of her crew of forty-six lost their lives. And so U-42's first war patrol, and Rolf Dau's first voyage in command, ended in defeat; a defeat that was largely brought about by the refusal of the crew of a British tramp to bend the knee to the enemy.

After disposing of U-42, *Imogen* and *Ilex* took station on the damaged *Stonepool*, and the three ships set course for the Bristol Channel. As darkness was closing in that evening, a keen-eyed lookout at the *Stonepool*'s masthead reported a submarine on the surface on the port beam. They were being shadowed again.

The escorting destroyers peeled off to attack, but before they could open fire the submarine had dived. An Asdic search was carried out, but no contact was made. Herbert Schultze – if it was U-48 – must have been already demoralised by his encounter with the *Heronspool*, and was unwilling to risk a fight with two destroyers and another armed tramp.

The *Stonepool* reached the safety of the South Wales port of Barry on 16 October, battered and bruised, but able to continue her voyage after repairs. Her end came in the icy waters off Greenland in the autumn of 1941, when she was caught up in the dreadful massacre of Convoy SC 42.

The first autumn of the war had proved to be a testing time for the U-boats. Vice Admiral Dönitz's daily war diary made gloomy reading:

On the subject of U-boat losses: of the Atlantic and North Sea boats, U 27, U 39 and U 12 are definitely lost, U 42 and U 45 probably, U 40 possibly. U 27 reported on 19.9 that she was leaving the operations area. There is no information on U 39 since she sailed. One major part of both crews are prisoners of war. This means that the boats were probably surprised on the surface and attacked with gunfire and possibly also by a/c. It is possible that they were so damaged as to be unable to dive, so the crews had to abandon the boats in the face of the enemy and sink them...

Nothing has been heard of U 42 and U 45 since they sailed. They did not reply to orders to report their positions. Enemy broadcasts and enemy press indicate that there was an anti-S/M hunt on 13th October during which 2 large boats were sunk. One report mentions S.S. "Stonepool" as having contributed to the destruction of the U-boats. On the 13th she had reported that she was in action with a U-boat. On the 15th she reported another U-boat; 2 destroyer flotillas (or at least part of them), were sent out from Portland to this position. According to another report, part of the crew of a U-boat, including the C.O., were on board a destroyer, which had picked up survivors from S.S. "Bretagne". Yet another report says that a member of the crew of a steamer, who had fired on a U-boat with his gun, observed that later on destroyers came up and sank the U-boat, which was no longer able to dive. (This cannot be S.S. "Stonepool".)

Actions are therefore said to have been fought between steamers and U-boats. Both steamers got away and in both cases the U-boat is said to have been destroyed, at least one of them on the surface.

Commenting on the risks taken by a U-boat challenging an armed merchant ship on the surface, Dönitz wrote:

One hit may render the boat incapable of diving and therefore the certain prey of destroyers. (It is not surprising that circumstances are different from those in the world war. At that time steamers were only gradually being armed; today all this has apparently been carefully planned and the effect of this form of defense must therefore be expected to be greater).

All twenty-four British merchantmen sailing with HX 84 were armed with a stern-mounted 4-inch anti-submarine gun and some also carried a HA/LA 12-pounder for defence against attacking aircraft. They all, with one exception, made some attempt to fight back as they sought to escape from the guns of the *Admiral Scheer*.

Having crippled the *Jervis Bay*, Kapitän Krancke then turned his sights on the largest ship in the convoy, the two-funnel liner *Rangitiki*. Weighing in at nearly 17,000 tons gross, the New Zealand Shipping Company's cargo/passenger liner inevitably stood out like a floating leviathan among the run-of-the-mill cargo ships making up HX 84.

Krancke had assumed, wrongly, that she was either a second armed merchant cruiser, or a troopship. If the former, she constituted a real danger to the *Scheer*, and either way she was a prime target to be sent to the bottom without delay.

Back in the halcyon days of peace, the *Rangitiki*, a 16-knot twin-screw motor ship, product of John Brown's shipyard on the Clyde, had run a regular service between London and New Zealand carrying general cargo outward and frozen lamb and wool home. In her heyday, she had carried 600 passengers and a crew of 350; now, with the war into its second year, only cargo mattered. Her holds were full to the hatchtops with 8,000 tons of refrigerated and general cargo, and her reduced crew of 220 were caring for just twenty-five passengers, all civilians, a number of women and children amongst them.

At the convoy conference before leaving Halifax each ship had been given a course to steer and a rendezvous to make for in the unlikely event (and it was stressed that it was most unlikely) of the convoy being attacked by a surface raider. When the signal was given by the Commodore, they were to alter away from the danger and spread out in a fan-like pattern to divide the enemy's fire.

When the 'unlikely event' suddenly became reality, and the signal to scatter was hoisted at the *Cornish City*'s masthead, the *Rangitiki* went with the others, running to the south-east at maximum speed. Unfortunately, the emergency had come at an inopportune time for the liner, her engineers being engaged in stripping down one of the cylinders of the main engine which was giving trouble. As a result she was hard pressed to work up to 13 knots. Her master, Captain Keith Barnett later reported to the Admiralty:

> *As we turned the "JERVIS BAY" drew out at full speed - about 13 knots - and steamed towards the enemy. The "RANGITIKI" did not open fire as I realised we were hopelessly outranged. The last signal we received from the Commodore was the emergency turn, then the convoy started to scatter to the S.E. The Raider then fired her second salvo which fell just in front of the "JERVIS BAY". The Escort had immediately opened fire but her shots fell short. The third salvo from the enemy hit her amidships and she appeared to stop, but continued to fire. The Raider, having got the range, hit the "JERVIS BAY" with another two salvoes, one forward and one aft, then she caught on fire.*

Dr Firth, passenger aboard the *Rangitiki*, commented:

When I got below the passengers had gathered on the starboard side, according to orders. We knew we were probably for it, as the Rangitiki was the biggest ship in the convoy. We all had our lifejackets on and most of us had a little package with our most treasured possessions. Mine happened to be just a folder of papers. Some of the faces were a bit pale and strained, but we smiled at one another and lit cigarettes. I don't want to sound patronising, but all the women were magnificent, both stewardesses and passengers.

By this time the raider had turned around and we heard a shell burst uncomfortably close. Suddenly there was one terrifying bang and a thud that shook the whole ship. It was on the side where we were, so we all moved over to the port alleyway...This was the shell that splashed the bridge and left some of its bits on the deck. Then we waited for the next one. Those of us who had seen the Jervis Bay knew how good the enemy's gunnery was and there wasn't much doubt as to what was happening. But the next shot didn't come and we were left waiting. We sang 'Roll Out the Barrel' and some other songs and we got along all right...

...I should like to say here how much we owed to the commander, Captain Barnett, his officers, and to the whole ship's crew. The work of the men of the Merchant Navy is particularly hard, because they can't hit back. Their first job is to see to the safety of their ship and cargo. They deserve all the admiration and protection they can get...

The *Rangitiki*'s Chief Radio Officer told of how he was playing table tennis when the attack started:

We had won a set each and were just on the final set when there were certain noises and the 2nd Officer looked out of the veranda café window and said, 'Good Lord! They're practising emergency night attacks.' Well, when the next bang went off we realised it wasn't in fun. I think I beat the world's speed record along 'A' Deck and went up to my wireless house. I got there, and in just a few minutes the Captain was on the phone. It appears we were being attacked by a raider of the Graf Spee type...The other thing I was worried about was would this particular set of ours reach England and America...I got it out, then we ran away from them – thanks to the Jervis Bay making a jolly good scrap of it with impossible odds.

Unknown to the *Rangitiki*'s radio officer, his transmission was picked up by the powerful commercial station Mackay Radio, on New York's Long Island, which then broadcast the following to all stations:

Intercepted message that British liner Rangitiki, 16,698 tons, being shelled by enemy ship of Graf Spee class in North Atlantic, halfway between Ireland and Newfoundland.

Even as the liner took refuge in the smoke screen the world was being informed of the German attack on Convoy HX 84.

On the bridge of the *Rangitiki* Captain Barnett recorded the sequence of the attack:

The second and third salvoes straddled the ship, and one shell fell about 50 yards off and covered the ship with spray and shell fragments. All this time the other ships in the convoy were using smoke floats. In the darkness we managed to get away. We didn't use our gun as it would have given our position away. Later we could see the German using star shells. It took five hours from the outset before we saw the last of the German flashes on the horizon. It was nothing short of a miracle that we had no casualties. The crew behaved jolly well, so did all the passengers...

The *Scheer* now brought her secondary armament into play, the first target for her 5.9s being the 8,000-ton Shell tanker *Delphinula*, bound Manchester with a cargo of gasoline. The first enemy ranging shots neatly straddled the fleeing tanker, and it seemed certain that her voyage was about to come to a sudden end. Then the ingenuity and sheer grit of the British merchant seaman came to the fore. The *Delphinula*'s Master dropped a smoke float, which drifted astern creating a fog that partially masked the tanker's movements. He then had a second float ignited on deck at the stern, which glowed red, sending out clouds of black smoke giving a fair impression of a ship on fire. Three more smoke floats were ignited on deck, and the smoke and flames given off must have persuaded the *Scheer*'s gunners that the tanker was done for, and they ceased firing at her. The *Delphinula* escaped undamaged, except for her badly scorched after deck.

Chapter 6

SCATTER

Viewed from the bridge of the *Admiral Scheer* in the half-light of the dying sun, the chaotic scattering of Convoy HX 84 was an incredible sight. Ships were steaming in all directions with smoke floats being hastily bundled over the side creating a curtain of oily-black smoke that was already blotting out the horizon. One by one the ships faded into the dark pall like ghosts leaving the stage, their exit marked by flashes of gunfire as they fired defiantly at their pursuer. At least a dozen of them were using their 4-inch anti-submarine guns, but this could only be a token gesture of defiance. The ancient guns, relics from more distant wars, were pitted against the massive centrally controlled armament of the *Scheer*. It was a no contest.

At that point Theodor Krancke must have felt like a huntsman unexpectedly disturbing a covey of partridge. Never before had the guns of the *Scheer* been presented with so many helpless targets. The temptation to go after them with all guns blazing was very great, but Krancke, with the fate of the *Scheer*'s younger sister *Admiral Graf Spee* in mind, kept a cool head. Barely twelve months had elapsed since the *Graf Spee*, challenged by three British cruisers off the River Plate, had chosen to fight. Her heavier guns had won the day at first, but she sustained serious damage in the action, and was forced to seek sanctuary in neutral Montevideo. The bones of *panzerschiff Graf Spee* lay gathering rust in the entrance to the Plate, where she had been scuttled by her crew.

At this point it should have been easy for Krancke to use his superior speed and the advantage of radar to pick off the merchantmen at his leisure. Not one of these slow, heavily-laden ships attempting to hide in the smoke should have got away. However, the *Scheer* had not escaped entirely unharmed in her clash with the *Jervis Bay*. The thunderous blast and violent recoil of the German's 11-inch guns had cracked the crystal of her delicate radar apparatus, rendering it completely useless. Krancke still had his stereoscopic range finders and bearing directors, but he had lost the ability to see through the smoke and in darkness. He was also anxious to get the *Scheer* onto a south-westerly course, so that when the time came, he would be able to make his own escape. Meanwhile chaos still reigned, with ships running wildly in all directions, and the *Scheer* steaming blindly at 23 knots, the risk of collision with one of these ships was very great. The consequences of that alone were too enormous to contemplate. Yet Krancke was keenly aware of the need to act quickly. Any hesitation would give the enemy ships more time to spread out and disappear into the night. Those manning the bridge of the *Scheer* and the lookouts on deck and aloft were all straining their eyes and ears to penetrate the smoke and the darkness, which with the moon now behind the clouds, was complete. Krancke was sorely tempted to fire star shell, but in illuminating the night he would be giving away his own position, perhaps putting the *Scheer* at the mercy of the enthusiastic, and often accurate fire of the merchant ships' gunners. This was a risk he dare not take.

Then the moon broke through the clouds revealing the small Ellerman & Papayanni Line steamer *Castilian* racing for the cover of the smoke. The 3,000-ton, 21-year-old steamer, snatched from the gentle idyll of her peacetime Mediterranean run by the exigencies of war, was sagging under a full load of steel and slow to move. She was saved from a sudden end by the timely appearance of a more desirable target. Third Officer J.R. Cooper of the *Castilian* recalls the escape:

> *After dark, we thought we were safe; around 1830, after having a sandwich and a mug of tea, we were stood down from the gun platform. The pitch darkness was suddenly broken as his (the Admiral Scheer's) searchlight was trained on us, we never saw him. Just as suddenly, it went off. We had 400 tons of high explosives in magazines in our tween decks. We were lucky he did not shoot at us, but we had just overtaken a tanker called the San Demetrio which was his next victim...*

The unwitting saviour of the *Castilian* was the Eagle Oil motor tanker *San Demetrio*, on passage from Galveston, Texas to Avonmouth with 11,200 tons of high-octane aviation spirit. The 8,073-ton tanker, under the command of Captain George Waite, was no stranger to the transatlantic run, having made numerous voyages between the United Kingdom and the West Indies oil ports. Early in the current voyage the *San Demetrio* had dropped out of the convoy with engine trouble, and had not rejoined until the evening of the 4th. In view of what was about to happen, it might have been better if she had continued to straggle.

Captain George Waite, Chief Officer Wilson, and a young Welsh apprentice John Lewis Jones were on the bridge of the tanker when the raider was first sighted. Young Jones, an enthusiastic ship spotter, realised that the unidentified warship – and by the shape of her she was almost certainly a man-of-war – resembled the photograph of the German pocket battleship *Deutschland* which he kept in his cabin. When he communicated his fears to Captain Waite, the captain agreed the stranger looked suspiciously like a warship, but preferred to wait until she came closer before making up his mind. The decision was made for him moments later when the *Scheer* opened fire, and the Commodore hoisted the signal for the convoy to scatter.

With no further hesitation, Waite called for as much speed as the engine-room could produce, and instructed Chief Officer Wilson to swing out the lifeboats. Later in the war, British ships would have their boats permanently swung out ready for lowering when at sea, but at that time boats were normally stowed inboard, except in submarine waters. The order to swing out created some excitement, but no panic. The *San Demetrio*'s crew donned their lifejackets and manned the guns. It could easily have been a routine exercise.

When the *Scheer*'s guns opened up, Chief Engineer Charles Pollard was in his cabin aft changing into uniform for the evening meal, which he ate in the saloon amidships with the other officers. Dashing out on deck, he saw the horizon astern aflame with gun flashes and realised at once that the convoy was under attack. Instinctively, he ran for the engine-room and slid down the ladders to the control platform. There he found Second Engineer Duncan and his two juniors had the situation well in hand. Duncan was at the throttle, and as he advanced the lever the *San Demetrio*'s eight-cylinder Kincaid diesel responded willingly. The heavily loaded tanker began to gather momentum. Satisfied that all was well in Duncan's hands, the Chief went back on deck, and from there to the bridge to be on hand should he be needed.

Second Officer Arthur Hawkins, who was the ship's gunnery officer, had meanwhile gone aft to the poop, where the 4-inch gun's crew was assembling. As soon as the full crew was on hand, Hawkins gave the order to load and fire. He had fired only two rounds when the order came from the bridge to cease fire. The range was far too great for the 4-inch and, as Captain Waite pointed out, the flash of the gun would only draw attention to the ship, making her a target for the raider's shells.

In later years John Lewis Jones, then captain of his own ship, wrote:

Although the San Demetrio was steaming away from the raider, we were still in the line of fire, and the Master, Captain Waite, decided to alter course to starboard and get clear of the main body of ships. At the same time, a ship on the starboard bow altered course to port and a collision seemed inevitable, but the seamanship and quick decision of Captain Waite avoided this fate, the ships sailing clear of each other and steamed on their original courses. Immediately after that the vessel was heavily hit by shells, and I could see her bow rising out of the water. She was close enough for us to hear the screams of the injured across the water and one of her lifeboats ran out of control on the falls, with bodies falling into the water...

The stricken ship Jones referred to was the 7,908-ton Brocklebank steamer *Maidan*, commanded by Captain C.L. Millar, and manned by a crew of nineteen British officers and seventy-one Lascars. She was carrying a 7,900-ton cargo of steel, iron, copper, brass, solder and Army trucks, and consequently slow to manoeuvre. She presented an easy target for Krancke's gunners, and they literally blew her apart. Every gun that could be brought to bear on the *Scheer*'s starboard side opened up on the British merchantman effectively silencing her single gun before it could be used in anger. Within minutes the *Maidan* was a blazing inferno, and listing heavily as the sea poured into her breached hull, she capsized and sank in a cloud of hissing steam. With her went her entire crew, most of whom must have already died in the fierce bombardment she had been subjected to. As the *Maidan* went down the moon came out in all its glory, lighting up the scene for the *Scheer*'s gunners with its brilliant yellow light.

And now *San Demetrio*, steaming hard for the cover of the smoke screen, came under the enemy's guns. Second Officer Arthur Hawkins wrote in his report:

We now changed our course steering to E.N.E., and when I went on to the bridge I could still see the raider who was now on our port quarter, at a distance of about 8 to 8½ miles, and consequently just a blurred shape. However, he opened fire on us commencing with a salvo which fell clear on our port side. The next salvo went right over the ship, but he registered a hit with the third shell which struck us on the bow about 2 ft above the waterline. It was quite dark by this time, so, although of course we could see the shell fire, we could not judge how large the salvos were...

The raider was using her 5.9s on the tanker, firing probably in salvos of four, and easily penetrating her unarmoured hull and superstructure. It was only too obvious that it was just a matter of time before a shell went home in one of her cargo tanks filled with high-octane. If the *San Demetrio* did not then vaporize, at the very least she would be turned into a floating inferno, from which no one would escape alive. Judging the situation to be hopeless, Captain Waite stopped his engines and ordered his crew to abandon ship. Second Officer Hawkins' report continues:

The shelling had become very heavy and shrapnel was flying around thick and fast, but I think the raider was out of range because at that particular time there were no direct hits on our vessel. I made my way to the bridge and from there went to the midship starboard boat, but I continuously had to take shelter because of the flying shrapnel. I got 9 men into the boat, and then as there didn't appear to be anyone else wanting accommodation I climbed in myself, and was just about to lower away when someone shouted for me to hold on for a moment. I waited and then took another 6 men on board whom I believe were the overflow from one of the other boats. The Captain, who was still on deck, told me to carry on, and so I lowered away. At this time, although the engines had been stopped, the ship was still doing about 8 knots but we managed to get the boat into the water successfully...The shell fire was getting heavier and so we thought it best to get away from the ship, and in doing so we lost contact with the other boat and never saw it again.

As the three lifeboats pulled away from the ship's side, the raider hit the tanker with a full salvo of shells. She immediately burst into flame, the fire running swiftly from end to end as the volatile aviation spirit in her tanks went up. There could be no going back now.

Close by the burning *San Demetrio*, and also presenting her stern to the *Scheer*'s gunners, was the London-registered *Trewellard*, with Captain L. Daniel on the bridge. The *Trewellard*, a 5,200-ton general trader owned by the Hain Steamship Company, was on her winter marks with 7,800 tons of steel ingots and pig iron. This was a truly deadweight cargo, occupying less than a quarter of the total cubic of her holds, an uncomfortable load at the best of times, making a ship so stiff that she had a heavy, shock-like roll in a swell. In wartime, such a cargo was seen as a one-way ticket to Davy Jones' locker. A single torpedo blasting open the *Trewellard*'s thin hull plates would flood her almost empty cargo spaces in minutes, immediately destroying her ability to float. She would inevitably go to the bottom like the proverbial stone, and it was very unlikely that any of her 39-man crew would survive.

Captain Daniel had lived with the dangerous vulnerability of his ship since sailing from Halifax eight days earlier, and when the *Scheer* came storming over the horizon with her guns blazing, his immediate reaction was to beat a hasty retreat. He altered course with the other ships and, following the example set by the *Rangitiki*, began dropping smoke floats over the side. Most of the other ships were doing the same, successfully creating a dense wall of smoke, behind which they hoped to escape. It was fortunate for them that the *Scheer*'s radar, with a range in excess of 10 miles and accurate to within 75 yards, was out of action.

As the *Trewellard* steadied up on a southerly course and worked up speed, Captain Daniel ordered his 4-inch gun's crew to open fire. He later reported:

> The raider at this time was about 5 miles away and I started firing at extreme range of 6 miles. We were carrying 6 smoke floats and we put these over before opening fire, but one of them did not ignite. We fired 9 shots in all, but by this time the raider was firing at me. We were struck in the stokehold, another shell struck in No.4 hold and I think the third went into the engine room on the port side and this blew parts of the engine through the skylight, killing everybody in the engine room. The ship started making water badly and the stern commenced to settle down. I tried to communicate with the engine room but the telegraph would not work and the telephones had gone.

Contrary to Captain Daniel's fears, the *Trewellard* did not go down with a rush. She settled quickly, but for some reason unexplained, she remained afloat when her decks were awash. His report continues:

> *I ordered the ship to be abandoned and this was accordingly done. The starboard forward boat capsized, it became waterborne forward and as we were unhooking the forward falls, turned round and capsized. The after port boat had been blown to pieces and completely disappeared, but we managed to get away the other two boats quite satisfactorily. I told the 3rd Officer in his boat to hang on and I had another look around the ship. I found the 2nd Engineer badly burned in the starboard alleyway. I managed to get him into the boat and then I found the Donkeyman in the same condition – very badly burned – and I managed to get him into the boat too. By this time the Trewellard was pretty low in the water and I got into the boat myself.*
>
> *When I got into the boat I found that it contained no oars, water, sails, equipment or any gear, so we pushed off with some loose floor boards.*
>
> *The raider was now on our starboard side at a distance of about 3 miles, but she was too far away for me to recognise her. He opened fire on the Trewellard and put about 30 shells into her amidships and she sank...*

It was a quiet time aboard the *Kenbane Head* when the German raider appeared. Another day at sea was winding down, another day nearer home. Work on deck was finished for the day, and in the galley the cooks were preparing the evening meal.

On the bridge, Chief Officer Bill French had just taken over the watch and was idly running his binoculars over the next ship in line ahead in the convoy. She was the Greek-flag *Anna Bulgaris*. During the crossing she had been behaving suspiciously, breaking radio silence twice a day, sending short bursts of unintelligible Morse. Only that morning, the *Jervis Bay* had closed the Greek ship within hailing distance and ordered her to shut down her wireless room. There may have been a perfectly innocent explanation for the forbidden transmissions – a first-trip wireless operator trying his hand on the key, perhaps – but foreign-flag ships sailing in British convoys were always under suspicion. The great fear was that someone might be giving away the convoy's position to the enemy, although it was never quite clear what their motive might be. The U-boats were no respecters of flag when they fired their torpedoes.

The 5,225-ton *Kenbane Head*, owned by the Ulster Steamship Company of Belfast was a seasoned North Atlantic trader. From the time she came out of the yard in 1919, one of a series of standard ships built as replacements for losses in the Great War, she had been employed on a regular service to Canada and the USA. She was the archetypal British tramp, blunt in the bow, with four cavernous holds, built to carry maximum cargo at minimum cost, and with a triple-expansion steam engine that gave her a service speed of 9 knots on 25 tons of coal a day. Her accommodation was barely up to Board of Trade standard, with her deck and engine-room ratings living in a comfortless, rat- plagued fo'c'sle right in the bows of the ship. Her officers lived amidships under the bridge, her engineers abaft the funnel, in cabins only marginally more luxurious than the crews' fo'c'sle. She carried a crew of forty-three, predominantly Ulstermen who, despite the ship's many shortcomings, still came back voyage after voyage. Under the command of Captain Thomas Milner, a brusque, no-nonsense 65-year-old who had held the rank of lieutenant commander in the naval reserve in the First World War, the *Kenbane Head* was considered to be a good ship to sail in.

After landing a cargo of china clay from Fowey in Three Rivers, the *Kenbane Head* had loaded general in Montreal for Belfast. As nearly half her crew lived in Belfast, this was a bonus voyage, on which homeward-bound really meant just that. There was a discernable air of anticipation on board.

When the *Scheer* attacked, and the *Cornish City* hoisted the signal to scatter; whilst the other ships elected to go to the north, east or south, Captain Milner decided that his best chance of escaping lay to the west. His decision was influenced by the *Kenbane Head*'s position in the convoy. She was sailing as rear ship of Column 9, with no ships to starboard or astern. It was a simple matter to haul out under full starboard helm and reverse course, while adding to the growing smoke screen by dropping smoke floats over the side as they went. Milner reasoned that in the general confusion and falling visibility he would be able to slip past the raider unseen.

Milner and French had been joined on the bridge by Second Officer George Lecky and Third Officer Bell, and the four men now stood transfixed looking back over the frothing wake, silent witnesses to the terrible firestorm that had suddenly engulfed HX 84.

Out on the starboard quarter, to the north, the evening sky glowed blood-red over the *Jervis Bay* which lay helpless on her side at the mercy of the fires consuming her. Close by, Captain Daniel's *Trewellard*, whose 4-inch gun's crew had dared to defy the *Scheer*, was another burning wreck, the waves already lapping over her bulwarks. A few miles to the east, the tanker *San Demetrio*, the aviation spirit in her cargo tanks now well alight, was a gigantic flaring torch.

To port, against the backdrop of rolling smoke clouds, jagged spurts of flame and the rumble of gunfire marked the path of the escaping ships, most of whom were now heading to the south and east. Captain W.H. Lawrence, commanding France, Fenwick's deep sea tramp *Briarwood*, bound for the East Coast with 6,500 tons of steel and timber, recorded the scene:

> *...Most of the ships could do 14 knots, but we could only do 9 knots, so we were rapidly left behind. I therefore decided to stay in the smoke. As the ships scattered to the S.E. the Raider turned, steering first E. veering to S through S.W. and to the W., hoping to cut off the convoy. The wind was blowing from the N.E., there was a black cloud to the S.W. and the smoke screen was blowing behind us, between us and the enemy.*
>
> *I came out of the smoke screen, had a look round and then went back into the smoke. I went down into the engine room, screwed down the safety valves, took the rings out, and got 12½ knots out of my ship, which is a lot for a 9-knot vessel. The stokers needed no encouragement and, assisted by the sailors, I have never seen coal put on a fire so quickly in my life...*
>
> *We had opened fire also, but the total range for my gun was 7 miles and I could see our shells falling 1½ miles ahead of the enemy, and we stopped. The "ERODONA" also opened fire, the "LANCASTER CASTLE", and some 10 or 12 other ships...*

The gunfire of the merchantmen could never be any more than a thumbing of the nose to the enemy, but for the men on the threatened ships it did much towards satisfying their urge to hit back. Furthermore, Kapitän Krancke, with the ghost of the *Graf Spee* hovering at his shoulder, was very wary of giving chase. He could not take the chance of a stray shell from one of these antique guns finding a vital spot in his ship.

Racing for the cover of the darkness to the west, Captain Milner had taken the *Kenbane Head* to within 2 miles of the *Scheer* and inadvertently put her at the mercy of the raider's guns. In a desperate bid to escape, Milner ordered his 4-inch gun's crew not to open fire for fear that the flash of the gun would give his position away. He might have succeeded if Krancke had not thought, mistakenly as it transpired, that the *Kenbane Head* was in fact firing at him. After the war, Krancke wrote in his book *Pocket Battleship*:

Suddenly there was a bang followed by a tongue of fire aft. That was not a hit. The ship's single gun was firing back at the Scheer. Almost as soon as those on board realised it a heavy column of water rose amidships and a shower of spray slashed the faces of those on the bridge, who tasted salt on their lips. That shell had exploded not more than twenty yards off its mark. A slightly greater elevation and the gun crew would have scored a direct hit on the Scheer...

Shocked by the near miss, but unable to see where the threat to his ship was coming from, Krancke ordered the 24-inch searchlight to be switched on. There was a loud click, and the brilliant white beam stabbed the darkness, swept around, and then caught the *Kenbane Head* and held her. Like a frightened animal, the British ship twisted and turned, but she could not escape the blinding light.

The *Scheer*'s forward turret followed the searchlight beam, and at Krancke's order the smoke-blackened 11-inch guns thundered out. Three huge shells, each packed with 600lbs of high explosive, went spinning across the water.

The range and bearing had been correctly calculated, and three quarters of a ton of high explosives homed in on the *Kenbane Head* hitting her in the stern, wrecking the after accommodation and blowing her steering gear to pieces. On fire and unable to steer, she was easy meat for the *Scheer*'s 5.9s, which completed the destruction of the helpless ship. Her yet-to-be-used stern gun was smashed, gaping holes were blown in her hull on the waterline, the starboard lifeboat was reduced to matchwood, and several shells exploded in the engine-room with devastating results. The *Kenbane Head* was being systematically destroyed piece by piece, and Captain Milner could do nothing to save her. And amidst all this frightening mayhem, Radio Officer Paddy Cahill remained in the wireless room abaft the bridge tapping out frantic SOS messages. Unfortunately, his calls for help were falling on deaf ears.

Tom Milner, reluctantly accepting that his ship was finished, ordered all the secret code books to be dumped over the side in their weighted canvas bags. He then mustered his crew on the port side of the boat deck alongside the one remaining lifeboat. As they assembled, another enemy salvo crashed into the bridge, sending shards of red-hot shrapnel slicing through the air. Men were cut down, and the teakwood boards of the deck ran red with their blood.

Despite the chaos reigning, the lifeboat was lowered, only to fill as soon as it hit the water. Darkness was hiding the fact that the hull of the boat was riddled with holes from shell splinters. There was a scramble to get back on board the ship before the boat sank, but the wind and sea were rising, creating a nasty chop on the water. This, combined with the ever-present Atlantic swell, was slamming the waterlogged boat against the ship's side, and of the forty-five men on board only twenty-two, including Captain Milner, succeeded in re-boarding. The others, many of whom were wounded, either fell back into the sea, or lay helpless in the bottom of the boat as it drifted away.

Back on board his ship, Captain Milner found that much of her main deck was already awash, and she obviously had not long to go. One wooden life raft was found to be undamaged, and this was launched and secured alongside. Further investigation showed that the two jolly boats on the bridge deck had also escaped the shelling. These 16ft boats, little more than dinghies, were normally used as workboats, and as such had no food, water or equipment, other than a rudder and two pairs of oars, on board. But at least they would offer some protection from the elements. They were lowered to the water and lashed to the raft, one on each side. The survivors boarded their makeshift rescue craft, and the *Kenbane Head* was abandoned to her fate. As they rowed away, they passed close to the damaged lifeboat, which was now floating on its tanks, with the bodies of two firemen inside. They were only a few hundred yards off the *Kenbane Head* when she lifted her bows in the air, and with an almost human-like sigh, sank stern first.

It was only when they lay back on their oars to watch their ship sink that the survivors realised what now faced them. They were a thousand miles from the nearest land, they had no food and only a small supply of water; and there was little hope of early rescue. Many of them, particularly firemen and stewards, had on only the minimum of clothing, and as the night came on the weather was worsening. Their hopes of survival were extremely poor. A head count revealed that they were thirty-seven out of the *Kenbane Head*'s total complement of forty-four. Captain Milner was on the liferaft, Chief Officer French had one of the jolly boats, and Second Officer Leckey the other.

While the burning ship was still above the waves, the light from the flames gave some comfort to the survivors, but when she sank and the flames were quenched, the complete darkness made their situation all the more frightening. The wind had reached near gale force, the swell was enormous, and the boats were continually lashed by spray. The night was bitterly cold, and those without proper clothing were suffering agonies. It seemed likely that many would not survive until morning. Then, at about 0300 on the 6th, to the joy of those still conscious, there was suddenly light again. Their joy turned to horror when they realised that a burning ship – it was the abandoned *San Demetrio* – was drifting remorselessly down on them.

In desperation, some of the survivors suggested boarding the tanker, but in view of the weather, and the possibility of the boats and raft being dashed against the burning ship's side, Milner overruled them. Instead, he ordered Second Officer George Leckey to cast off and take his boat around the stern of the tanker to see if it might be possible to board on the other side.

With four men at the oars, Leckey set off and disappeared around the stern of the *San Demetrio*. That was the last ever seen of George Leckey and his 9-man crew. The likely explanation of their loss is that, in attempting to find a place to board, the jolly boat was thrown against the ship's side and capsized.

When dawn finally came next morning, after enduring a night of horrors, Milner found that eight more of his men had perished, killed by the cold and wet that penetrated deep into their bones. Their bodies were committed to the deep with as much dignity as the heaving sea would allow.

Those remaining on the raft now transferred to the jolly boat, and the raft was cast off. Crowded into the tiny boat, the twenty men, all that was left of the *Kenbane Head*'s crew, settled down to await their fate.

Chapter 7

HEROES ARE MADE

Third Officer Bill Fellingham of the Hain Steamship Company's *Trefusis* reported:

Masters of ships in convoy were given scattering procedures according to various textbook patterns but, due to the presence of the ADMIRAL SCHEER on the port side of the convoy, HX 84's scatter was by no means a textbook affair.

HX 84 was, in fact, in total disarray. Three ships had been sunk and one, the tanker *San Demetrio*, damaged and on fire. The armed merchant cruiser *Jervis Bay*, the convoy's sole escort, lay broken and in flames, most of her gallant crew dead. The remaining merchantmen, taking advantage of the smoke screen and the cover of encroaching night, were steaming for all points of the compass, running like chickens before a fox. The scene was one of total confusion. This great fleet of ships, once in orderly columns; now shrouded in smoke and darkness, was in complete disarray. Signal lamps flashed, whistles shrieked, and several near collisions were in the process of occurring. Second Officer R.L. McBreaty, of the *Lancaster Castle*, carrying a full cargo of grain from the St. Lawrence, wrote:

The master of the Lancaster Castle, Captain Hugh Williams, called his officers together on the bridge and it was decided that every time we saw a gun flash we would turn our stern to it and make as much speed as possible. Many other ships must have had similar plans and with many alterations of course in the darkness there were some near collisions.

One ship came so close to us going in the opposite direction that we could hear them shouting at us as she slid down our starboard side....

Third Officer Fellingham elaborated:

With many ships, including the TREFUSIS, dropping smoke floats, the gathering dusk, some ships (not the TREFUSIS) firing their aft guns and all ships having the same thought in mind, to put their sterns to the ADMIRAL SCHEER and all speed on their engines, chaotic would be a fair description of the scatter. The TREFUSIS had several 'near miss' encounters with other ships of the convoy during the scatter and, to me, it is remarkable that there were no collisions. The TREFUSIS was, probably, the slowest ship in the convoy and also a coal burner and many ships passed us at close quarters, some very close...

Despite all the frenzied activity, the *Scheer*, 28½ knots and armed with an array of big guns rarely seen on the high seas, had all the advantages. On the face of it, even without her radar, she was capable of catching and sending every one of those fleeing ships to the bottom before another dawn came.

Convoy HX 84 was in mortal danger, and threatening to go down in history as the only convoy ever to be completely wiped out by the enemy. For Britain, this would be the culmination of a wretched year in which over 800 British and Allied merchant ships and their cargoes had already been lost. This was against a background of impending defeat at home. London was under siege from the air, suffering saturation bombing by the *Luftwaffe* every night for eight long weeks without let-up. Long after the war had ended, when he was able to speak freely, Winston Churchill spelled it out:

Our armies were known to be almost unarmed except for rifles. There were, in fact, hardly 500 field guns of any sort and hardly 200 medium or heavy tanks in the whole country. Months must pass before our factories could make good even the munitions lost at Dunkirk...the German Navy found itself in possession of the whole European continental coast from the North Cape to the Spanish frontier. The implications were clear: never before in her history had Great Britain found herself faced by enemy forces on all sides except the West, a loophole which the German Navy attempted to close and then isolate this country from the rest of the world.

HX 84 had come through that loophole in the west carrying a quarter of a million tons of the materials so desperately needed in the beleaguered British Isles. The tankers alone were bringing in over 100,000 tons of oil fuels, while the rest were deep with steel, timber, food, guns, aircraft, and enough munitions to fill the country's sorely depleted arsenals. The fourteen British dry cargo carriers each had enough high explosives in their holds to blow them out of the water twice over.

It now seemed certain that the *Scheer*'s big guns would prevent much, if not all, of this vital cargo reaching the waiting ports of Britain. And that is precisely what would have happened had not Captain Hugh Pettigrew taken up the sword laid down by the now late Captain Edward Fogarty Fegen. This night, which in happier days had seen the celebration of Guy Fawkes and his Gunpowder Plot with fireworks and bonfires, was becoming a night on which heroes were made.

The near miss Krancke had attributed to the *Kenbane Head*'s gun had, in fact, been fired by the Canadian Pacific ship *Beaverford*. Like the rest of the convoy, when the Commodore hoisted the signal to scatter, she had sheered away from the raider and headed south, racing for the cover of the smoke screen. But when her master, Captain Pettigrew, saw the merciless way the *Kenbane Head* was being gunned down by the *Scheer* his Glaswegian ire was aroused.

The *Beaverford* had no pretentions to be a warship. She was not even, like the *Jervis Bay*, a merchant ship masquerading as a warship. She was a commercial cargo carrier right down to her keel plates; a cut above the usual, perhaps, but a merchant ship manned by merchant seamen, nothing more. She made her maiden voyage from Glasgow to Montreal in January 1928, and spent the next twelve years criss-crossing the stormy waters of the North Atlantic with the manufactured products of Britain's busy factories outwards, and steel and timber home. For her crew it was a hard trade, but rewarding.

The Canadian Pacific Railway was the brainchild of a group of Scottish Canadian businessmen whose dream it was to join together the various separate settlements of North America. They were faced with an engineering project of mammoth proportions, but with the help of 9,000 Chinese labourers the enterprising pioneers carved a railway through nearly 3,000 miles of dense forest and prairie, conquering the Rockies through Kicking Horse Pass, 5,339 feet above sea level, and with a gradient of 1 in 23. The construction of the railway began in February

1881 and was completed in November 1885, six years ahead of schedule, joining for the first time Montreal on the Atlantic coast to Vancouver on the Pacific.

From connecting the two ports, the natural progression was to join the two oceans, and in 1886, three weeks after the first train had crossed Canada, a contract was taken out for the carriage of mails and cargo by a joint rail and sea service. The first ship to be involved, the wooden barque *W.B. Flint*, arrived in Vancouver from Yokohama on 26 July 1886, with 670 tons of tea consigned to New York. This was delivered by rail in New York only forty-nine days after leaving Japan. Previously, the fastest tea clipper, routed around Cape Horn, would have taken up to four months to deliver the same cargo.

On 13 June 1887, the Cunard steamer *Abyssinia* arrived in Vancouver from Yokohama with mail, passengers and cargo for Chicago and New York, along with a small trial consignment of tea for London. In New York, the tea was transferred to another steamer, the *City of Rome*, and delivered in London on 29 June, twenty-nine days after it had been loaded in Yokohama. At the time, ships sailing from Japan to London via the newly opened Suez Canal normally took nine to ten weeks for the voyage. The rail/sea link firmly established, the Canadian Pacific Steamship Company was set up in the winter of 1887. When the Second World War broke out, Canadian Pacific had a fleet of twenty vessels, fifteen of which were large passenger liners; the remaining five were straight cargo ships. The 'Beaver boats' were well known and respected on both sides of the Atlantic.

In February 1940 the *Beaverford* and her four sisters were chartered by the Admiralty to carry government cargoes. The *Beaverford*'s status as a merchant ship did not alter in any way. She still sailed under the Red Ensign, but she now carried two guns, the usual 4-inch anti-submarine gun mounted aft and a 3-inch in the bows. At the time, both sides were still adhering to the Geneva Convention, which prohibited merchant ships from carrying heavy guns forward of the bridge. Strictly speaking, the *Beaverford*, with her 3-inch mounted in the bows, had assumed the role of aggressor, which was certainly not the Admiralty's intention. She carried only two trained DEMS gunners, so both her guns were almost entirely manned by crew members, sailors, firemen and stewards, with any officers that could be spared. Thirty-nine-year-old Second Officer Charles Morris, who had attended a three-day gunnery course in

Glasgow, was designated as Gunnery Officer. To call the *Beaverford* a battle-hungry man-of-war would be an overstatement, but she was prepared to fight, as Theodor Krancke was about to find out.

When she sailed out of Halifax with HX 84, the *Beaverford* was under the command of Captain Hugh Pettigrew and carried a crew of seventy-three, which included the two Navy gunners. Sixty-year-old Hugh Pettigrew, a stocky, fresh-complexioned Glaswegian, had sailed with Canadian Pacific for many years, as had the majority of his crew. These 'Company' men had stayed with Canadian Pacific throughout the dark days of the Depression, taking a cut in pay and often dropping a rank rather than end up on the beach, jobless and penniless.

In the inter-war years, 1929-1932, Britain, like most industrialised countries, had run into a severe economic recession, in Britain's case mainly due to the huge financial drain of the First World War. British industry, then largely dependent on the export of steel, coal and manufactured goods to countries abroad, was hard hit when those countries stopped buying. Old established businesses, particularly the coalfields and heavy manufacturing, collapsed; millions lost their jobs, and families faced starvation. In some areas of the country unemployment rose to 30 per cent of the working population. The government of the day was reduced to a state of panic. Income tax was raised to an unprecedented five shillings in the pound, and savage cuts were made in the public sector. Wages in all government departments, including the Armed Forces, were slashed by 10 per cent, as was unemployment benefit. The pay cuts resulted in a mutiny in the Royal Navy, which was as futile as it was misguided.

Amongst the worst hit was Britain's merchant fleet, which had already suffered grievously in the war. Hardly a creek or navigable river in the country was without its sorry collection of laid-up ships, and British shipowners, already renowned for operating their ships on a shoestring, were forced to cut back even further. In contrast to the recent war days, when trained seamen were at a premium, there were now queues of men waving Master's and First Engineer's certificates at every shipowner's door. Men who had served long years in command were reduced to signing on as junior mates, or even as able seamen, ex-chief engineers were to be found trimming coal and firing boilers. It was a sad and degrading situation, which still prevailed to some extent when war broke out again in 1939.

Typical of the era was 28-year-old Warwick Brookes, sailing as writer to the *Beaverford*'s chief engineer, John Sinclair. Surrey-born Brookes had begun his sea-going career as a cadet aboard HMS *Conway*, the elite pre-sea training school ship from which many of the top shipping companies drew their potential deck officers. Joining Canadian Pacific in the summer of 1929, Brookes had served three years as a cadet before sitting and passing his Second Mate's Certificate, the essential first rung on his long climb to command. Had the times been normal, he would then have been expected to join his next ship as Third or Fourth Officer. Unfortunately, there were hundreds ahead of him, many of whom held superior qualifications and all desperate to take any job afloat, no matter how lowly the rank. Warwick Brookes, qualified on paper to take charge of the watch on the bridge, found himself sailing with Canadian Pacific as a humble able seaman, and grateful for the opportunity.

After two years on deck, a frustrated Brookes tried his hand ashore, working as a capstan hand for a small engineering company in Surrey. Inevitably, the lure of the sea drew him back, and in June 1937 he rejoined Canadian Pacific. The effects of the worldwide depression were still being felt, and again Brookes was unable to gain officer status. In fact, he found himself on the bottom rung of the ladder, signing on as coal trimmer, a dirty, back-breaking job. Many men would have given up after one voyage, but Warwick Brookes was not one to be deterred by events. By the time he married his 21-year-old fiancée, Mary, shortly after the outbreak of war, his ability with words had landed him a post as Chief Engineer's Writer; not highly paid, perhaps, but the job carried status.

The decision to challenge the German raider was spontaneous, and that of Captain Hugh Pettigrew alone. He was well aware that his ship, with her brace of small calibre guns, unsupported even by a rangefinder, was no match for this enemy pocket battleship; and there was the matter of the cargo he carried in his tween decks. There was enough high explosive under the hatch boards to blow him and his crew into eternity should one of the enemy's massive shells find a vital spot. In point of fact, Pettigrew had little choice. The *Beaverford* was clearly visible to the Germans in the light of the burning *Kenbane Head*, and as the raider was obviously so much faster than his ship, Pettigrew saw no point in running. And the more he weighed up the tremendous odds he was facing, the more determined he became to fight back. He passed the word for the forward gun to open fire.

The firing of the *Beaverford*'s 3-inch was really only an act of desperation, and no one was more surprised than Captain Pettigrew when his first shell burst close alongside the *Scheer* sending a column of water high in the air. Evidently, the rifling of the old gun was not so badly worn after all, and certainly the DEMS gunlayer, sighting the gun entirely by eye, was a true professional.

If the mood aboard the *Beaverford* was one of surprised elation, on the bridge of the *Scheer* there was consternation. After disposing of the *Jervis Bay* with comparative ease, and with no other escorts in sight, Kapitän Krancke had assumed that he would be free to sink the helpless merchantmen at his leisure. They might be scattering like frightened rabbits, but there appeared to be method in their apparent confusion. They had very cleverly laid a smoke screen to cover their escape, and some were even showing contempt for him by firing back with their stern guns. Now one of them, with a gun mounted forward, actually had the audacity to attack him.

Although his ship was protected by armour plate, 80mm thick on the hull and 40mm on the main deck, Krancke was still fearful that one of these enemy ships lobbing protest shells at him might hit a vital spot. The *Scheer* was over 1,000 miles from her nearest friendly port, and serious damage could spell a premature end to her first Atlantic foray. To have to run for one of the Biscay ports with his tail between his legs could not bear contemplation, but it was a distinct possibility. By now Krancke was beginning to have serious doubts about the wisdom of tackling this troublesome convoy.

The *Scheer* had already suffered some damage, and that from the tremendous concussion caused by firing of her 11-inch turrets. To quote Krancke:

The upper companionway on the starboard side looked almost as though it had had a direct hit. Doors had been lifted off their hinges, flooring was torn up and broken, dry paint had flaked off bulkheads and was lying over the carpets. One of the new boys had obviously overlooked his job of closing a bulkhead, not a particularly important one, but with it open the heavy guns of the nearest turret had created havoc with the blast of their salvoes.

And now this suicidal belligerent merchantman seemed determined to pick a fight. In reality, there could be only one end to such an unequal contest, but nevertheless Krancke was more than a little apprehensive.

Krancke ordered his Gunnery Officer to illuminate the target with star shell, and to open fire when ready, using the forward 11-inch turret. He was determined to put an end to this aggressive stranger without delay. The firing began with star shell from one of the forward 4-inch guns. Meanwhile, in the *Scheer*'s forward 11-inch turret, the breeches of the great guns were open and the automatic hoists purred as they brought fresh shells up from the magazine below.

The star shells, three in quick succession, burst directly over the *Beaverford*, the brilliant white flares turning night into day as they slowly floated down on their parachutes. Now, for the first time, Krancke was able to see his opponent clearly. She was a substantial cargo ship, nine or ten thousand tons, and she was very heavily loaded with a high deck cargo covered by tarpaulins. Canadian timber, Krancke presumed. She looked like easy meat for his big guns.

The eerie lights hanging in the sky also allowed those on the *Beaverford* to see their enemy, and the enormity of what they were facing was enough to make their blood run cold. Pettigrew had altered course to allow both his guns to bear, but the range was still too great, and his shells were falling well short of the *Scheer*. As he watched, he saw the yellow flash of the raider's big guns, and seconds later three giant shells were spinning through the night air towards the *Beaverford*.

Hugh Pettigrew was no Navy man, but he was also no fool, and before the *Scheer*'s guns had begun their recoil he had his ship turning under full helm, and was racing for the safety of the smoke screen. The *Beaverford* was running for her life, her twin turbines screaming in protest as Chief Engineer John Sinclair thrust the control levers hard up against the stops.

Pettigrew's manoeuvre had been almost too late. As she surged forward the British ship was neatly bracketed by the German shells, one falling ahead and one on each beam. The triple blast turned the sea around the *Beaverford* into a seething cauldron, and a squall of icy water and shrapnel swept across the ship.

There were no casualties, and the only damage to the ship came from the hot shrapnel which started small fires on deck. The evil-smelling smoke of the burning smoke floats now enveloped the *Beaverford* hiding her from her enemy, and for the moment she was safe. No one will ever know what went through Captain Hugh Pettigrew's mind then, but he surely must have been tempted to keep running to the south, away from this awesome monster intent on destroying Convoy HX 84. As captain of a merchantman his primary duty was to ensure the safety of his ship and his crew, but now there were overriding considerations. It seems certain that his subsequent actions must have been influenced by the pitiful sight of the *Jervis Bay* lying on her side, smashed and burning, her scuppers running red with the blood of her dead and dying. Five ships had already gone down under the guns of the German raider, and there was nothing to stop her disposing of the rest, unless someone took on the mantle of Captain Edward Fogarty Fegen. And that someone had to be Hugh Pettigrew, whose ship, with her two guns, twin-screw manoeuvrability and superior speed was the only one able to challenge the enemy. Unless he created a diversion – and he realised he could do no more – then the raider would hunt out every last ship, sending them broken and burning to the bottom of this deep ocean along with their precious cargoes. With no more deliberation, Pettigrew took the *Beaverford* back out of the smoke screen and steered directly for the enemy. The battle lines were drawn, the gauntlet flung down.

Having made the decision to take over as protector of HX 84, Hugh Pettigrew began to play a dangerous game of cat and mouse with the *Scheer*. Steering erratic zigzag courses to avoid the raider's shells, he dodged in and out of the smoke screen, firing his guns each time he emerged, and then running for cover again. It was an outrageously one-sided contest. The *Beaverford*'s shells did not so much as blister the raider's paintwork, while Krancke's guns were inflicting real damage on the British ship. Each time the *Beaverford* emerged from the smoke to trail her coat across the *Scheer*'s path, she was met with a wall of shells from the raider's heavy and medium armament. The merchantman was soon on fire and shipping huge quantities of water through holes in her waterline. But as long as she was still afloat she was drawing the *Scheer*'s fire and allowing the other ships to escape. In retrospect the *Beaverford*'s defiance was nothing short of suicidal, but at the time it was a magnificent spectacle to behold.

The *Beaverford*, a humble Atlantic trader which through the exigencies of war just happened to have two guns on board, was proving to be a very tough nut for *panzerschiffe Admiral Scheer* to crack. Under the command of a fearless Scot, Captain Hugh Pettigrew, she was fighting a clever diversionary action worthy of the finest tradition of any fighting Navy.

Although Pettigrew tried every trick in the book, and more, to evade the storm of shells homing in on him, the *Beaverford* was hit hard time and time again. In the fierce running fight that seemed to go on and on forever, the raider fired twelve rounds from her 11-inch turrets and seventy-one from her 8-inch guns. Inevitably, some of these shells found their target. In all, three 11-inch and sixteen 8-inch shells hit the *Beaverford* with devastating effect. The British ship was slowly and deliberately being reduced to a burning hulk, spurting clouds of angry steam as the sea washed over her red-hot decks. Only her deck cargo of timber was keeping her afloat. And yet Hugh Pettigrew continued to command from his battered and burning bridge, and the *Beaverford*'s guns continued to fire. Pettigrew was achieving his object, for while he continued to defy Krancke's guns, the other ships of the convoy were escaping into the night.

For more than four hours the *Beaverford* held the *Scheer* at bay, during which time her radio officers John Fraser and Charles Morris maintained contact with the outside world, sending out detailed reports of the attack on the convoy. Their transmissions were acknowledged, but there was no help near at hand.

Finally, consumed by frustration, Krancke ordered his torpedo gunner to administer the *coup de grâce*. This was an order the *Scheer*'s torpedo officer obeyed with alacrity, for he had rarely been called upon to fire his tubes in anger. And the *Beaverford*, brilliantly lit by the flames on board, was a target not to be missed. The *Scheer* leaned slightly in recoil as the torpedo left its tube, hit the water in a welter of spray and accelerated towards its mark.

An observer on the deck of the *Scheer* described the end of the *Beaverford*:

A great fountain of water leapt out of the sea, shining with a cold silvery light in the moonbeams. There came the roar of an explosion and the sound of smashing wood and a great volume of water falling back into the sea. The torpedo had hit the fore part of the ship and lifted it right out of the water. Water now rushed into her gaping side and the deck cargo slipped as she heeled over. There was a great sound of bursting and cracking now as the wooden cases broke up. The ship's stern rose higher out of the water and then the whole vessel slid under the surface and once again the drama was over. When the first shells burst around the doomed ship the Wireless Officer sent out his last message: 'It's our turn now. So long. The Captain and crew of s.s. Beaverford.'

Radio Officer John Fraser died at his Morse key, alone and far from his village home in the foothills of the Grampian mountains. Throughout the action he had remained at his post, transmitting detailed reports of the attack on the convoy and the destruction of each ship by the *Scheer*.

They all died heroes, those brave men who had followed Captain Hugh Pettigrew into the mouth of Hell when he challenged the mighty *Admiral Scheer*. From the youngest, 16-year-old Steward's Boy Eric Crowhurst on his first voyage, to Fireman Tom Anderson, sixty-one years old, and with a lifetime of ocean seagoing behind him: they gave their lives for others.

There were no survivors to tell of the end of the *Beaverford*, but it seems most likely that when the *Scheer*'s torpedo went home the bombs and shells stacked in the British ship's tween decks simply blew her apart.

The following tribute appeared in the London Evening Standard in 1944:

I do not think the story of how the gallant 'Beaverford' fought to the last has ever been told. There were no survivors for the whole crew perished. Like the 'Jervis Bay', the 'Beaverford' went down with her flag flying – not the White Ensign worn by the 'Jervis Bay' as one of HM ships, but the Red Duster of Britain's Merchant Navy, and in the words of the Captain of the ship next to her in the convoy, 'She did not disgrace the British Merchant Navy.' It was from this Captain that the story was obtained. The 'Beaverford' took the brunt of the raider's attack as her fate shows, after the 'Jervis Bay' had gone down.

At 5 pm on that unforgettable date, Nov.5th 1940, in the North Atlantic, the enemy raider encountered the British convoy. Instantly the 'Jervis Bay' headed for the foe, her guns blazing. The whole weight of the raider's guns were concentrated upon her, but the desperate twenty minutes of her noble effort to draw the raider's fire gave the convoy time to disperse. The 'Jervis Bay' went down at 5-20 pm., and immediately the raider turned to attack the nearer ships of the scattering convoy. Vengefully, the foe singled out the 'Beaverford' for concentrated attack. So it fell to her to take the place of the 'Jervis Bay' and to carry on the delaying action against the enemy, by which so many of the convoy were saved.

Both she and her nearest neighbour in the convoy had thrown out a smokescreen to shield the other ships in their vicinity. These ships then parted company – the CPR ship steaming south and the other going north.

From his bridge and with his aft guns firing the master of the northbound ship could watch the fight almost to its end. For more than 5 hours the 'Beaverford' stayed afloat firing and fighting to the last, pursued by the raider. Using the big reserve of engine power for speed, and superb seamanship for steering and manoeuvring to baffle and evade the enemy's aim, for all that time she held her own, hit by shells but hitting back, and delaying the raider hour by hour while the rest of the convoy made their escape into the rapidly gathering gloom.

It grew so dark during the battle that the raider had to use star shells to illuminate his target and to maintain the range for his guns – a dreadful display of fireworks for Nov.5th. The unequal engagement lasted until 10-45 pm when there was a burst of flame from the 'Beaverford' and her splendid fight was over.

It is thought that her end was due to the firing of a torpedo from the raider. There are none left of her officers and crew to tell what caused that fierce final explosion which sent her to the bottom. She went down in a glare of red flame with a great shower of enemy star shells above her as she sank. She had fought a good fight; she had finished her course.

Further than that, the *Beaverford* and her gallant crew are mentioned only in passing in the many books, articles, poems written to tell the story of HX 84 and the *Admiral Scheer*. The *Jervis Bay* and those who sailed in her, on the other hand received all the accolades a grateful nation could bestow on them, even though their suicidal challenging of the enemy raider was always doomed from the start. The Admiralty's version of the action, which makes no mention of the *Beaverford*'s part, is contained in the citation to Captain Fegen's Victoria Cross, which appeared in the London Gazette on 22 November 1940:

The King has been graciously pleased to approve the award of the VICTORIA CROSS to the late Commander (acting Captain) Edward Stephen Fogarty Fegen, Royal Navy, for valour in challenging hopeless odds and giving his life to save the many ships it was his duty to protect. On the 5th of November 1940, Captain Fegen, in His Majesty's Armed Merchant Cruiser Jervis Bay, was escorting thirty-eight Merchantmen. Sighting a powerful German man-of-war he at once drew clear of the convoy, made straight for the Enemy, and brought his ship between the Raider and her prey, so that they might scatter and escape. Crippled, in flames, unable to reply, for nearly an hour Jervis Bay held the German fire. So she went down, but of the Merchantmen all but four or five were saved.

On 18 November 1940, Mary Brookes, wife of Coal Trimmer/Chief Engineer's Writer Warren Brookes, received a telegram from Canadian Pacific Line informing her that her husband of just twelve months was reported missing at sea, believed killed. On Christmas Eve she received a parcel from the Company. It contained all the letters she had written to her husband since he sailed. They had not been delivered. In July 1941 she received a communication from the Ministry of Pensions informing her that as from August of that year she would receive a widow's pension of fifteen shillings and six pence per week, providing she did not marry again.

In acknowledgment that her husband had given his life for his country, Mary Brookes received the following cyclostyled tribute from Buckingham Palace:

The Queen and I offer you our heartfelt sympathy in your great sorrow.

We pray that your country's gratitude for a life so nobly given in its service may bring you some measure of consolation.

George R.I

This message of condolence, repeated seventy-two times, was circulated to the next of kin of the men of the *Beaverford*, who had willingly given their lives to save others. No medals, not even a commendation or a single word of praise; just silence. It was as though this ship and her crew of unrecognised heroes had never existed.

Chapter 8

THE ONE THAT ALMOST
GOT AWAY

It was just over an hour to midnight on 5 November 1940 when a cataclysmic explosion blew the *Beaverford* apart and she went to the bottom with all her crew. Her loss was a grievous one; 8,000 tons of valuable cargo and seventy-three brave men, but she had played a crucial role in the unfolding drama of that terrible night. Through the skill and tenacity of Captain Hugh Pettigrew she had held off the mighty *Scheer* for almost five hours; dodging, feinting, taunting, all the while firing her two puny guns in defiance. Her sacrifice was not in vain, for as she engaged in this crazy, one-sided duel with the German raider, thirty-three ships and their cargoes escaped into the night.

Having at last disposed of the troublesome *Beaverford*, Kapitän Theodor Krancke found time to take stock of the situation. What had at first promised to be a simple turkey shoot had turned out to be a harrowing confrontation lasting nearly six hours in all, during which time the sun went down and darkness closed in. The cost to the *Scheer* in ammunition alone had been a heavy one. In subduing the *Jervis Bay* she had used up 335 heavy and medium shells, while the whole operation so far had taken a third of her total supply for all guns. And now Krancke's Meteorological Officer was at his elbow anxiously warning of the approach of bad weather. A howling gale that would not only restrict his speed but drain his fuel tanks, adding to the problems he already faced, was something Krancke could well do without. In the action with HX 84 the *Scheer* had suffered significant minor damage on deck, but that could be repaired easily. Losing the radar was a blow, but Krancke was confident he would be able to obtain a new crystal from one of the supply ships. Now, however, it had been discovered that the Arado spotter aircraft, which was stowed on a catapult between the mast and funnel, had also been severely damaged by the blast of the big guns. The aircraft's fuselage was buckled, several frames were broken, and the rudder and ailerons were smashed. Krancke's engineers were confident that they could repair the damage to the seaplane, but it would take some considerable time. Meanwhile, the *Scheer*'s visibility range was seriously restricted.

Throughout the action the *Scheer*'s wireless office had been listening in to distress messages sent by the ships under attack, and there could be no doubt that the British Admiralty was fully aware of the situation. Retribution would almost certainly already be on its way. There had been no reports from Berlin as to the disposition of the British fleet, but there was every possibility that some heavy units, battleships perhaps, were within striking distance.

It so happened that Krancke need not have feared pursuit. The Royal Navy had no big ships handy, and it would be several days before anything capable of challenging the *Scheer* arrived on the scene. However, for Krancke, unaware of what was happening outside his immediate sphere, the threat was very real. His radar was still out of action, his ammunition severely depleted, and his fuel was not unlimited. He decided that he must content himself with five ships sunk and one possible, the tanker *San Demetrio*, last seen drifting abandoned and on fire. As to those that got away, it would be pointless and time consuming to continue to seek them out with star shell and searchlight.

By far the largest of the escaping ships, New Zealand Shipping Company's liner *Rangitiki*, had been straddled by the *Scheer*'s big guns, but reached the cover of the smoke screen unharmed. Captain Barnett reported:

The smoke screen proved most effective and I really do not think we should have got away without it...The San Demetrio seemed to be making a lot of smoke so we took cover in that, and then in the smoke put out by ships ahead of us...

We continued through South to West, it grew dark and cloudy, we passed the Cornish City, and two other ships, but did not see the Fresno City. One of our cylinders was out of action and we were only able to do 13 knots at the best. After dark we steered West and North, realising that the raider would not be likely to stay for long in that vicinity. We turned South, crossed our own track, and on the morning of the 6th turned North again...

Captain Barnett sent out a signal reporting that his ship was being attacked by a German raider, probably of the *Graf Spee* class, but he had resisted the temptation to use his gun, reasoning, correctly as it turned out, that the flash of the 4-inch would immediately pinpoint his position for the *Scheer*'s gunners.

Captain Fraser, of the motor tanker *Erodona*, adopted similar tactics:

...it was pretty obvious that the Raider would, after silencing the escort, make South after the scattering convoy. Therefore, owing to this vessel being last, I decided to take full advantage of the smoke screen left behind by the others and ourselves. The main motors were turning at their utmost capacity, and I steered W through the smoke and ultimately N round it and thus eluded the Raider by steering in a Northerly direction, this being the direction the Raider approached the convoy in the first place...

Third Officer Fellingham, of the *Trefusis*, wrote:

Darkness was by now almost total and the ADMIRAL SCHEER started using a searchlight with which to find its targets. So, every time we saw the flashes of its guns or its searchlight we put our stern to that position and steamed away as fast as our engines could take us. We saw several explosions when the ADMIRAL SCHEER'S guns scored a hit but, thankfully, we noticed that the action was taking place further and further from us. By 2200 the gun flashes and the flames of the ships on fire had all dipped below the horizon. We found that we were heading northwards and we decided to continue on that course for the rest of the night.

The *Trefusis*, a 7-knotter of First World War vintage, described by Fellingham as 'probably the slowest ship in Convoy HX 84', was extremely lucky to have escaped the raider's guns. The same could not be said for Reardon Smith's *Fresno City*, sister to the commodore ship *Cornish City*. A 14-knot motor vessel of just under 5,000 tons gross, the *Fresno City* carried a crew of forty-seven under the command of Captain R.L.A. Lawson. She was down to her Winter North Atlantic marks with 8,129 tons of Canadian maize.

The *Fresno City*, the third ship of Column 2 in HX 84, had a grandstand view of the closing moments of the fierce duel between the *Scheer* and the *Jervis Bay*. Captain Lawson later wrote in his report:

> *Convoy was now turning to starboard and this vessel's engines going full speed ahead – 14 knots. The second salvo, which immediately followed the first, struck the Escort on the port side, a few feet above the water line as she was turning to port to face the enemy. Fire was observed to break out almost immediately. The third salvo hit the bridge and superstructure. I saw no more of this action as my attention was directed to manoeuvring vessel past the slower moving vessels ahead...*

By this time the convoy had come round onto a westerly heading, and the *Fresno City*'s powerful Doxford engine was straining at the leash, its pistons thumping out a mad tattoo and producing more revolutions than they had ever done in eleven years of tramping the oceans.

As he broke clear of the other ships, Lawson ordered smoke floats to be dropped and instructed his 4-inch gun's crew to open fire. This order went out in the heat of the moment, for the raider, although clearly visible, was well beyond the range of the *Fresno City*'s gun.

Taking cover in the smoke screen, to which he had just added his own contribution, Lawson began to alter to the south in easy steps of ten degrees at a time. Finally, when the ship was steadied up onto a south-south-westerly heading, he made a dash for the horizon. By this time it was dark, and with the gun flashes and dancing flames of the burning ships fast dropping astern, it seemed that the *Fresno City* had escaped to sail another day.

For more than an hour the heavily laden ship raced through the night steadily increasing the miles between her and the scene of the attack. By 2230, the flames of the Dante's Inferno created by the *Scheer*'s guns had finally dipped astern. Only then did Captain Lawson allow himself to relax and consider that he had indeed made good his escape. His assumption was to prove premature.

Ten minutes later, the darkness on the starboard quarter was split apart by the brilliant white beam of a powerful searchlight. The beam moved from side to side, probing, and lighting up the tops of the rising waves, which were now beginning to tumble and foam as the wind rose. Before Lawson was able to take avoiding action, the searchlight swept

11-inch gun turret in action – Three giant shells were spinning through the night air. (Helepolis)

A four-stacker Town-class destroyer – The most dubious gift since the Trojan Horse. (Vallejo Naval & Historical Museum)

Admiral Scheer bottom up, Kiel April 1945 – An ignominious end for a once-proud ship. (Foto Gallerie)

S.S. BEAVERFORD
OUR SHIP
LOST WITH ALL HANDS
IN ACTION
5TH NOVEMBER 1940.

Beaverford memorial plaque – Anybody's for a few shillings. (Downhills Central School)

Captain Sven Olander (left) – An unlikely hero. (William Oag)

Convoy in mid-Atlantic – The barometer was falling steadily. (Merchant Navy Association)

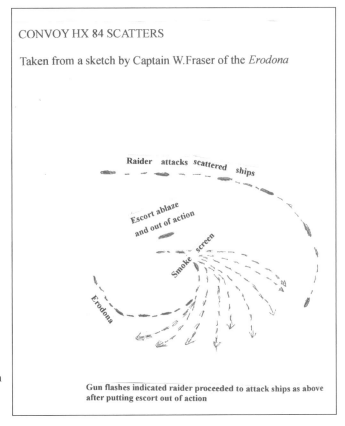

CONVOY HX 84 SCATTERS

Taken from a sketch by Captain W. Fraser of the *Erodona*

Raider attacks scattered ships

Escort ablaze and out of action

Smoke screen

Erodona

Gun flashes indicated raider proceeded to attack ships as above after putting escort out of action

Convoy scatters – From sketch by Captain W. Fraser of the *Erodona*.

HMS *Jervis Bay*'s officers – Acting Captain Edward Fogarty Fegen seated fourth from left. *(Telegraph Journal*, Saint John, NB, Canada)

HMS *Jervis Bay* – An ageing ex-passenger liner. (Aberdeen & Commonwealth Line)

Jervis Bay survivors on board the *Stureholm* – British sources did not comment on the rescue. (William Oag)

M.V. *Stureholm* – The Good Samaritan of HX 84. (Photoship)

Theodor Krancke (left), promoted Vice Admiral, with General Rommel and others inspecting Atlantic Wall defences prior to D-Day. (Photo Bundesarchiv)

Panzerschiff *Admiral Scheer* – Came over the horizon with a bone in her teeth. (Hilchebach)

S.S. *Beaverford* – Assumed the role of aggressor. (Canadian Pacific Steamships)

S.S. *Mopan* – Dinner would be late. (Elders & Fyffes)

San Demetrio – A wonderful propaganda coup for Britain. (Helderline)

Stern-mounted 4-inch – Many dated from the turn of the century. (Dept. of National Defence/Library Archives, Canada)

across the *Fresno City* then locked on to her, bathing the escaping ship in a blinding blue-white glare.

Every man aboard the *Admiral Scheer*, from their Captain on the bridge to the lowliest powder boy below, had been at their action stations for ten hours since first sighting the *Mopan*. They were tired, and looking forward to a new dawn undisturbed by the crash of gunfire and the stench of burning cordite. Having decided that no more could be gained by chasing after the remaining ships of HX 84, Krancke's intention was to seek clear sea-room to the south, and then rendezvous with the *Nordmark*, his supply ship, in the region of 23° North. This was based on the premise that the Royal Navy would be expecting him to either continue raiding in the North Atlantic or head directly for a French Biscay port at full speed. It was just by pure chance – or 'Sod's Law' as any seaman would have it – that the *Fresno City* was also going south, and on a collision course with the *Scheer*.

Once again the alarm bells rang out on the raider, and her heavy-eyed gunners were jerked back into immediate readiness. Lookouts on the bridge had sighted what was described as 'a modern motor-ship of about 8,000 BRT'. After examining the stranger through his binoculars, Krancke made a small alteration of course to close with her, and when about 2 miles off, ordered his searchlight crew to illuminate the target.

Captain Lawson describes subsequent events:

At 2240 on the 5th November, in position 51° 47 N 33°29 W, without anything having been seen, suddenly a searchlight was directed upon my vessel by another ship close up on the starboard quarter. Travelling at high speed, this vessel opened fire from about 200 feet when just abaft the beam; three shots were fired in rapid succession from an upper midship turret, three from starboard and one from a port turret. The guns were fired in rapid succession, not in salvoes. The shells were directed in the order engineroom aft, engineroom forward, No. 1 Hold, No. 2 Hold, No. 2a Hold, No. 4 Hold and No. 5 Hold. The seventh shell did not explode though the shock of impact was felt. The engines stopped immediately the first shell struck the vessel. I remained on the starboard side of the bridge during the action, but was unable to see anything of the enemy vessel as I was blinded by the searchlight. The only thing about which I am quite certain is that she had three gun turrets forward.

Later, from the lifeboat, I observed the shell hole in the fore part of the engineroom was almost cleanly drilled and appeared to be about 12 in diameter. I would have thought, and I express this opinion as a layman, that guns of this calibre would make much louder reports. Immediately the shells exploded hatch covers, etc. were blown skyward and the forward hatch tarpaulins were draped over the cross-trees. All compartments, except No.5 Hold, immediately caught on fire. When No.2 Hold was struck an object hit and demolished the starboard wing of the bridge.

Dazzled by the *Scheer*'s powerful searchlight perhaps, Captain Lawson grossly underestimated the distance between the two vessels as 200 feet. The raider had, in fact, opened fire from a distance of 1¾ miles, but this was close enough for her shells to hit home with a devastating effect on the startled merchantman. Theodor Krancke wrote in his book:

From the foremast of the motor ship flew a long canvas windsock used for ventilating the cargo holds (maize in bulk is notorious for sweating, and the Fresno City's cargo was obviously no exception). Flames rose up to it from the deck and set it alight. Another heavy shell had torn open the ship's side and caused fires in the interior. Framed by the ripped and blasted plates the fierce fires made the water glow red like burning lava. The vessel was obviously lost and the Scheer sailed on, leaving her last victim behind her.

The *Fresno City*'s engine-room, being Krancke's primary target, was reduced to a smoking shambles. Her main generator received a direct hit, resulting in an immediate loss of all power. Other shells holed the ship below the waterline in several places, and before she drifted to a halt she was already sinking.

When he received reports of the extent of the damage, Captain Lawson decided the time had come to abandon ship. Unfortunately, when he hit the button to sound the customary six shorts and a long on the air whistle, it produced only a faint hiss of escaping air. The supply of compressed air to the whistle had been cut off. Lawson turned to Chief Officer Payne, who was beside him on the bridge, and instructed him to muster the crew on the boat deck. Payne left the bridge at a run.

Captain Lawson remained on the bridge until the way was off the ship, then, having thrown all code books and secret papers over the side in their weighted bag, he left the bridge and went to join the others on the boat deck. Much to his surprise, when he reached the boat deck he found it deserted. The port lifeboat had already left the ship's side, and the starboard boat was suspended bow-down from its after fall. Obviously, in the rush to launch the boat the forward fall had run away, resulting in disaster.

Lawson set off to search the ship for survivors, and within minutes met Second Officer Gleghorn and eight others, who had been sheltering in the saloon alleyway while the ship was under fire. With the aid of these men Lawson was able to re-secure the starboard boat and make it ready for launching. He then continued his search for survivors.

The engine-room, which had suffered the brunt of the *Scheer*'s bombardment, was still on fire and too hot to enter. Of Fourth Engineer Hopper and Junior Engineer Muir, who had been on watch below, there was no sign. The midship's accommodation was deserted, and moving forward, Lawson found that one of Krancke's shells had wrecked the crews' quarters, which were also still burning. On the foredeck lay the badly mutilated body of Ordinary Seaman D.R. Smith, and as Lawson examined him, Able Seamen Mackie and Finnis, both seriously injured, came staggering down the deck. They had escaped from the burning accommodation through a hatch on the forecastle head.

The injured men were made as comfortable as possible in the remaining lifeboat, which was then launched with some difficulty owing to the heavy swell now running. Lawson and the others boarded, and bent their backs to the oars to take the boat clear of the ship. Just half an hour had elapsed since the beginning of the attack.

Once clear of the ship, the missing port lifeboat was sighted. Under the command of Chief Officer Payne, this boat contained twenty-three men, all uninjured. With the thirteen in Lawson's boat, this accounted for all the *Fresno City*'s crew, with the exception of the unfortunate Ordinary Seaman Smith.

Despite strenuous efforts to keep the two boats together, they drifted apart during the night, and when daylight came on the 6th, Lawson found that he was alone on an increasingly hostile sea. During the night they had watched the death throes of their ship. She had burned fiercely until 0400, offering a comforting light for the men in the tossing boat, then, at 0435, her superstructure was seen to collapse, and the flames were quenched as she sank.

Reasoning that any rescue ship that might be on the way would probably go to the position of the initial attack on the convoy, some 80 miles to the north, Lawson set course for that position. After thirty-six hours of hard rowing and sailing, the approximate position was reached at noon on the 7th. There was nothing to be seen, no ships, not even a scrap of wreckage from the recent battle.

Swallowing their disappointment, the survivors set course to the eastwards, and home, facing up to the possibility that a very long and hazardous voyage lay ahead of them. During the night that followed the weather deteriorated rapidly, and by dawn of the 8th it was blowing force 8 from the west, with high seas and heavy rain squalls. Fortunately, the gale was to their advantage, and the boat was able to sail steadily before the wind with only a small jib sail rigged.

By daybreak on the 9th Lawson estimated they had covered some 200 miles since striking out for the land, with another 600 miles to go. There had been no let-up in the weather, and with the spray blown off the rough seas continually lashing the occupants of the boat, morale was at a low ebb. Then, as the sky lightened in the east, smoke was seen on the horizon to starboard followed by the masts and funnel of a ship. Lawson at once altered course to cross the track of the ship, and at noon they were picked up by the Greek steamer *Mount Taygetus*. Captain Lawson later wrote:

> *Captain Samathrakis and his crew received us warmly and did everything they possibly could for us. No more thoughtful care and attention could have been given us by our own families. The wounded men, Mackie and Finnis, were put to bed in the ship's hospital to rest before having their wounds dressed. The Chief Officer, Mr Domanicos, had some medical knowledge and was most assiduous in his attention to the men.*

Luck had been with Captain Lawson and his crew. Not only had they escaped the destruction of their ship by the *Admiral Scheer* with only one man lost, but they had been extremely fortunate in their chance meeting with the *Mount Taygetus*. Another week or so exposed to the wrath of the elements and few of them would have survived to see their native land again.

Dawn on 6 November found the *Scheer* heading south in a rising gale. During the day Krancke wirelessed a report to Berlin giving details of his attack on Convoy HX 84. Rather optimistically it would seem, he claimed to have sunk nine ships with a total of 86,000 tons gross, with four others damaged. Eager for news of a significant victory, Berlin seized on Krancke's report and enlarged on it. The following appeared in the New York Times on 9 November:

BERLIN Nov. 8 – German surface warships operating in the North Atlantic along the British shipping lanes to North America have attacked and destroyed a British convoy, the High Command reported today. A total of 86,000 tons of British shipping, it is asserted, was sent to the bottom.

This is the first official German report of the naval action in which, according to reports received here yesterday from the United States, the British vessels Rankitiki and Cornish City were sunk. The communiqué on the action, however, did not mention the ships' names or their number, but reports complete destruction of the entire convoy.

(Unofficial but informed sources in Berlin were quoted by the Associated Press as saying fifteen or twenty ships were destroyed. The number believed to be in the convoy at the time of the first reports of the incident here Tuesday was forty. According to The United Press, they had a naval escort. In London the story was called 'not likely').

News of this success of the German high seas patrol was received with frank elation in Berlin. It is called the outstanding success so far reported by the German surface warships, which month by month are said to patrol the ocean shipping lanes far from their home ports. Together with German submarines and bomber planes they form the triple threat blockade instrument which at the present stage is one of Germany's most important weapons in the war against Great Britain.

The significance of the action reported today, German quarters point out, lies in the fact that the convoy was attacked and destroyed at its source. Thus, they state, it is evident that Germany not only is able to blockade Britain in her own waters, catching her convoys as they approach their port of destination, but also in overseas lanes.

(The SOS messages from the ships being attacked Tuesday gave their position as in mid-Atlantic, half way between Ireland and Newfoundland.)

It is now said here that Germany's navy has proved itself capable of operating successfully at long as well as short range, which brings up a new significant factor in blockade warfare.

In fact, the newspaper Angriff tonight asserts that 'a new chapter of naval warfare has begun'.

Details of the naval action are lacking in Berlin. The German press repeats reports from the United States that the engagement took place about 1000 miles east of Newfoundland. Nor is there any indication here as to the type of vessels that carried out the German attack. (The shelled freighters themselves reported their attacker as a pocket battleship of the Admiral Graf Spee class, presumably the Luetzow or Admiral Scheer.)

BERLIN, Nov. 8 (UP) – The official DNB news agency said today the convoy sunk by surface warships Tuesday was taken by complete surprise. So sudden was the attack, it added, that only two ships were able to send out distress messages before they were sunk. The others were said to have gone down before they could call for help.

The agency said the convoy was on a "most important" transport route. It was escorted by strong units of the British fleet, DNB said, and therefore apparently considered itself in no danger.

LONDON, Nov. 8 (UP) – A British naval spokesman, commenting on today's German High Command assertion that German surface raiders in the Atlantic had destroyed an entire British convoy, said:

The Admiralty, as well as Mackay Radio, has received a message that one ship was being shelled. It is not known which ship was being shelled or how many ships were in the convoy.

In his book published in 1956, Kapitän Theodor Krancke states:

The general investigation and the sifting of all reports gave the following picture which also includes those targets which were bombarded only for a short time and not persistently, whereby the target numbers are those previously used in the description of the action. The tonnage is that estimated on board the Scheer. In brackets after the target are the name and actual tonnage of the ship in question as revealed by published evidence after the war, whereby with regard to targets 9 and 10 the question remains open as to whether they really were Admiralty vessels. Further, with regard to target 9 it is possible that it is the same as target 12, whilst target 10 may be the target 2 already bombarded and in any case not sunk.

Target	Sunk	Gross BRT	Damaged
1. Auxiliary cruiser *Jervis Bay*	14,200	14,164	–
2. A tanker (*San Demetrio*)	–		8,000
3. A freighter (name unknown)	–		3,000
4. Troop transport (*Rangitiki*)	–		16,700
5. A freighter (seen at angle from aft)			–
6. A freighter (*Andalusia*)			3,000
7. A freighter (*Maidan*)	10,000	7,008	–
8. A freighter (*Trewellard*)	6,000	5,201	–
9. A freighter (Admiralty ship?)	10,000		–
10. A tanker (Admiralty ship or possibly target No.2 *San Demetrio* again)			
11. A freighter (*Kenbane Head*)	7,000	5,225	–
12. *Beaverford*	10,000	10,042	–
13. A freighter (*Fresno City*)	10,000	4,955	–
And in addition the *Mopan*	5,389		

When the official count was made, it was revealed that although Krancke had dealt HX 84 some hard knocks, the net result of his attack on the convoy was a lot less serious than he claimed. The *Scheer*'s guns had in fact sunk, in addition to the *Jervis Bay*, five merchant ships out of thirty-seven with a total of 33,371 tons gross. And of the seventeen tankers with the convoy, only one, the *San Demetrio*, had been set on fire – and she was still afloat. As to the cargo lost, some 40,000 tons of steel, timber, grain and munitions had gone down with the ships, but the granaries and arsenals of the Americas were bottomless, and so long as Britain provided the ships the cargoes would flow.

With typical aplomb, the Admiralty sought to turn what can only be described as a first class disaster into another heroic tale illustrating the Royal Navy facing up to impossible odds. To them the pot was always half full. Late on the evening of 12 November they issued the following communiqué:

> *It can now be stated with certainty that all except nine of the ships in the convoy attacked by an enemy surface raider on the night of November 5 escaped. The convoy consisted of 38 ships of which one had dropped astern. It will be remembered that the German High*

Command announced that the whole of this convoy had been destroyed.
It is possible that some of the ships still missing may be safe. That
nearly three-quarters of this large convoy escaped destruction at the
hands of the powerful German raider was due to the high degree of
efficiency shown by the captains of the merchant vessels in scattering
and making use of smoke and to the very gallant action of H.M.S.
Jervis Bay (Acting Captain E.S.F. Fegen, R.N.) which was escorting
the convoy. H.M.S. Jervis Bay steered for the enemy and engaged her
with greatly inferior armament, thus enabling the majority of the
convoy to make good their escape. H.M.S. Jervis Bay continued to
engage the enemy after she had been hit and was burning furiously.
Nearly two hours after the beginning of the engagement an explosion
was seen to take place on board H.M.S. Jervis Bay, and it is regretted
that she must be considered as lost. It is known that 65 of the survivors
of H.M.S. Jervis Bay are on board a merchant ship.

The *Scheer*, meanwhile, was heading for a rendezvous with the tanker
Eurofeld some 600 miles to the north-east of the West Indies. The
meeting was long overdue for the *Eurofeld*. On the outbreak of war in
September 1939 she had been in Aruba loading a cargo of oil, on
completion of which she received orders from Berlin to make for the
Canary Islands. There, with the blessing of the Spanish authorities, she
had lain undisturbed in Santa Cruz, Tenerife, until she was ordered to
sea again in the late summer of 1940.

By this time the *Eurofeld*'s engines were in a poor state thanks to the
lack of proper maintenance and spares, and when she ventured out into
the Atlantic, her top speed was in the region of 5 knots. Her meeting
with the *Scheer* on 12 November consequently had a double purpose.
She was to refuel the raider, in return for which the *Scheer*'s engineers
would do their best to repair the *Eurofeld*'s engines. When the *Scheer*
sailed from the rendezvous on the 20th of the month, she was well
placed to make another, more profitable, rendezvous.

The 7,448-ton British ship *Port Hobart* sailed from Liverpool on 4
November, bound New Zealand via the Panama Canal. She had left the
convoy when abeam of the Straits of Gibraltar on the 20th, and
continued unescorted towards the Caribbean. Unfortunately for her,
after leaving the convoy she ran straight into the arms of Kapitän
Theodor Krancke.

At 1115 on the morning of 24 November, the *Port Hobart* sighted smoke on the horizon to the north-west, and soon the mast and funnel of a ship approaching at speed were visible from the bridge. As the stranger breasted the horizon it could be seen that she was a warship, and as the Master of the *Port Hobart* had not been notified of the presence of British warships in the area, he immediately sent out an RRR signal.

At three minutes before midday, Krancke opened fire with his 11-inch guns at a range of 2 miles, leaving the *Port Hobart* in no doubt of his intentions. What followed was predictable. The British ship hove to, she was boarded by an armed party, and her crew taken prisoner. The *Scheer* then sank their ship by gunfire. Krancke continued on his way, well satisfied that his first Atlantic sortie, which had not begun well, was at last beginning to pay dividends.

Chapter 9

THE RESCUE

The dying moments of HMS *Jervis Bay* were chaotic and bloody. Able Seaman Sam Patience, manning a gun on the port side of the AMC's forecastle head, wrote many years later describing the carnage:

The shells were coming over. You could hear the whine of the shells. You didn't know where they were going to land. First of all the bridge got hit, and the radio room. The ship was on fire and the salvoes were coming over and blokes standing beside you were getting killed, burned alive, and all this, and heads blown off where I was standing, or P1 Gun, which was my action station...

After we'd turned towards the battleship a salvo came over and blew S1 Gun (that was on the opposite side), the gun, the mounting and the crew right off the focsle. We were subjected to that fire more than necessary really, because the ship stayed afloat for a long time. I didn't feel frightened at the time because I was too busy doing what I had to do on P1 Gun and there was no time to think about fear. I was too occupied to feel frightened. Later on, as the ship was sinking and most of the people had been killed, then I was thinking not so much frightened but how to get out of it. That was the main objective. Self-preservation. The ship was smashed to bits and started sinking. She took a long time...

The *Jervis Bay* was on fire, her bridge in ruins, her hull holed like a colander above and below the waterline, and many of her crew were dead or dying. Yet, steering from aft with the emergency gear and floating on the empty drums in her holds, she fought on. Then, a flurry of shells from the raider destroyed her after steering position, blasted open her engine-room, and silenced her forward guns. Without power or steering, she drifted to a halt, unable to train her remaining guns, and sinking slowly by the stern. It was all over.

Fegen was dead, and so was his first lieutenant, Lieutenant Commander George Roe, who had sailed as Chief Officer in the *Jervis Bay* before the demands of war ended her carefree cruising days and turned her into a fighting ship. It now fell to Lieutenant Commander Keith Morrison, the only senior navigating officer left alive, to take command of the armed merchant cruiser in her dying moments. Thirty-eight-year-old Morrison, another merchant seaman who had answered the call to arms, had in another life been First Officer sailing with the Orient Line to the Far East. He was a professional seaman and navigator of the highest calibre, and now he was facing the ultimate challenge.

Before sailing on this his last voyage, Morrison must have had a premonition of death, leaving behind a letter to be handed to his wife in the event of his death. In it he wrote: 'If I have to die I am not afraid to do so & I know I will have died supporting a righteous cause. Don't let my death affect the attitude towards the war; and we must win for the sake of civilisation. If we were to lose, my death & those of many others would have been in vain...' In his letter, quite unintentionally perhaps, Keith Morrison expressed the sentiments of most British seamen of his day.

There was, in fact, very little left for Lieutenant Commander Morrison to command. The German gunners had done their work well: the *Jervis Bay* was lying on her side, her lee rails under and in danger of blowing up any minute as the flames spread towards her magazines. Her guns were now silent, and she would fight no more. It only remained for her new commander to save those few who were still alive. Morrison gave the order to abandon ship. He was last seen standing on the foredeck with his great friend Surgeon Lieutenant Commander Tyrrell Evans. Both men were severely wounded and they died with their ship.

Every one of the *Jervis Bay*'s lifeboats was shot through with holes, and completely unusable. All that could be organised was the ship's jolly boat – and that was holed – and one large Carley float. To make matters worse, with the coming of darkness the weather had deteriorated dramatically. The wind had freshened to near-gale and a dangerous sea was building up. It was only with great difficulty that the jolly boat and the Carley float were launched. They were followed by a second raft that had been found. This was constructed of 40-gallon drums and wooden sparring, and was most probably the ship's painting raft, crude but strongly made. While the survivors, many of whom were wounded, abandoned ship, the *Scheer* continued to fire on them, filling the air with lethal shrapnel. More men were dying.

Sam Patience takes up the story again:

> *I realised the ship was going down. I couldn't swim. I thought, well, I've got to take a decision here. Either you go down with the ship or you go over the side. I got hold of a ship's lifebuoy. I had a good look around. There was only one guy who was still alive with me at the time. There were only two of us both fishermen. He came from Hull. I said, 'Come on, Bill, let's get over the side.' He said, 'But I can't swim.' I said, 'Neither can I, but I'm off. I'm going.' And I went over the side and got away from the ship before she went down. And I thought I could survive. I thought I was strong enough to survive until morning with the lifebuoy, thinking I would get picked up in the daylight. I would never have survived all night. It was too cold in November 1940, and while I was sliding over the side I could see I had injured my hand, all my fingers were hanging off. I didn't notice it at the time.*
>
> *I got in the water and started paddling about, then all of a sudden a lifeboat came up. It was the only boat that got away. I didn't know any boats had got away. They dragged me on board, lifebelt and all...*

Leading Seaman James (Slinger) Wood, gunlayer on one of the midships guns, was caught in a hail of shrapnel:

> *I looked down and saw my left leg was skinned and that I had stopped a piece in my right leg. We were helpless, but we kept our guns firing as long as we could. It wasn't much use but it was something to occupy our minds...*

It was with some relief that at last Wood received the order to abandon ship. Throwing off his heavy duffel coat and boots he went over the side, and for the second time since the outbreak of war he found himself treading water as his ship went down. The first occasion had been in the relatively calm waters of the Thames Estuary in November 1939, when the destroyer *Blanche* had been sunk by a magnetic mine. Then he had been picked up within minutes by another destroyer. This time it was different. This was the icy Atlantic, it was blowing a gale, and there were no other ships in sight. Wood remembers:

I could see a raft tossing on the rough seas about 200 yards away – my wounds were bothering me, and I don't know how I ever made it. But I did. Jerry wasn't satisfied with getting our ship. He tried to get us while we were in the water, firing shrapnel at us…

In retrospect, it seems unlikely that the *Scheer*'s gunners were deliberately firing at the men in the water. Theodor Krancke, for all that he was an enemy to be feared, was a humane man – as he would demonstrate in his dealings with other ships during the voyage.

Able Seaman Tom Davison – 'Davo' to his shipmates – survived the shrapnel and took to the water when it became obvious that the *Jervis Bay* was about to go down. Twenty-eight-year-old Davison, married with a young daughter, had every reason to live, and was confident he could survive in the water. Steeled by the strict regime of the Gravesend Sea School, he had begun his sea-going career as a deckhand in a coastal collier, unquestionably one of the toughest and most unrewarding berths at sea. He later graduated to deep-sea ships, sailing with the Bristol City Line until, as a naval reservist, he was called to the colours when war broke out.

Swimming clear of the sinking ship, Davison found himself in a sea of floating debris, but none of it large enough to support his weight. He swam on, his body numbed by the icy grip of the Atlantic. The flames from the burning ship were now extinguished, and the darkness all around him was impenetrable. But despite the rough seas and the stinging spray that constantly lashed at his face, he kept swimming and searching: he knew that if he stopped he would die.

Gradually, but inevitably, the extreme cold, fatigue, and the trauma of the night began to sap Tom Davison's strength, and he found himself longing for a quick death. The prospect of giving up, of just sinking below the angry waves into the dark womb below, became very tempting. Then he heard voices, and he was wide awake and fighting again. He had found the only Carley float to survive the *Jervis Bay*.

Davison's elation was short-lived. There were so many men on the raft that they were literally shoulder to shoulder; a groaning, cursing mass of sodden humanity. The raft was so overloaded and so low in the water that the waves were breaking clean over it. There was no chance of climbing aboard, and Davison had to be content with hanging on to one of the grab lines. Now, at least, he could stay afloat, but how long would it be before the sea took him?

Slinger Wood was one of the lucky ones to find a place on board the Carley float. In later years he remembered: 'We were on the raft for nine and a half hours, sitting in water up to our chins most of the time. All I had on was a pair of trousers and a jersey. The sea was pretty rough and there was a north-easterly blowing. There were 34 of us on our raft out of a crew of about 250, but many had been killed in action.'

There was only one seaman officer on the raft, Midshipman Ronald Butler. He had been in the water for several hours before boarding, but immediately took charge, showing 'outstanding leadership and initiative'. Butler still had his torch, and he used this to good effect flashing SOS all around the horizon in the hope of attracting a rescue ship. Meanwhile, Slinger Wood, despite his terrible wounds, was having some success in raising morale by encouraging the survivors to sing, leading them in raucous choruses of 'Roll Out The Barrel' and 'There'll Always Be An England'. At any other time Slinger Wood would have been ridiculed, but on that night he saved many a life.

Drifting near the Carley float, but unseen in the darkness, was the *Jervis Bay*'s jolly boat, which although holed in the stern, carried another twenty survivors, including Sam Patience. And beyond that was the ship's painting raft, also damaged by shellfire, but supporting twelve men. It is said that at least another thirty men were out there clinging to floating wreckage.

There seemed to be little hope of rescue for these unfortunate men. They were 800 miles from the nearest land, and it might be days before help came, by which time most of them would have died from exposure. As for the other ships of Convoy HX 84, they had scattered to the four winds, the primary duty of their various masters being to save their ships and their cargoes. They would not be coming back to pick up anyone.

But the hapless *Jervis Bay* survivors were not completely alone. To the south, where the guns still thundered and flashed, the heroic *Beaverford*, by this time a burning wreck, was still fighting her desperate rearguard action swopping shell for shell with the *Admiral Scheer*. And with her, somewhere hidden in that dark stormy night, was a ship destined to become the Good Samaritan of HX 84. She was the Swedish-flag *Stureholm*.

The *Stureholm*, a 4,575-ton motor vessel of the Swedish America-Mexico Line of Gothenburg, built in 1919, was one of the first diesel-engined ships on the transatlantic run. Sailing under a neutral flag, she was carrying 6,850 tons of steel and scrap iron loaded in Boston for Grangemouth and had joined HX 84 at Halifax. In command was 60-year-old Captain Sven Olander, plump, amiable and balding, an unlikely hero. Despite his unassuming appearance, Olander was a shrewd leader of men, and a humanitarian to the core. His crew, a mixed bunch consisting of nineteen Swedes, six Danes, two Norwegians, one Finn, one Dutchman and a lone Scot, held him in high respect.

When the *Admiral Scheer* had first appeared on the scene, the *Stureholm* made her break under the cover of the smoke with the other merchantmen, but after witnessing the way the *Jervis Bay* sacrificed herself to save the convoy, Captain Olander decided that if any of her crew survived, he could not leave them to die in the water.

As was customary in Swedish merchant ships when there was a crucial decision to be made involving the safety of the crew, Olander called his men together and asked them if they were prepared to go back to look for survivors. He made an impassioned plea, saying, 'You saw what the *Jervis Bay* has done to save us all. She was right in the guns of the enemy. She did not have a chance and we all knew it. But she rode like a hero and stayed to the last to give us a chance to run for it. Now I would like to go back and see if there's anyone still in the water. I shan't do it without your agreement. Those who agree put up their hands.'

Seen in the cold light of day more than seventy years on, Captain Olander's proposal was nothing short of suicidal. Nevertheless, although many Scandinavian crews were pro-German, the men of the *Stureholm* voted almost unanimously to go back. Before he turned his ship about, Olander had large Swedish flags hung from the bridge and illuminated by floodlights. Then, by watching the gun flashes and the sweeping searchlight of the *Scheer*, he established the position of the raider, and keeping below the horizon, carefully skirted around behind her. He was taking a fearful risk, but he hoped that if the *Stureholm* was spotted her neutrality might be respected.

As the Swedish ship embarked on her errand of mercy the North Atlantic was beginning to show its true winter face; the wind was freshening from the south, already up to force 5, the waves were steepening and the swell taking on a ponderous roll.

On board the *Jervis Bay*'s jolly boat, loaded down to her gunwales with twenty men, some of them wounded, conditions were becoming unbearable. The boat was holed in the stern, and taking on water at an alarming rate. Although every effort was being made to head up into the wind, the boat was constantly drifting beam on to the waves and rolling so violently that it was in danger of capsizing. There was no shelter from the weather, and the icy spray torn off the breaking wavetops saturated their clothes and lashed at their faces with cruel insistency. There was no escaping the wrath of the ocean.

It was approaching midnight when a young seaman in the bows of the boat called out that he had seen a light ahead. The horror of the night momentarily forgotten, every eye strained to penetrate the darkness, but the light did not show again. Later they became aware of a vague shadow crossing their bows. The shadow became the outline of a ship, and the slow, steady beat of an engine was heard. As weak as they were, the half-drowned survivors raised a cheer.

The stranger came closer, then the beat of her engine was stilled. The sound of voices was heard, calling out in English; but to the absolute horror of the British survivors the accent was unmistakeably Germanic. After all they had endured, they were about to be taken prisoner.

It was then that they heard above the noise of the wind and waves, 'Aye, ye're all right now, boys.' This time the accent was pure Glasgow. The caller was the *Stureholm*'s Scottish greaser.

The crowded boat came alive again. Oars were dipped with a will, and they crossed astern of the ship, and came up on her lee side. Rope ladders rattled down from the deck of the *Stureholm*, and those who were able climbed up the ship's side. The wounded and exhausted were hauled aboard by some of the Swedish seamen. Even though the rescue was carried out in darkness and with the jolly boat rising and falling crazily on the heaving waves, not one man was lost.

Once aboard, the twenty survivors were taken below, stripped of their clothes and rubbed down until their circulation returned. They were given dry clothes, hot coffee and generous tots of schnapps. The injured were made comfortable and their wounds dressed.

On being told that other survivors had got away on two rafts and that there might be men still alive in the water, Captain Olander manned the *Jervis Bay*'s jolly boat with his own men, and sent it away in charge of Second Officer Berner.

After more than eight hours drifting aimlessly in rapidly worsening weather, the occupants of the only Carley float to be launched from the *Jervis Bay* were almost past caring. They had survived the sinking of their ship, but to what end? Suddenly, at about 0330 on the 6th, 22-year-old Acting Sub Lieutenant Hugh Pattinson brought the raft alive again with a shout: 'Is that a ship?'

Pattinson, although gravely wounded, had sighted a shadow on the water which was now hardening into the outline of a ship. Midshipman Butler, whose torch was not yet exhausted, immediately began flashing SOS at the ship. It might be the enemy come back to finish them off, but who cared?

There was no answering signal, but after a while there was the creak of oars in rowlocks, and a small boat emerged from the darkness. None of those on the raft recognised the boat as the *Jervis Bay*'s jolly boat, and they were puzzled by the guttural accent of the oarsmen, but this was no time to pick and choose. There was a concerted sigh of relief when the boat came alongside the Carley float and the nationality of the rescuers was revealed.

The jolly boat took off fifteen of the more severely injured survivors and rowed back to the *Stureholm*, which was hove to within a few hundred yards. By this time, however, there was a very rough sea running, and it was only with great difficulty that the wounded men were taken on board the Swedish ship.

It was now obvious to Captain Olander that to attempt to rescue more men with the small boat was too dangerous, and he ordered his boat's crew back on board. The jolly boat was then abandoned to the elements, and Olander manoeuvred his ship so that the Carley float drifted alongside. Lights were put over the side, a rope ladder dropped, and with the raft heaving up and down on the waves, and slamming against the ship's side, one by one the survivors scrambled aboard the *Stureholm*. It was not an easy boarding, as most of the rescued were injured in one way or another, but under the direction of young Midshipman Butler, and with the help of the Swedish ship's crew, not one man was lost. Last on board were the bodies of three men who had died on the crowded raft during the night. They were 22-year-old Acting Sub Lieutenant (E) Hugh Pattinson RNVR, naval reservist Seaman Alexander Webster and one of the *Jervis Bay*'s original crew Second Cook Harold Hinstridge.

After having been unable to find room on board the Carley float, Tom Davison allowed himself to drift off into the darkness. His body was already becoming numb with the bitter cold, and it seemed that it would be only a matter of minutes before he must surrender to the sea. Then, for the second time that night, he heard the sound of voices, and a shadow on the water became the *Jervis Bay*'s painting raft. The frail structure, composed of 40-gallon drums and wooden spars, was already crowded with about a dozen men, but room was found for Davison, and he climbed on board.

Able Seaman Jack Barker, still in his teens, later described conditions on the raft:

> *Eventually, there were ten or twelve of us on this raft, pretty well shocked and feeling the effects of exposure: a gut-tearing pain, feeling of abandonment, of need to sleep. Older hands knew the danger and prodded us awake...*

The hours passed, no one knew how many, and they clung to the makeshift raft while the waves washed over them threatening to claw them back into the sea. But Tom Davison, for one, refused to give up. Although he had previously been in the water for many hours, he had held onto his torch, and this he was now using to flash distress signals into the storm-wracked night.

At 0440, almost ten hours after the makeshift raft was launched from the *Jervis Bay*, Davison's signals were seen from the bridge of the *Stureholm*. Once again, Captain Olander demonstrated his outstanding seamanship by putting his ship alongside the drifting raft. Through his efforts another thirteen brave men lived to sail again.

Of the others who took to the water when the *Jervis Bay* sank – and there were said to be thirty, or so – only one man survived. He was Stoker Warren D. Stevens, one of the Royal Canadian Navy reservists who had volunteered to sail with the merchant cruiser. When he went over the side from the burning ship, Stevens was lucky enough to find a broken wooden hatch cover amongst the floating debris. This was no substitute for a lifeboat, but there was enough buoyancy in the heavy timber planking to support his weight.

Stevens lost count of the hours he drifted, growing colder and more exhausted all the time. Then, at around midnight, he saw a ship moving slowly amongst the wreckage. He later told a reporter on the Halifax Mail, 'I yelled and they stopped, but I guess they didn't see me.'

Four hours later, having picked up survivors from the *Jervis Bay*'s jolly boat and two rafts, the *Stureholm* returned. Warren Stevens explained: 'I was wearing a naval duffel coat with the hood pulled down over my head. I threw back the hood and waved. They shone the light on me and then picked me up.'

Stevens was a lucky man, for although Captain Olander continued his search until daylight, there was no one else to rescue. The bone-chilling cold of the North Atlantic had done its work well.

By the bold and valiant action of Sven Olander and his crew, who had put themselves in great danger, sixty-five men, all that remained of the *Jervis Bay*'s complement of 250, had been saved from the sea.

In the dark hour before the dawn, on Wednesday 6 November, with the wind gusting to force 9 and the *Stureholm* rolling and pitching heavily in the rising sea, Captain Olander again called his crew to the bridge. He told them that it was his opinion that they could do no more, and with sixty-five extra men on board and insufficient lifeboat capacity for all, it would be wise to return to Halifax. Officers and crew were in unanimous agreement with him, and the ship was put about.

Olander's last sad duty of that day was to commit the bodies of Hugh Pattinson, Alexander Webster and Harold Hinstridge to the deep. Four days later, the *Stureholm* stopped briefly off Cape Race to signal news of her arrival, and at 1740 on the 12th she reached Halifax. The *Jervis Bay* survivors were landed, nine of the badly injured being taken to hospital, while the others were transferred to the armed merchant cruiser HMS *Cormorin* to await passage home. The *Stureholm* would set out to cross the Atlantic again with the next available convoy.

The following comments appeared in The Straits Times, Singapore's English language daily, on 30 October 1960:

> *...It is unlikely that any of the others who escaped would have survived for long – the Admiral Scheer made no attempt to pick them up – had not Captain Sven Olander, master of the Swedish vessel*

Stureholm, conscious of the great debt they owed to the survivors of the ship that saved the convoy, ignored all orders and turned back in the darkness of the night to search for the men of the Jervis Bay.

It was an act of the utmost courage, for all night long the Admiral Scheer, robbed of her prey, was prowling around the area firing off starshells as she hunted for the now scattered members of HX 84.

But the great risk Olander took was justified over and over again; they found and rescued from the freezing night waters no fewer than 65 survivors.

A hopeless sacrifice many people later called the loss of the Jervis Bay. Sheer senseless destruction to send in a cockleshell like the Jervis Bay against the might of a pocket battleship, a folly and a bravado that amounted to nothing less than madness.

No doubt such people are right. No doubt it was madness, but one feels that Fegen and his men would have been proud to be numbered among the madmen of the world.

And one feels too that it would be unwise, to say the least, to express such harsh sentiments in the hearing of any of the members of the 34 ships of Convoy HX 84 that came safely home again because Fogarty Fegen and the men of the Jervis Bay had moved out into the path of the Admiral Scheer and died so that they might live.

British sources did not comment on the rescue.

Chapter 10

THE FOUR-STACKERS

Quite coincidentally, while HX 84 was assembling in Halifax the first of the American destroyers handed over to the Royal Navy under the 'ships for bases' agreement were in port preparing for the Atlantic crossing. As might be expected, the possibility of these ships accompanying the convoy on passage was being discussed. The ocean crossing would provide an excellent opportunity for the four-funnelled, flush-deck destroyers, or 'four-stackers' as they were known by their new owners, to prove their worth and at the same time they would be a welcome addition to the convoy's meagre escort.

Unfortunately, the Admiralty had underestimated the amount of work to be done on the destroyers before they were ready for sea. Built towards the end of the First World War, they had never seen action, and had spent much of the intervening years laid up in the backwaters of the USA. If they had been properly 'mothballed' they would have been in good condition when brought back into service. However America was in the grip of a deep economic recession at the time, and any measures taken to preserve the surplus ships were largely superficial. As a result, their new British owners found them in what can only be described as a run-down state, particularly in the engine-room. Much of the electrical wiring was perished, and rust was everywhere in abundance.

Given time, the more obvious faults could have been rectified, but there was no easy solution to the poor sea-going qualities of the four-stackers. Even in the best of weather they were slow to answer to the helm, and in a heavy sea they were practically unmanageable. The main cause lay in the twin propellers, which instead of being opposed, as in British ships, both revolved in the same direction. This gave these destroyers a turning circle said to be only slightly less than that of a 30,000-ton battleship, an unforgiveable shortcoming in a warship designed for the chase. And perhaps the worst handicap suffered by the ex-American ships was a dangerous lack of stability. This was so critical that when a double bottom fuel tank became empty it was necessary to fill it with sea water in order to preserve positive stability. Even with all double bottom tanks full and pressed up, the destroyers were so 'tender' that they rolled alarmingly in a seaway. One unnamed British admiral is quoted as saying they were 'the worst destroyers I have ever seen', while a Canadian corvette commander called them 'the most dubious gift since the Trojan Horse'.

There is little doubt that in the 'ships for bases' exchange Britain struck a poor bargain. On the other hand, although the four-stackers were sadly lacking in many respects, for the Royal Navy they represented more guns, more depth charges, more hitting power in the fight against the U-boats. At a time when the country's very existence depended on keeping her sea lanes open, this was worth more than any gold.

The first of the ex-US Navy destroyers, now designated the Town-class by the Royal Navy, did not sail from Halifax until 1 November, four days after HX 84 left the port. They were to cross the Atlantic in two separate flotillas, the first consisting of HMS *Lincoln* (ex-USS *Yarnall*), HMS *Ludlow* (ex-USS *Stockton*) and HMS *Lewes* (ex-USS *Craven*); the flotilla being under the command of Commander Alan Sheffield, RN in *Lincoln*. They were followed by HMS *Leamington* (ex-USS *Twiggs*), HMS *Churchill* (ex-USS *Herndon*), HMS *Montgomery* (ex-USS *Wickes*), HMS *Leeds* (ex-USS *Conner*) and HMS *Stanley* (ex-USS *Macalla*). The second flotilla was commanded by Commander William Banks, RN in *Leamington*. Being critically short on bunker capacity, both flotillas were ordered to make the 2,800-mile passage at an economical speed, any attempt to catch up with HX 84 then being regarded as futile.

Originally designed for sub-hunting in US coastal waters, the Town-class destroyers were equipped with twin Parsons turbines developing 20,000 shaft horse power, giving them a top speed of 35 knots, and also a voracious appetite for oil fuel. While this might have been acceptable with a bunker station behind every other headland, an ocean passage of almost 3,000 miles was a quite different matter. It was estimated that with a call at St John's, Newfoundland to top up bunkers, and steaming at an economical 14 to 15 knots, the destroyers would have just enough fuel to reach Belfast, with perhaps thirty or forty tons in reserve. The latter represented less than a day's steaming, and to any prudent mariner would seem a very risky undertaking. But given the parlous state of

Britain's navy, these ships were urgently needed on the other side of the Atlantic, and in the eyes of the Admiralty it was a risk worth taking.

Things began to go wrong right from the start of the voyage. HMS *Sherwood* was not ready to sail from Halifax with the others, and followed on to St John's alone. While in St John's, HMS *Stanley* developed condenser trouble, and was unable to proceed further. *Lincoln*, *Lewes* and *Ludlow*, fully bunkered, cleared St John's on the morning of the 3rd, but had not been long at sea before *Ludlow* was forced to turn back with engine problems. Fortunately, she was able to rectify the fault and catch up with the flotilla later in the day. All this did not augur well for the proposed crossing.

The three destroyers, led by Commander Sheffield in HMS *Lincoln*, cruised in a rough 'V' formation, with *Lewes* and *Ludlow* keeping station close on *Lincoln*'s port and starboard quarters respectively. By this time Sheffield was better acquainted with the ships under his command. His conclusions, which he committed to paper, were scathing:

> *As regards sea-going efficiency, and making allowances for the strangeness of the layout, I think it might easily be summed up by saying that they were rather like what one would expect a ten-year-old motor car to be, had it been badly maintained. For instance, all valves appeared to leak, all the electrical wiring in the ship was perished, alarm circuits were burnt out, the steering was stiff, it took two men to work the manoeuvring valves, and there were no non-slipping surfaces whatever.*

At this point Commander Guy Sayer, in HMS *Ludlow*, advised Sheffield that his ship was burning oil at an alarming rate, almost 30 per cent more than normal. Furthermore, Sayer calculated that with a consumption of 48 tons per day, even at a conservative 14 knots, he would arrive in Belfast with as little as half a ton of oil in his tanks. And that was not allowing for adverse weather or emergency diversions. So far, the weather had been fair, with a light S'ly breeze and slight sea, but this was the 'broad Atlantic', liable to be lashed by howling gales summer and winter alike.

The second flotilla of Town-class destroyers, led by Commander William Banks in HMS *Leamington*, remained in St John's in the hope that the troubled *Stanley* might soon be ready for sea. However, it soon became clear that HMS *Stanley* would be out of action for some considerable time, and Banks decided he must sail without her. On the afternoon of the 4th, the five remaining ships, *Leamington, Leeds, Churchill, Sherwood* and *Montgomery* left St John's and set course for Belfast. Thirty hours later, late in the evening of the 5th, disaster struck again with *Sherwood* reporting both her evaporators out of action. Without these vital engine-room auxiliaries she would be unable to make fresh water for her boilers, and there could be no question of her continuing the voyage. She returned to St John's. With the crossing only barely begun, Banks had already lost two of his ships.

That same night events in the North Atlantic took a dramatic turn, when Commander Sheffield received an urgent signal from Whitehall which read:

ENEMY ARMOURED SHIP ADMIRAL VON SCHEER OPERATING IN NORTH ATLANTIC. LAST KNOWN POSITION 52° 50 N 32° 15 W AT 2003 OF 5TH NOVEMBER 1940.

Then, suddenly, the ether, which had been wrapped in wartime silence, became alive with the staccato squeal of high-speed Morse. The liner *Rangitiki* was reporting she was being 'gunned' by a vessel of the *Graf Spee* class, and a few minutes later the steamer *Cornish City* joined in, reporting that she was also under fire. Then came the plaintive cries of HMS *Jervis Bay* as she bravely fought back against the guns of a vastly superior enemy. Just 150 miles to the south of HMS *Lincoln*, Convoy HX 84 was facing extinction.

Commander Sheffield was now faced with a fearful dilemma. British merchant ships were under attack within reachable distance. His ships, mounting between them twelve 4-inch and six 3-inch guns, plus thirty-six 21-inch torpedo tubes, were, theoretically at least, well placed to go in and cripple, if not sink, any enemy ship, even if she was one of Hitler's finest. This being so, Sheffield might have been tempted to rush to the scene of the action, had he not stopped to consider the true state of affairs. His guns were of 1918 vintage, his ships were unarmoured, and their crews were still struggling to come to terms with their unfamiliar American equipment. And then there was, above all, the vexing question of fuel consumption. At 14 knots he had calculated that the flotilla would just reach Belfast, and no further. A high-speed dash to challenge the enemy attacking HX 84 would, assuming they survived the action, almost certainly leave his destroyers calling for tugs to complete their voyage.

Meanwhile, Commander Sheffield brought his flotilla to third degree readiness and altered course for the position given. He recorded in his log:

> *I considered whether I should increase speed but the slender chance of meeting the enemy coupled with the delicate fuel situation in Ludlow and the fact that 14 knots got me to the required position at dawn decided me against it. At the time, wind was freshening from the ESE and by midnight ships were beginning to work and soon afterwards green seas were coming over...*

Any doubts Sheffield still entertained were resolved when during the night the Admiralty signalled:

CLOSE CONVOY HX 84 ATTACKED BY BATTLESHIP IN POSITION 52° 57 N 32° 23 W. RESCUE SURVIVORS. ATTACK BATTLESHIP BY NIGHT IF OPPORTUNITY OCCURS.

The last part of the signal Sheffield felt he might safely ignore, as the enemy would be long gone before he reached the spot. The saving of lives was now paramount.

When a reluctant dawn finally came on the 6th, Sheffield had to conclude that if any survivors of the convoy battle still lived he had little hope of finding them. As the sun rose behind the heavy overcast, the wind stepped up to force 9, a whole gale from the ESE, and the rain was slanting down in blinding sheets. Visibility was at times nil, at best 2 miles. The swell had become heavy and shock-like, the spume coming off the tops of the mountain-sized waves like drifting snow. The three destroyers, battling to stay within sight of each other, resembled half-tide rocks, their open decks being swept by foaming green seas every time the bows went under. Inevitably, Sheffield was forced to reduce speed to 11 knots to avoid serious damage to his ships.

With the sky completely overcast and the visibility poor, it was impossible to obtain an accurate position, and Commander Sheffield was reduced to navigating by dead reckoning. At 0900, he estimated he had reached the position given by the Admiralty, and he then intended to make a sweep to the westward with *Lincoln*, *Lewes* and *Ludlow* in line abreast 2 miles apart. As he was about to pass the order to alter course, *Lewes* signalled that her bridge steering had broken down, and she was on hand steering from aft. A few minutes later, her starboard anchor broke adrift, and she had to run before the wind to secure it. In doing so, she lost sight of the other ships.

At sea bad fortune rarely travels alone, and no sooner had *Lewes* run into difficulties than *Ludlow* was reporting that her steering was also giving trouble. This she communicated to *Lincoln* by lamp, her main aerial having been brought down by the violent rolling.

The state of *Ludlow*'s bunker tanks was also giving cause for alarm. Commander Sheffield later wrote in his report:

> *I had therefore, to face the situation wherein prolongation of the search would most likely have resulted in Ludlow not being able to complete the journey. If the weather were to continue as it was, there would have been some risk of Lincoln and Lewes similarly placed. The enemy reports had indicated the possibility of survivors being spread over a wide area. The weather made it certain that boats, rafts, etc. would be considerable distances to the west. I considered the possibility of continuing the search and returning to St. Johns, but as we were practically in the middle of the Atlantic, and as on the westward passage the weather varies considerably, even in twelve hours, I might well have found myself steaming into a W'ly gale within 24 hours. In addition, Lincoln and Lewes each had on board an American officer and several packages of secret and important aircraft apparatus, which I had been informed was required in the UK as early as possible. Weighing all these considerations, namely, the very slight chance of locating survivors, compared with the very great chance of not getting the ships to harbour. I decided without much hesitation or doubt to abandon the search.*

Perversely, during the afternoon the weather began to improve, and by 2030 Sheffield was able to order an increase of speed to 14 knots. He did consider turning back to search again, but the fuel situation aboard *Lewes* was now beginning to give serious concern. Then, when she reported her gyro compass was out of action and that she was steering by magnetic compass, Sheffield's mind was made up. His primary concern was to get his three ships into a British port as soon as possible.

At daylight on 8 November the flotilla was 250 miles off the west coast of Ireland, and within a day's steaming of Belfast. It seemed to Commander Sheffield that at last his troubled voyage was almost over. Then, at about 0945, amongst an increasing stream of messages he was receiving from the shore came an urgent signal from Lands End Radio. The British steamer *Empire Dorado* was under attack by enemy aircraft some 40 miles to the north of the flotilla's position.

The 5,500-ton steamer *Empire Dorado*, owned by the Ministry of War transport and managed by the north-east coast tramp company Runciman & Co., had left Liverpool on 4 November in the westbound convoy OB 239. Less than forty-eight hours out from Liverpool the news of the *Admiral Scheer*'s attack on HX 84 had come flooding in, and the Admiralty immediately recalled OB 239. Meanwhile, Kapitän Krancke, frustrated in his bid to obliterate HX 84 by the stubborn resistance of HMS *Jervis Bay* and Hugh Pettigrew's *Beaverford*, had called for air support.

Largely due to the machinations of Reichsmarschall Hermann Goering, head of the German Luftwaffe, in 1940 air support for Hitler's Kriegsmarine ran to just a handful of Focke-Wulf FW 200 maritime reconnaissance bombers based at Bordeaux-Merignac in Brittany. The four-engined 'Condors' of *Kampfgeschwader* 40 had a range of 2,200 miles, and carried four 500lb bombs, along with a formidable array of machine-guns. In their war against British shipping they flew north from Biscay, taking a wide sweep to the west of Ireland, then on to Norway to refuel and rearm, returning along the same route a day or so later. In doing so, they were able to attack convoys to and from Gibraltar, and those crossing the Atlantic, all of which passed through the Western Approaches. By the autumn of 1940 KG 40 had sunk over 90,000 tons of Allied shipping. On 26 October, a Condor flown by Oberstleutnant Bernhard Jope crippled the 42,348-ton liner *Empress of Britain*, which was later sent to the bottom by Hans Jenisch in U-32. This was one of the few examples of successful cooperation between the Condors and the U-boat arm.

Commander Sheffield was reluctant to prejudice the completion of his Atlantic crossing by going to the aid of the *Empire Dorado*. Then an

SOS from the British merchantman was picked up. The *Dorado* reported she was sinking slowly, and as all her lifeboats had been smashed she had no means of abandoning ship. She added that she had casualties on board. This left Sheffield with no alternative but to render assistance to the sinking ship.

As both *Ludlow* and *Lewes* were now sucking on the dregs of their last bunker tank, Sheffield ordered them to carry on to Belfast, while he took *Lincoln* to the north at 20 knots. He later wrote:

At 1245 I sighted the ship whose hull appeared undamaged, although her funnel was down. At 1324 I took three men off a raft some two miles to westward of the damaged ship. It appeared that these three men had abandoned ship in a panic. At 1340 I sent Medical Officer in seaboat to Empire Dorado. Between this time and 1645 I embarked Master and all living survivors of the accident, eight men being left in the ship dead. I had intended to sink the ship as she might have been a danger to navigation but at about 1600 HM Trawler Man o' War arrived and wanted to take the ship in tow. This I approved, myself setting course 085° 20 knots at 1700.

The *Empire Dorado* spent some ten months in port under repair, returning to sea in September 1941. She was subsequently lost in collision while crossing the Atlantic in Convoy SC 53 in November 1941.

Commander William Banks, leading the second flotilla of Town–class destroyers in HMS *Leamington*, finally sailed from St John's at about 1300 on 4 November. He was already one ship short; HMS *Stanley* being held in port for engine repairs, and his flotilla was further depleted when HMS *Sherwood* dropped out on the 5th. This left Banks with just four ships, *Leamington*, *Churchill*, *Leeds* and *Montgomery*. Then, with the ocean passage barely begun, twenty-four hours of dense fog slowed the destroyers to a walking pace. By this time Banks must have been convinced that he had a Jonah in his midst.

And there was worse to come. The four destroyers had worked up to 15 knots when it was discovered that *Leamington* had a serious leak in her stern gland compartment which was threatening to flood the engine-room. The gland was tightened up, but the leak persisted, and slowly became worse. Commander Banks made the following entry in his log:

A suction was fitted to the compartment but neither steam pump would suck. The electric pump for pumping out the forward compartments was taken aft but this would not suck. On being stripped down it was discovered that the rotor clearances were 1/16 instead of, say, 4/1000 . This could not be rectified. The watch were for the following three days employed at intervals in baling out this compartment. By 8 November the watch were employed baling continuously. All seven valves on the pump line to aft were taken down and found to have rag and waste wrapped tightly round them and two valve glands were leaking badly in the line. The refit of these valves was completed by the evening of the 8 November, when the steam pump started to suck out the stern gland compartment...The general condition of the machinery, which can be attributed to bad maintenance, is not satisfactory.

The commander's concluding remarks appear to be something of an understatement. While *Leamington* was by no means in danger of sinking, she was lacking in seaworthiness, and this being so, her role as a fighting ship was severely impaired. Nevertheless, when, late on the 5th, Banks received the Admiralty's signal reporting the attack on HX 84 by a German pocket battleship, he put all his ships on a war footing.

At daylight on the 6th, the flotilla was in unusually fair weather, with a light SW'ly breeze, slight sea and maximum visibility, while 240 miles to the east Sheffield's ships were riding out a full gale. Banks had not increased speed, and in order to make best use of his small force had spread his ships in line abreast, 16 miles apart. The horizon was empty all round, and remained so until late afternoon when the British tanker *Sovac* was sighted. The *Sovac*, a survivor of HX 84, was making her way back to Halifax. She gave Banks the full story of the *Admiral Scheer*'s attack on the convoy.

Leamington, having lost touch with the other destroyers during the night, passed through the position of the attack shortly after dawn on the 7th. The weather continued fair, but nothing was seen. This was not surprising. Any survivors, from the *Jervis Bay* or other ships, who might have been in the water would have perished in the storm of the previous day, and by then the *Scheer* was several hundred miles to the south, and heading for a rendezvous with her supply ship.

Commander Banks considered calling in his other ships to make a thorough search of the area, but by this time *Leamington*'s stern gland was leaking so badly that the water could only be kept at bay by continuous hand baling. Banks was also receiving reports from HMS *Leeds* that she was running short of fuel, and had just enough oil remaining to reach Belfast. Banks decided to carry on to Belfast, where all four destroyers arrived on the morning of 10 November.

With the first seven flush-deckers safely across the Atlantic, the others followed at regular intervals, but never alone. In view of the problems experienced by Commanders Banks and Sheffield, thereafter the ex-American destroyers crossed in flotillas of not less than three ships.

The Town-class destroyers had an unremarkable war. Between them they sank four U-boats, and in return lost seven of their number to Dönitz's torpedoes. The only one to win any claim to fame was HMS *Campbeltown*, ex-USS *Buchanan*. She was used as a battering ram to break down and blow up the lock gates at St Nazaire, thereby denying access to the only dry dock in the Atlantic big enough to take the German battleship *Tirpitz*.

To say that the four-stackers were unloved by their British crews is another understatement, but with hard work and a great deal of improvisation their major faults were largely overcome. Nothing could be done about their seaworthiness, however. British-built destroyers of the same vintage were superb sea boats, highly manoeuvrable, completely stable, and strong enough to drive through the worst of weather. The American ships, on the other hand, were like highly strung racehorses, always to be handled with great care, and never pushed beyond their limits. An illustration of their vulnerability was provided by HMS *Roxborough*, ex-USS *Foote*. Escorting Convoy HX 222 in January 1943 *Roxborough* slammed into a wave that completely demolished her bridge structure, killing eleven men, including her commanding officer and his first lieutenant.

By the end of 1943 the Town-class destroyers had achieved all that had been asked of them, which was mainly to make up the numbers while the Royal Navy was being brought back up to strength. They were then phased out, a number of them being transferred to Russia to boost the Soviet Navy.

It may seem that Churchill was over generous in giving the Americans 99-year leases on bases in the British West Indies in exchange for a collection of old destroyers hurriedly taken out of mothballs. But, looking back, he obviously had no other option open to him. In the summer of 1940, there were powerful isolationist forces in America who were convinced that Britain would lose the war, and were strongly opposed to the transfer of the destroyers. Not least amongst them was the US Ambassador Joseph P. Kennedy, well known for his Irish Republican connections, who reported from London that a British surrender was 'inevitable'.

However, as always, the wily Churchill had ulterior motives which he did not reveal until after the war. He wrote in his memoirs:

The transfer to Great Britain of fifty American warships was a decidedly unneutral act by the United States. It would, according to all standards of history, have justified the German Government in declaring war upon them...It was Hitler's interest and method to strike down his opponents one by one. The last thing he wished was to be drawn into war with the United States until he was finished with Britain. Nevertheless, the transfer of the destroyers to Britain in September 1940 was an event which brought the United States definitely nearer to us and to the war, and it was the first of a long succession of increasingly unneutral acts in the Atlantic which were of the utmost service to us. It marked the passage of the United States from being neutral to being non-belligerent...

Churchill does not mention Bermuda, and this is where Britain did gain a significant advantage. Part of the deal he struck with Roosevelt included the handing over of the defence of Bermuda to US forces, thus releasing a considerable number of British servicemen for deployment where they were more needed. And there was also the new airfield to be built on the islands.

The Bermudas, or the Somers Isles as they were once called, are an archipelago of islands in the Atlantic 640 miles off Cape Hatteras. The islands are hilly with very little flat ground anywhere, and it was always considered impossible to build an airfield of any size in the colony. That was...until the US Army landed.

The Americans promised to build an airfield on the Bermudas capable of handling large landplanes. Hitherto, only flying boats had been able to operate in and out of the islands. With characteristic 'can do', the US Army bulldozed several small islands level and joined them by infilling the water between them with soil and rocks. This more than doubled the total land mass of Bermuda, and provided a level area large enough to build a runway capable of taking the big four-engined Liberators of the US Army Air Force and the Royal Air Force.

Kindley Airfield, named for the American pilot who flew with the Royal Flying Corps in World War I, was completed in 1943, and for the rest of the war provided, amongst other things, valuable long-range air cover for Allied shipping crossing the Atlantic. For this alone, all the faults of the four-stackers might be forgiven.

Chapter 11

SAN DEMETRIO

The voyage had not begun well for the Eagle Oil tanker *San Demetrio*. Four days out of Halifax with HX 84, she suffered a major engine breakdown and was forced to drop out of the convoy. For the next sixteen excruciatingly long hours she lay rolling in the swell, helpless and dangerously vulnerable. Deep in her bowels Chief Engineer Charles Pollard and his men sweated blood as they struggled to effect a repair, acutely aware that only the thin steel hull plates stood between them and the certain death an enemy torpedo would bring. For Captain George Waite, anxiously pacing the bridge deck of the 8,073-ton tanker, it was as though the memory of an earlier nightmare had come back to haunt him.

Eleven months before, on the morning of 9 December 1939, Waite had stood on the bridge of the Eagle Oil tanker *San Alberto* sniffing at the clean salt air as he set off on yet another Atlantic crossing. The *San Alberto* was westbound in ballast for Trinidad.

The tanker was only twelve hours to the west of Land's End when a torpedo fired by an unseen U-boat slammed into her hull, and with an explosion resembling the eruption of a volcano, split her in two.

It was now dark, and the North Atlantic was at its winter worst, blowing a full gale with a high sea running. Three lifeboats were lowered, one of which capsized and its crew of five were thrown into the sea. The other two boats cleared the ship with thirty-eight men on board.

Hove to and riding the waves in his crowded boat, Captain Waite watched as the forward half of his ship sank. The after part of the *San Alberto*, which contained her engine-room, remained afloat. Several hours later, the stern was still afloat, and showing no signs of sinking. Waite put it to his men, who were cold, miserable, and for the most part dreadfully seasick, that half a ship was better than none, and it was agreed to try to re-board the wreck.

The second lifeboat was located and, despite the very high seas and the danger of the boats being smashed against the ship's side, all thirty-eight men reached the deck of what remained of their ship. An inspection of the engine-room showed the main engine and auxiliaries to be in good order. First priority was given to a hot meal from the galley and a change of clothes, then the engine was started. The after half of the *San Alberto*, proceeding stern first, was on its way home.

Unfortunately, soon after they were under way the weather took a turn for the worse, and by midnight the remaining watertight bulkheads of the tanker were beginning to give way under the onslaught of the pounding sea. By dawn on the 10th, with no let-up in the weather, Captain Waite had to accept that the *San Alberto* must again be abandoned. He sent out a distress message, which brought the destroyer HMS *Mackay* racing out from the Western Approaches. When she arrived the sea was still running high and it was impossible for Waite to lower a boat. Finally, using two Carley floats attached to lines between the destroyer and the wreck, all thirty-eight men were taken off.

The *San Alberto*'s stern half finally joined the rest of the ship at the bottom of the Atlantic soon after the last man was rescued. Of the five whose boat had capsized when the *San Alberto* was abandoned, four were picked up by another destroyer and one was lost. For his leadership in this courageous attempt to save his ship and her crew Captain George Waite was awarded the OBE.

The *San Demetrio*, her engine repaired, rejoined HX 84 during the evening of 4 November. In view of what followed twenty-four hours later, there were those on board who were of the opinion that it might have been better not to have rejoined the convoy. And they could have been right.

Bound for Avonmouth from Aruba, the *San Demetrio* was carrying 11,200 tons of high-octane gasoline. This made her a prime target for any U-boat able to get within torpedo range, and all on board were acutely aware of their vulnerability. However, in these far distant waters they considered they were reasonably safe. And they were, until the *Admiral Scheer* put in an appearance and Captain Waite found himself, for the second time in his career, ordering his crew to abandon ship.

It was the *Scheer*'s third salvo that finally crippled the already burning *San Demetrio*. Two of the shells went home, one blowing a huge jagged hole in her bow plates just above the waterline. Able Seaman

Ernest Daines, unfortunate enough to be on lookout in the bows, was killed instantly. The second shell scored a hit amidships, destroying the wireless room and killing both radio officers, who were then attempting to get out an SOS. In his book, Kapitän Krancke described the havoc wreaked by his big guns as perceived from the *Scheer*'s bridge:

> *...seconds later a terrific mass of black smoke and a great sheet of flame shot three hundred feet and more into the air...Flames were licking up the masts, running along the bridge and racing towards the ship's bows. Direct hits had been scored on all oil tanks and they were exploding one after another. Further direct hits were scored in the tanker's sides along the waterline and everything went very swiftly. Rockets were shooting up from the bridge and bursting in the sky above the inferno...*

It being dark, and with the convoy's smoke screen thickening, Theodor Krancke can be forgiven for his somewhat colourful description of the scene. Nevertheless, the British tanker had taken a terrible pounding. Krancke's shells had completely destroyed her bridge and after accommodation, and her upper decks were in flames. Miraculously, however, only three of her 42-man crew had been killed or injured, and perhaps more miraculously still, none of her cargo tanks, each containing highly inflammable spirit, had yet caught fire. But now, in the opinion of Captain Waite, it was time to go. He rang the engine-room telegraph to 'Finished with Engines' and sounded the abandon ship signal on the ship's whistle.

The *San Demetrio* was being hit repeatedly, and hot shrapnel was scything across the decks, but there was no wild rush for the lifeboats. The tanker's crew were conscious of the volatile nature of their cargo, and they knew they were in a race against death: the exit from the ship was disciplined, if fast and vocal.

Chief Engineer Pollard had started back for his cabin to collect his steel helmet, but halfway along the catwalk he thought better of it, and was just in time to join his boat as it was being lowered. The night was dark and the boat was swinging wildly in the swell, and in an unguarded moment Pollard's right hand was crushed between the ship's side and the boat. Although he was bleeding profusely and in great pain, he was able to carry on. Two men following the Chief jumped from the tilting deck and fell heavily into the boat. Both appeared to be badly injured, but this was not the time for licking wounds.

Three lifeboats cleared the burning tanker, and they were only yards off when fire engulfed her bridge house and after accommodation. One boat, with Chief Officer Wilson in charge, contained nineteen men; another, under Second Officer Arthur Hawkins, had sixteen on board, including Chief Engineer Pollard and the two injured men. The third, which was last to leave the ship, was crewed by Captain Waite and three others. The shells were still raining down, and to exacerbate an already dire situation, the raider had opened fire with machine-guns and tracer bullets were arcing across the water. Describing the confusion many years later, 19-year-old Apprentice John Lewis Jones, who was in Second Officer Hawkins' boat, wrote:

We rowed for our lives. Vessels seemed to be coming at us from all directions. In avoiding being run down, we lost all contact with the other lifeboat, neither could we recognise our own ship from the other vessels on fire in our vicinity. The German raider continued firing until about midnight. The sound of the gunfire had been receding all the time; taking into account the devastating effect of his attack up to our turn, I did not think many vessels escaped unharmed...

As the night wore on the weather became even worse, but Hawkins and Jones were lucky enough to have two young Shetland Island men, McNeil and McLennan, in their crew, both of whom were ex-fishermen and well accustomed to handling a small boat. Under their direction, with a sea anchor out and a canvas canopy rigged in the bows to give shelter from the breaking seas, they rode out the rest of the night in comparative comfort. When daylight came on the 6th, the weather was beginning to moderate, which helped to raise spirits in the boat. Then a ship was sighted close by, and there was a great flurry of excitement. Flares were broken out and burned, but the ship disappeared in a rain squall without apparently seeing them.

Another hour went by, then hopes were raised again when a second ship, this time a tanker, was seen at about 6 miles. She appeared to be stopped, and at Hawkins' urging the oars were shipped, and they rowed towards her. It was a long, back-breaking pull, and by the time they were nearing the drifting ship darkness was coming in again. The survivors, who had been taking turns at the oars, were now nearing exhaustion, but one final burst brought them close enough to see the tanker clearly. Jubilation was followed by disappointment when they recognised her as their own ship, the *San Demetrio*, and she was still on fire. Second Officer Hawkins wrote in his report:

> *She was still burning furiously and there was a lot of oil on the water, so I decided that, due to the fierceness of the fire, it was unsafe to board her that night, hoping that the fire would have abated by morning. We were all feeling a bit under the weather as everyone had been seasick, but there was a little opposition to my decision to wait until the morning before boarding the ship, everyone being anxious to get on board at once. However, we pulled up to windward and decided to lay to until morning.*

In the early hours of the 7th, as their small boat rolled drunkenly in the heavy swell, the survivors were horrified to see the fire suddenly flare up in the stern of the tanker. In the light of the flames they could see she was settling by the head. When full daylight came and the ship was nowhere to be seen, it was assumed she had sunk. Disappointment lay heavily on the boat, and Hawkins came in for a great deal of criticism for not attempting to board during the night. However, Arthur Hawkins was clear as to where his duty lay, and he refused to believe that the *San Demetrio* had gone. He ordered the sails to be hoisted, and running before a stiff breeze, six and a half hours later his optimism was justified. Their ship was in sight again.

This time, with plenty of daylight left, Hawkins decided to attempt to board at once. This was not going to be easy. The tanker was drifting down on them, and there was a very real danger that the steel lifeboat might be thrown against the ship and cause a shower of sparks. The sea around the *San Demetrio* was covered in petrol, and if that was ignited by a spark they would all be roasted. But needs must. It had rained heavily during the night, and in addition to the constant seasickness, everyone in the boat was cold and wet. There were no dissenting voices when Hawkins announced that they must board without delay.

As they approached nearer, the prospect of a successful boarding receded. Black smoke was pouring from the tanker's poop and midship accommodation, she was well down by the head, and green seas were sweeping her decks with every roll. Wisely, Hawkins left the approach in the capable hands of the two Shetlanders, McNeil and McLennan, both skilled in small boat handling. With split-second timing they brought the boat alongside the burning tanker without a bump.

Reboarding the ship was not easy as the boat was rising and falling on the swell like a fairground roller coaster, and the only access was by the broken remnants of a pilot ladder that had been left hanging over the side. Furthermore, there were three injured men in the boat. Chief Engineer Pollard had crushed his right hand, and John Davies, the storekeeper, and the greaser John Boyle, had fallen into the boat when boarding. Pollard was in great pain, and Davies and Boyle appeared to have cracked ribs, and possibly internal injuries. It was a hard struggle but, one by one, the sixteen survivors hauled themselves up the ship's side. In his memoirs, Apprentice John Lewis Jones described the situation that awaited them on deck:

She was still on fire, but no one objected to re-boarding…Anything was better than remaining in the lifeboat, and it was obvious that further time spent in the boat was going to be a futile attempt to survive. We were only partially successful in recovering our lifeboat, which was left hanging in the falls about six feet clear of the water. From the boat it was seen that the ship was badly damaged; after boarding, the damage found was appalling. A shell had entered the port bow just above the waterline, exploded, and splinters had holed our collision bulkhead, resulting in our fore-hold making water, which was settling the ship by the head. The bridge and all the midships accommodation was a mass of twisted steel, the main deck under the structure was buckled with heat from the fire, which had been so intense that the brass and glass of the portholes had melted and fused, resembling icicles. Part of this mess was still burning. The main deck abaft the bridge had a number of splinter holes, and the petrol cargo was flooding from this as the ship rolled. All the after accommodation on the port side had been destroyed, also the decks. This area was still on fire…

Once aboard the ship, Arthur Hawkins made a thorough inspection of the decks, finding a number of fires still burning, with much of the steelwork adjacent to these glowing red-hot. He was amazed to find that although the main deck was awash with petrol, which had a flash point below 73°F, none of it had caught fire. In fact most of the highly inflammable cargo in the tanks appeared to have survived. As a precaution, Hawkins put his men to work with fire extinguishers to subdue the worst of the fires still raging. While they were thus engaged, their lifeboat, which they had been unable to hoist aboard, broke adrift and was lost. From then on, they had no option but to bring the ship under control. Apart from a small jolly boat, which had been holed by shellfire, the ship was now their only lifeboat.

Meanwhile, Chief Engineer Pollard, with Third Engineer George Willey, Greaser John Boyle and Storekeeper John Davies, had gone below to investigate the state of the engine-room. They found the floor plates awash with three to four feet of water, but the auxiliary machinery, pumps, generators, etc., appeared to be undamaged. They fired up the boiler, and by nightfall they had sufficient steam to run the pumps and a generator, giving light and water on deck to fight the fires. They then turned their attention to the main engine.

At 0230 on the morning of the 8th, Pollard was able to tell Acting Captain Hawkins that his ship was ready to proceed. Unfortunately, by this time the weather had again deteriorated and it was blowing a full gale from the west. This did not deter Hawkins, who was determined to get his burnt and broken ship and her cargo into a British port. This was not going to be an easy passage. The *San Demetrio*'s bridge had been gutted by fire; her compasses, charts, signal flags and steering gear and wireless room completely destroyed. A spare compass was found, but this proved to be so wildly inaccurate as to be useless.

Undaunted, Hawkins connected up the emergency steering gear, and steering from aft with the few spokes left on the poop steering wheel, and keeping the wind astern, he set off in what he judged to be an easterly direction. At best, he hoped to make a landfall somewhere on the west coast of Ireland, at worst, they would end up in Occupied France. Acting Captain Hawkins wrote in his report:

> *Things looked a bit bad particularly as she was shipping a lot of water in the fore hold, which was originally empty. The wind was force 8 and she was rolling very badly and was down by the head. Every time she rolled petrol came gushing up on deck as the petrol tanks were badly holed. Luckily, I had No.6 tank empty and so decided to run petrol*

*from for'ard and so throw her head up a little. The Chief Engineer and
the Apprentice went down to the pump rooms which were full of gas and
we ran petrol from No.9 which gave her a starboard list and lifted her
head considerably. She rode much better after that and shipped less
water.*

In working in the gas-filled pump room Chief Engineer Charles Pollard
and Apprentice John Lewis Jones put their lives on the line, for the
tiniest of sparks from the pumps could have blown them into oblivion.
But, like everyone else on board, they had been through so much, and
were determined to see this desperate enterprise to a conclusion. There
was no more room in their lives for fear.

By the morning of 9 November, the weather had eased a little, and
the *San Demetrio* was as seaworthy as the efforts of her skeleton crew
could ever hope to make her. Occasional glimpses of the stars through
breaks in the heavy overcast confirmed that she was roughly on course,
and Hawkins, ever the optimist, predicted they would make a landfall on
the Irish coast on the 12th. It was now time to think of other things.

Since reboarding the tanker, the survivors had been living on cold
tinned food, Hawkins being loath to light the galley fire for fear of an
explosion. On top of everything else, four days without hot food or drink
was a hard cross to bear. When the ever-resourceful Charles Pollard
produced an ingenious way of cooking onions and potatoes by injecting
steam into a bucket there was great jubilation. In different circumstances
this would have been a very basic, unappetising meal, but to men who
had been through so much, boiled onions and potatoes had never tasted
so good. When three bottles of rum were found intact in the stores, the
survivors felt they were at last winning their private war against the sea.

But it was not all joy. During the day 28-year-old John Boyle, the
engine-room greaser who had played a major part in restarting the *San
Demetrio*'s engine, complained of feeling unwell. He had injured himself
jumping into the lifeboat when abandoning ship, and had been in pain
ever since, although he had not previously complained. Boyle's
condition worsened during the night, and he died before dawn on the
11th. Only after his death was it discovered that he had been suffering
from an internal haemorrhage, which eventually proved fatal.

To the great disappointment of all on board, land was not sighted on
the 12th, as Hawkins had predicted. However, his navigation, even

though he had no instruments or charts, was not that much in error. At first light on the 13th, there it was, a dark line on the horizon ahead; the west coast of Ireland. Hawkins wrote in his report:

> *...we sighted land on the 13th November. The fact that we had no compass made it very risky...Our greatest risk was the probable presence of mines but we just had to trust to luck, although we didn't relish the idea of trying to land without the assistance of a boat, and we only had a very small boat that had been badly holed by the raider's gunfire. We knew it was Ireland, and made for Black Sod Bay to make anchorage, but the water was looking suspiciously broken and so we moved a little further down. We thought if we could carry on until night time we would put the holed boat over the side and try to attract the attention of the keeper of the lighthouse which was visible in the distance. We waited until nightfall and signalled with our torch but, getting no reply, we decided to cruise around in the bay for the remainder of the night.*

Unknown to Hawkins, as the *San Demetrio* idled off the coast she had been sighted by a coast watcher who responded to the 'SOS' and 'HELP' in large letters they had painted on the bridge sides. However, communications in this remote corner of Ireland were poor, and a lengthy delay followed. The watcher telephoned the Lloyd's Agent in Queenstown, who in turn telephoned the British Naval Attaché in Dublin. The attaché then attempted to notify the Admiralty and Eagle Oil in London, but failed. Determined to help this ship so obviously in distress, he contacted a friend in Maidenhead, who was then able to pass the message to the Admiralty. The Lloyd's Agent also sent a boat out to the *San Demetrio* with a doctor on board, but the weather was so bad that the boat had to turn back.

Captain Hawkins had correctly identified his landfall as Blacksod Bay, a large sheltered bay on the north-west tip of Ireland, but contrary to his assumption, the bay was clear of all obstructions, and would have provided a safe anchorage for the night. It is probable that the *San Demetrio* ended up in Clew Bay, some 15 miles to the south. It was here, during the night, that the body of John Boyle was committed to the deep. It was a sad end for a brave man.

At daybreak on the 14th, the naval salvage tug *Superman* arrived off the bay, sent by the Admiralty to take the damaged tanker in tow. If Hawkins had agreed to the tow, any salvage money awarded for bringing the ship in would have gone to the Admiralty. This Hawkins was not prepared to accept. Having fought so hard and so long to save their ship, he put it to his crew that if anyone was going to claim salvage, it should be them. The decision to carry on alone was unanimous. Before they left the bay, they were joined by the destroyer HMS *Arrow*, which had been sent to escort them to the Clyde. *Arrow* sent across a party of volunteers to help the *San Demetrio*'s depleted crew, who were by now on the point of exhaustion. They included Second Officer Morfee, Second Engineer Caizley, Third Engineer Drever and Fourth Engineer Semple, who had been rescued by *Arrow* after their ship the *Empire Wind* had been sunk by a German long-range bomber. The destroyer's doctor also came across to attend to the injured on board the tanker, particularly Chief Engineer Pollard, whose crushed hand was festering. John Lewis Jones wrote in his memoirs:

> *At 1830 we proceeded towards the Clyde escorted by the destroyer, which was later joined by others; we were also given continuous air cover during daylight. I doubt that any single merchant ship had up to that time enjoyed such a strong escorting force. The San Demetrio anchored in the Clyde on the 16th November.*

On the 19th, the *San Demetrio* went alongside an oil berth in the Clyde under her own power, and was moored by her own crew. These same men then connected up the pipes, and discharged their cargo of petrol with their own pumps. Of the 11,200 tons of petrol originally loaded, only 200 tons had been lost. In view of the dangers the men had faced, this was a truly outstanding achievement, for which they were duly rewarded.

As Hawkins and his crew had brought their ship into port without the aid of tugs or any other ship, they were entitled to claim salvage money. The courts valued the *San Demetrio*, which was just two years old, at £250,000 and her cargo at £60,000. Neither her owners, Eagle Oil, nor her insurers contested the claim, and the sixteen men involved in the epic voyage were awarded £14,700, a great deal of money at a time when a senior ship's officer would be earning around £20 a month. Acting Captain Arthur Hawkins, whose calm and reasoned judgement was the driving force behind this desperate enterprise, received £2,000. He was also given the ragged, salt-stained Red Ensign that had flown proudly at the *San Demetrio*'s stern while she was under fire and throughout her momentous voyage home. And, rightly so, there were medals, too. Second Officer Arthur Hawkins and Chief Engineer Charles Pollard each received an OBE, while Third Engineer George Willey was given an MBE. Storekeeper John Davies, Boatswain Walter Fletcher, Seaman Oswald Preston and Apprentice John Lewis Jones were each awarded the BEM, while Greaser John Boyle received a Posthumous Commendation. The Shetland islander Calum MacNeil, who was largely responsible for the handling of the lifeboat, also received a Commendation. Later, John Lewis Jones and Charles Pollard were awarded Lloyd's War Medal for Bravery at Sea in recognition of the fearful risks they took in working in the *San Demetrio*'s gas-filled pumproom.

The incredible story of the *San Demetrio* went around the world, a richly deserved tribute to those involved; a wonderful propaganda coup for Britain which helped to divert attention from the shame of Convoy HX 84. Books were written, and a memorable film was made which is still shown today. The saga of the tanker *San Demetrio* and the modest heroes who saved her will be remembered long after the last of Britain's merchant ships has gone from the sea.

In March 1942, after a long spell in dock under repair, the *San Demetrio* was back at sea, down to her marks with 11,000 tons of motor spirit and alcohol, and homeward bound across the Atlantic. In command was Captain Conrad Vidot, and back in the Chief's cabin was the indefatigable Charles Pollard, the only one of the tanker's original crew to remain with her.

The *San Demetrio* sailed from Baltimore on 15 March, and by the afternoon of the 16th had cleared Chesapeake Bay, and was heading north to join a convoy at Halifax. For America, the war was only three months old, still 3,000 miles distant, and for much of the country it was business as usual. The coastal towns were still brilliantly lit, lighthouses and buoys had not been dimmed and ships still advertised their presence with full-strength navigation lights. And, as in peacetime, a constant stream of shipping was making its way up and down the coast, every ship an easy target, silhouetted against the bright lights of the shore. Admiral Dönitz was quick to take advantage of this mistaken complacency, sending in twelve of his biggest and best U-boats, which, needless to say, were having a veritable field day. In the first two months of 1942, attacking always at night, they had sunk seventy-three merchantmen, totalling 429,891 tons gross. 'Like shooting fish in a barrel', was the expression being used by the U-boat men.

On 8 February, Dönitz made the following entry in his War Diary:

Lt. (SG) Hardigen, commander of U-123, being the first commander to return from the east coast of America, made a report on his experience in this unknown area. The expectation of encountering many independently routed ships, clumsy handling of ships, slight, inexperienced sea and air patrols and defences was so truly fulfilled that conditions had to be described as almost completely of peacetime standards. Independent operations by submarines was therefore correct.

The commander found such an abundance of opportunities for attack in the sea area south of New York to Cape Hatteras that he could not possibly utilize them all.

At times there were as many as 10 ships in sight that were sailing with lights on peacetime course. Thus there were numerous opportunities for two or even three boats to attack at one spot alone.

U-404, a newly commissioned Type VIIC, commanded by Kapitänleutnant Otto von Bülow, made her appearance on the coast on 15 February 1942. Lying on the bottom during the daylight hours and surfacing at night, she was soon making her presence felt. Bülow sank the American freighter *Collamer* on 5 March, the Chilean-flag *Tolten* on the 13th, and another American, the *Lemuel Burrows*, on the 14th. Then the *San Demetrio* came his way.

Von Bülow had been shadowing the Eagle Oil tanker since she cleared Chesapeake Bay, and at 0216 on the morning of 17 March he ended her long run of luck with two torpedoes.

One torpedo slammed into the *San Demetrio*'s engine-room, destroying her engine and killing the watch below; the other exploded in her No.2 cargo tank, which erupted in a fireball that quickly engulfed the ship.

Nineteen men lost their lives on that St Patrick's Day off the coast of Maryland. Showing considerable bravery and calm judgement, Captain Vidot mustered his remaining men and supervised the launching of two lifeboats. As they pulled away from their burning ship she took a heavy list to starboard, lifted her bows high, and sank by the stern. With just two torpedoes, U-404 had done what the *Admiral Scheer* and all her great array of guns had failed to do sixteen months earlier. If ever proof was needed of the superiority of the U–boat over Germany's big ships, the *San Demetrio* had provided it.

The survivors of the *San Demetrio* were picked up two days later by the US merchant ship *Beta*. Chief Engineer Charles Pollard was among them. He returned to sea again, but died two years after the war ended at the comparatively young age of fifty-nine. It is conceivable that the stress of his traumatic voyages in the *San Demetrio* hastened his death.

For bravery shown in saving thirty-one men from certain death, Captain Conrad Vidot was awarded an OBE (Civil Division) and the Lloyd's Medal for Bravery at Sea.

Chapter 12

END OF PASSAGE

No one, not even the Admiralty in all its great wisdom, had been prepared for the *Admiral Scheer*'s audacious attack on Convoy HX 84. When Commodore Maltby, in the *Cornish City*, gave the order to scatter there was a plan in place to reform the convoy when the danger was past, but in the melee that followed he seems to have been ignored. The need to clear the area was so urgent it was left to each individual ship to choose her own avenue of escape. Later, when it was realised that the majority of the merchantmen had escaped the raider's guns, the Admiralty signalled the surviving ships to reassemble at a rendezvous point 300 miles to the north-west of Bloody Foreland on the west coast of Ireland.

By the morning of 8 November, Maltby had rounded up eight ships, and others were homing in on the *Cornish City* from all points of the horizon. Steaming in single line astern, the reforming convoy was then making for a rendezvous with corvettes of Western Approaches Command which would escort them into the North Channel. The weather had moderated during the night, but was deteriorating again as the sun rose. Thickening cloud and a wind that was round to the west and freshening were sure signs of another Atlantic gale on the way. But the promise of a good blow did nothing to dampen the growing optimism of the men in the ships. They were convinced that their recent nightmare was at last over – and so it would have been if the *Luftwaffe* and some of Admiral Dönitz's new-found allies had not taken a hand.

For the unescorted merchant ship the danger area was edging ever further westwards, as illustrated by *Kampfgeschwader* 40's spectacular success with the crippling of the troopship *Empress of Britain*.

Only two weeks earlier, the 42,500-ton Canadian Pacific liner, commanded by Captain Charles Sapsworth, was inbound for Liverpool with 205 military personnel and their families on board, when she was ambushed by KG 40. A Focke-Wulf Condor, piloted by Oberleutnant

Bernhard Jope, pounced on the liner before her escorts arrived, first machine-gunning her, then hitting her with two 250kg bombs. She was extensively damaged on deck, fires were started that could not be brought under control, and her engine-room had to be abandoned. Captain Sapsworth ordered his passengers and most of his crew into the boats, remaining on board with a skeleton crew of volunteers.

As his ship did not appear to be in danger of sinking, Sapsworth decided to attempt to make port. Help was at hand with the naval tugs *Marauder* and *Thames*, who put tow ropes on board, and escorted by the destroyers *Broke* and *Sardonyx*, with Sunderlands of Coastal Command covering by day, the *Empress of Britain* headed for the North Channel at 4 knots.

An entry in Dönitz's War Diary for 26 October read:

A successful air attack was made on 'Empress of Britain', 42,000 tons. Radio Intelligence and air reconnaissance confirmed that the ship was on fire and unable to proceed. Radio Intelligence established that extensive rescue operations had been started. Ship's position was AM 5455 (55° 03 N 10° 45 W) and U-boats were informed. U 32 is nearest.

U-32, under the command of Kapitänleutnant Hans Jenisch, had sailed from Lorient three days earlier, and was then within easy reach of the position given. Jenisch sighted the tugs and their tow and attempted to attack by day, but was forced under by patrolling Sunderlands. He re-established contact using hydrophones, and made his approach submerged, surfacing after dark. The 42,000-ton *Empress of Britain*, under tow at 4 knots, presented an unmissable target, and Jenisch hit her amidships with two torpedoes. The escorting destroyers believed the double explosion had been caused by fire reaching the liner's fuel tanks, and took no action, leaving Jenisch free to escape.

At 0205 on the 28th, the *Empress of Britain* took a heavy list, rolled over and sank. She was the biggest Allied ship sunk so far in the war. Of her total complement of 623, twenty-five crew and twenty passengers lost their lives in the two attacks.

Retribution was swift for U-32. Two days later, on 30 October, she was caught and sunk by the destroyers *Harvester* and *Highlander*. Nine of her crew died with her, while Hans Jenisch and thirty-seven others were taken prisoner.

KG 40 struck again on 4 November, when one of their patrolling Condors sighted the 19,000-ton liner *Windsor Castle*, inbound for the Clyde off the west coast of Ireland. This time fortune was with the British ship. The Condor scored a direct hit with a 500lb bomb, but the bomb, which landed in the First Class smoking room, failed to explode. Had it done so, the damage and casualties would have been considerable. As it was, the *Windsor Castle* reached an anchorage at Greenock under her own steam, and the bomb was defused.

At about 1000 on the morning of 8 November, the bridge of the *Cornish City* observed an aircraft circling low on the horizon some 15 miles ahead. It was assumed this must be a patrolling Sunderland of Coastal Command, a forerunner of HX 84's coastal escort. This assumption was proved wrong only minutes later, when a dirty black smoke cloud mushroomed up from the horizon, to be followed by the rumble of a heavy explosion. Immediately afterwards, radio silence was broken by the urgent rattle of Morse, a cry for help from the Swedish ship *Vingaland*, reporting she had been bombed and was on fire.

The 2,719-ton motor vessel *Vingaland*, carrying steel and general cargo from New York to Glasgow, another HX 84 escapee, had been approaching the rendezvous position when a Condor of KG 40 swooped and lobbed a bomb into her engine-room. The blast killed the men on watch below, smashed the main engine, and started fires amidships. The *Vingaland* was abandoned at once, nineteen men taking to the boats, and leaving six dead on board. The survivors were picked up by the ex-French flag steamer *Danae II* on Commodore Maltby's instructions.

The attacking Condor, one of the squadron that had swooped on the westbound convoy OB 239 earlier in the day, made off as soon as it saw the other ships approaching, but it left alarm bells ringing throughout HX 84. It was with some relief that, later in the day, the convoy was joined by the destroyer HMS *Hesperus*, with the tanker *Oil Reliance* in company. The relief would have been short-lived had it been known that another danger was now threatening.

In June 1940, when Italy entered the war on Germany's side, the Italian Navy offered Admiral Dönitz a detachment of its own submarines to help out in the North Atlantic. Dönitz did not have a high opinion of Italian submariners. He is quoted as saying: '...they are not sufficiently hard and tough for this type of warfare. Their way of thinking is too sluggish and according to rule to allow them to adapt themselves clearly and simply to the changing conditions of war. Their personal conduct is not sufficiently disciplined and in the face of the enemy not calm enough.' Nevertheless, Dönitz desperately needed more submarines, even if only to carry out reconnaissance for his U-boats, and in the months that followed a flotilla of twenty-seven Italian boats arrived in Bordeaux. Among them was the *Guglielmo Marconi*.

The 1,200-ton *Marconi*, under the command of Giulio Chialamberto, was one of the Italian Navy's more successful boats. Sailing from Naples on 6 September, she arrived in Bordeaux on the 23rd, venturing out into the Atlantic a month later. She reached her operational area off the west coast of Scotland on the night of 6/7 November, where she was joined by another of the Italian flotilla, Giulio Ghiglieri's *Barbarigo*. The two boats had been warned of the imminent approach of an eastbound convoy, presumably HX 84, but although they searched to the west they sighted nothing. Then, on the 8th, the *Marconi*'s radio operator intercepted a message sent by the *Cornish City* regarding the bombing of the *Vingaland*. Chialamberto set course for the position given, and just before sunset sighted the burning ship. The *Vingaland* was an easy target, and Chialamberto's torpedo went home. Unfortunately for the Italian commander, the destroyer HMS *Havelock* was in the vicinity, and her Asdic operator picked up the *Marconi*. *Havelock* attacked, raining down depth charges on the submarine, forcing her to go deep. Chialamberto took her down to 125 metres, far deeper than any British submarine could dive. This led *Havelock*'s commander to believe he had sunk the Italian, and he withdrew.

The *Vingaland* was last seen with her decks awash, and it was assumed she sank that night. After the war, her wreck was found in 700 fathoms in position 55° 41 N 18° 24 W.

After escaping the depth charges of HMS *Havelock*, the two Italian submarines appeared to have become involved with the reassembled convoy HX 84. Captain Lawrence, of the *Briarwood*, reported:

On the afternoon of Sunday, 10th November, at 1320 we appeared to pass very close to a submarine, in fact I thought we had struck something. The Master of the ERODONA also said he thought he struck something and that it felt like the explosion of a depth charge. Shortly afterwards a torpedo was seen to pass between the stern of the ERODONA and the bow of the BRIARWOOD, although I never saw it.

The *Cornish City* reported similarly, although the timing is different:

> *At 0945 BST November 10th when in position 55° 46 N 09° 42 W
> track of torpedo was seen passing through the centre of convoy.*

It was never established who, or what was attacking HX 84 so near to home, but as there were no German submarines in the area at the time, it was almost certainly one of the Italians.

When Captain Lawson took his lifeboat away from the burning wreck of the *Fresno City* at around midnight on 5 November, he was confident that rescue would soon be on the way. As soon as the gunfire had died down, he decided to go back 30 miles to the spot where the raider first attacked, fully convinced that British rescue ships would already be there. His boat's crew consisted of just twelve men, two of whom were badly injured, and could take no part in handling the boat. It was a long sail, and it was noon on the 7th before they reached the scene of the attack; only to face bitter disappointment. Where Lawson had expected to find other lifeboats and rescue ships busy taking on board survivors, there was only emptiness. Not even a scrap of wreckage remained to tell of the carnage that had been wreaked.

The temptation was to heave to, put out a sea anchor and wait for help – which is what the Admiralty advised for survivors – but this was the North Atlantic, they were nearly 800 miles from the nearest land, and it was the height of winter. After giving the matter some thought, Lawson concluded that if they stayed in the area they were more than likely to die of exposure before rescue came. He decided to sail east for Ireland.

The Atlantic reverted to form during the night, and by dawn on the 8th it was blowing westerly force 8, with a very rough sea. The open boat offered no protection from the elements, and its occupants were constantly being lashed by icy spray and driving rain. They were cold, wet and miserable, but running before the wind with only a light jib sail rigged, the heavy boat fled eastwards like no ship's lifeboat was ever meant to do. By dawn on the 9th they had covered 200 miles, a remarkable feat of seamanship taking into account the fact that the average merchant ship's officer, although adept at handling a big ship, is the complete amateur when it comes to sailing a small boat.

As the war at sea progressed, it became apparent that in the event of an attack on a convoy the escorts were spending far too much time picking up survivors when they should have been chasing the enemy. This gave birth to yet another innovation, the convoy rescue ship.

Initially, rescue ships were chosen from the ranks of the merchantmen, ideally small vessels with well experienced crews. In the event of an attack, it was the function of the rescue ship to drop back and pick up survivors from sunken ships. A typical rescue ship of her day was Bristol City Line's *Gloucester City*.

The *Gloucester City*, a 3,071-ton North Atlantic trader commanded by Captain Sydney Smith, was not a ship to turn heads. Built in 1919, she was a no-nonsense cargo carrier with a maximum speed of 9 knots, but in the eyes of the Admiralty she was a handy little ship suited to their needs. On the outbreak of war in 1939, she was requisitioned and fitted out as an ammunition ship for the British Expeditionary Force. When the Allied campaign collapsed in June 1940, and France fell to Hitler's *Wehrmacht*, the *Gloucester City* resumed her place in Britain's Atlantic supply chain. As she was on the Admiralty's books, she soon found herself with the dual role of cargo carrier/rescue ship, sailing with the westbound convoy OB 191.

Twenty-four hours out of Liverpool, Dönitz's top U-boat ace Otto Kretschmer slipped through the convoy's escort screen and torpedoed the 6,322-ton *Jersey City*, one of Reardon Smith's of Cardiff, a company which at this early stage of the war was suffering heavy losses. Two crew members of the torpedoed ship were killed in the explosion, but thanks to the prompt action of Captain Smith and the *Gloucester City*, who immediately went to her aid, the *Jersey City*'s master and forty-two others were saved.

By the time the *Gloucester City* joined Convoy OB 237 to cross the Atlantic in November 1940, Captain Sydney Smith and his crew were well practised in the arts of rescue, and once again they were stationed at the rear of the convoy, ready to pick up survivors. OB 237 was an important convoy, and heavily escorted; the thirty-six merchant ships being covered by three destroyers, a corvette and two armed trawlers. However, it was then Admiralty policy to disperse westbound convoys in 25 degrees West, this being considered the maximum range of the U-boats based in the French Biscay ports. This was a risky policy, but in view of the shortage of escort vessels, it was considered to be a risk worth taking.

OB 237 dispersed on 2 November, and on the evening of the 5th the *Gloucester City* was crossing south of the Denmark Strait when her radio officer picked up the SOS sent by the *Rangitiki* reporting that HX 84 was being shelled by an enemy battleship. Other reports came flooding in of ships sunk, the position given being only 290 miles to the south-west, just thirty-two hours' steaming for the 9-knot *Gloucester City*. The Admiralty's standing advice to merchant ships was to stay clear of other ships sunk by enemy action, for obvious reasons; but Captain Sydney Smith, knowing there might be men in the water needing help, decided to intervene. He altered course to the south-west and increased speed.

The *Gloucester City* was no ocean greyhound, but Smith estimated he would be able to reach the scene of the attack in the early hours of the 7th. Then the Atlantic again turned nasty. After dark on the 6th, the wind suddenly freshened, ratcheting up to storm force 10 from the west by midnight. Slamming into the mounting head seas, the elderly *Gloucester City* took a heavy pounding during the night but, fortunately, towards dawn the wind eased. By 0600 on the 7th she was in the position given by the *Rangitiki*, but conditions for a search could not have been worse. It was still dark, the rough seas were slow to subside, and driving rain squalls were shutting the visibility down to zero at times.

Allowing for wind and current, Captain Smith assumed any boats or rafts would have drifted in a south-easterly direction, and with extra lookouts posted, he began a square search. The possibility that the German raider might be still in the vicinity either did not occur to him or, more likely, he thought the risk worth taking.

Smith's decision proved to be the right one. An hour later, a small boat was sighted. It was the *San Demetrio*'s after port lifeboat, manned by Chief Officer Wilson and eighteen others. They were taken on board and given hot food and dry clothes. Smith continued to search, and two and a half hours later his perseverance was rewarded when the tanker's other missing boat, with Captain Waite and three men aboard, was found. Of the *San Demetrio*'s third boat, in charge of Second Officer Arthur Hawkins, there was no sign, and no one was aware of the incredible adventure Hawkins, Pollard and the others had embarked upon.

Two more hours passed while Smith continued to criss-cross from horizon to horizon. Then, around noon, two small sails were observed to the south, which proved to be all that was left of the *Trewellard*'s crew. Captain Daneil and twenty-four very cold and exhausted men.

Encouraged by his success, Captain Smith persisted in his search for survivors, and that afternoon two more lifeboats were found. One contained Captain Milner and nineteen of the crew of the *Kenbane Head*, the other was the missing boat from the *Fresno City*, containing her Chief Officer and twenty-three men.

The search was called off at nightfall, when it became obvious to Captain Smith that no one else was alive in the area. His humanitarian mission, undertaken on the spur of the moment, had been a spectacular success, and in the finest tradition of the sea. The *Gloucester City* had saved from almost certain death no fewer than ninety-two men. They were landed in St John's, Newfoundland on 13 November, all none the worse for their ordeal. Captain Sydney Smith was later awarded the OBE (Civil Division) for his 'outstanding courage and leadership during the war'.

The question that must now be asked is how a small, elderly tramp like the *Gloucester City* was able to locate and rescue seven boatloads of survivors when seven British destroyers were said to be in the same area at the same time and found nothing.

Despite the numerous technical problems that had plagued the four-stackers, they were still infinitely better equipped to carry out an extensive search and rescue operation than an ageing Bristol Channel tramp. Steering by gyro compass, they were constantly in touch with each other by radio, they carried powerful searchlights, and were manned by enough men to keep a lookout on every point of the compass with binoculars at all times. *Lincoln*, *Ludlow* and *Lewes* reached the position of the attack on HX 84 by 0900 on the 6th. They were followed twenty-four hours later by *Leamington*, *Leeds*, *Churchill* and *Montgomery*. Commander Sheffield and Commander Banks claimed bad weather and fuel shortages limited their ability to search, but both divisions of destroyers passed through the area on the 6th and 7th; and yet they saw no survivors, no wreckage.

The *Gloucester City*, on the other hand, with minimum crew and nothing more sophisticated to guide her than a magnetic compass and a sextant, not only reached the correct spot, but also searched the area for more than nine hours. Captain Smith's dogged perseverance resulted in the rescue of ninety-two men who might otherwise have died.

Captain (D), Devonport reported to the subsequent Board of Inquiry, held on 19 November 1940:

*HMS Leamington's division, which included HM ships Churchill,
Leeds and Montgomery, received no instructions whatever to search
for survivors but their orders to spread out and search for the Admiral
von Scheer took them through the area in which Convoy HX 84 was
attacked. Visibility was good and all ships kept a good lookout, but
sighted neither survivors, nor any sign of wreckage.*

HMS *Lincoln*, accompanied by *Lewes* and *Ludlow*, specifically ordered to
search for survivors, likewise found nothing, even though Commander
Sheffield reported the weather as 'fair'.

Furthermore, not one of the destroyers reported seeing the
Gloucester City, or, for that matter, the *Stureholm*, both of which were in
the area at the same time. It is to be wondered whether, as a result of
some serious navigational error, the destroyers might have been
searching in the wrong area.

Fresh out of William Doxford's Sunderland yard in 1918, the
5,299-ton *Trefusis* produced a commendable 11 knots on her trials. In
November 1940, after twenty-two gruelling years in the cross-trades,
she was hard-pressed to make 9 knots. When the *Admiral Scheer*
turned her guns on Convoy HX 84, the *Trefusis* scattered with the rest;
but in view of her lack of horse power, Captain Parmee elected to make
his escape to the north, where the horizon was dark and beckoning.
Only five hours later, when the flash of the guns and the dancing
flames of ships on fire had dipped below the horizon, did he feel
reasonably safe.

When dawn came on the 6th, the *Trefusis* was alone on an empty, but
increasingly hostile sea. Ironically, she had left one danger behind, only
to be confronted by another. During the night the bottom had dropped
out of the glass, and it was blowing a full gale from the north-east with
a sea gone wild. The *Trefusis*, deep-loaded and awkward with steel in her
lower holds and timber stacked high on deck, was soon taking a severe
pounding, pitching heavily and shipping green seas overall.

Like all ships in convoy, the *Trefusis* carried sealed orders giving her
a route to be followed should she be forced to go her own way. When
opened, the orders showed a rendezvous point off Bloody Foreland,
where it was hoped the scattered ships would be reassembled under the
protection of escorts from Western Approaches Command. This would
entail the *Trefusis* altering onto an easterly course, but fearing that the

German raider might also be heading east, Captain Parmee decided to continue to the north.

Over the next four days the *Trefusis* struggled to make headway against the weather, but her progress was painfully slow, her average speed being a little over 6 knots. At noon on the 9th, she was some 150 miles north-west of Rockall and at last in position to turn south to make her approach to the North Channel. However, taking into account that he was so far to the north, and heeding reports of U-boat activity near the North Channel, Captain Parmee decided to pass north of the Outer Hebrides, and enter British waters via the Minches. In view of the foul weather and uncertain visibility this was not an easy approach. And one which was not recommended by the Admiralty for unescorted vessels. The Minches, or Skotlandsfjord in the Old Norse, are a 100-mile-long strait separating the Outer Hebrides from mainland Scotland. In 1940 it was a busy stretch of water, used by convoys north- and southbound from the assembly point at Loch Ewe. Submerged rocks, powerful tides and currents, wildly fluctuating weather, lighthouses dimmed or unlit, and fleets of unpredictable fishermen, all combined to make the Minches a serious navigational hazard.

There is a legend, repeated even today, that a tribe of supernatural sea creatures known as the 'Blue Men of the Minches' inhabit these waters lying in wait for the unwary mariner. Half human, half fish, the Blue Men are said to lure ships to disaster, and can only be deterred by the sea captain with a sharp tongue and a talent for unsolvable riddles. It must be that on the dark November night in 1940 when the *Trefusis* entered the Minches, Captain Parmee had no such riddle to offer. The following is an eyewitness account of events written in later life by Captain (then Third Officer) H.C. (Bill) Fellingham:

Shortly before 2000 on 11th November I went on the bridge to relieve the 1st Mate. It was a wild night with a strong easterly wind and frequent rain showers in between which the moon would briefly appear. The Mate told me to be on the lookout for fishermen as he had seen several, so, as soon as he had left the bridge, which was about 2002, I took up the binoculars and started scanning the horizon, starting on the port beam. When I got to about one point on the port bow I saw a dark shape which, at first, I thought was land but then realised was a ship. I put my hand into the wheelhouse to put our navigation light master switch on but found that it was already in the on position, shouted 'starboard' to the helmsman and blew one short blast on the ship's whistle. The other ship then put its navigation lights on from which I could see that it was crossing our bow finely from port to starboard. I then shouted 'hard to starboard', gave another short blast on the whistle and put the engine room telegraph to 'full astern'. To my consternation the other ship then blew a two short blast signal signifying that it was turning to port and, at 2008, the TREFUSIS struck the other ship, at a nearly 90° angle, between her bridge and her funnel (which was aft).

Our engines had not been going astern until after we hit so the full momentum of the Trefusis went into the collision. After we had drawn away from the other ship, which proved to be THE DUCHESS, a 1200 dwt coaster, straggling behind a northbound convoy through which the TREFUSIS had unknowingly steamed (during the 1st Mate's watch and which he thought were fishermen), she morsed to us 'sinking – send boat'. I asked our Captain if I should take a boat away and he agreed.

I need to relate why I found it impossible to put on our navigation lights, the master switch being already in the on position. The TREFUSIS was one of those ships which, when the degaussing coils were energised, had insufficient electrical capacity to provide any other electrical facilities apart from emergency navigation lights. Because the Captain wanted a light in his cabin to do the ship's accounts, he got an engineer to take a lead from the navigation light circuit. However, this meant that the master switch had to remain on and the individual navigation light switches off. The individual light switches were on the lower bridge which meant the officer of the watch leaving the bridge to put them on – an impossibility in a swift emergency, as this collision was.

Launching the heavy old wooden, oar propelled lifeboat in total darkness into a lumpy sea was difficult to say the least. I got six volunteers to man the boat with me, four firemen, a steward and one AB. Our Captain had taken the TREFUSIS up to windward of THE DUCHESS, which was still afloat with its lights on, so that we could row downwind to her. However, as soon as we had left the lee of the TREFUSIS, I heard cries of 'help' coming from the water to windward of us. I tried to head towards the cries but in the weather circumstances and sea state, we didn't have enough muscle power to pull the heavy boat to windward, the boat's head fell off the wind as each wave hit it. We tried our utmost but, tragically, the cries got weaker and weaker until we heard them no more.

THE DUCHESS was still afloat to windward and we saw some of her lights flashing on and off so I concluded that someone was still on board and made for her. On manoeuvring alongside we saw, as her stern rose in the seas, that her propeller was still turning and getting the boat alongside her without being struck by it was quite tricky, she was only 190ft long and had a large wooden rubbing band just above the waterline. When alongside, one man jumped into the boat. When I yelled 'tell the rest to hurry along', he said that he was the only one left on board. It appears that he was the Cook/Steward and was in his bunk when the collision occurred. By the time that he got on deck he found that the other 11 men in the crew had (in spite of having asked the TREFUSIS to send a boat) launched their lifeboat but it had overturned as soon as it left the ship's lee and all were thrown into the water. We returned to the TREFUSIS from which we had been away for 3 hours.

We passed Ailsa Craig in the evening of 12th November, a week had already gone since the ADMIRAL SCHEER had attacked HX 84, and anchored in Rothesay Bay in the morning of the 13th after suffering another collision when an outward bound Swedish ship struck us amidships, fortunately in our bunker spaces. The TREFUSIS was one of the last ships to reach the UK, the last being the SAN DEMETRIO which we all stood at the rail and cheered as she went past with SOS painted on her shell damaged deck houses, a sight I will never forget.

Chapter 13

THE AFTERMATH

Late on Sunday afternoon, 12 November, seven days after the *Admiral Scheer*'s savage assault on Convoy HX 84, watchers at the entrance to Halifax harbour saw a rust-streaked Swedish tramp emerge from the fog. A flag signal at her yardarm indicated that she had survivors on board. The *Stureholm* had returned to her port of sailing.

News of the attack on HX 84 and the sinking of HMS *Jervis Bay* had travelled ahead of the *Stureholm*. It had been thought that every man on board the British AMC had perished, and port workers were astonished when the sixty-five survivors, some still in their salt-stained naval uniforms, filed down the gangway of the Swedish ship.

By the time the *Jervis Bay*'s men had been taken care of, many of them finding beds in the local hospital, news of the epic rescue had spread around the town, and the celebrations were in hand. Captain Olander and his men were treated to the full force of Nova Scotian hospitality. They were wined and dined, photographed from every possible angle, and generally feted like the heroes they were. The partying had not finished when Sven Olander found himself faced with yet another dilemma.

The *Stureholm* still had nearly 7,000 tons of steel on board urgently needed in Britain, and was scheduled to return across the Atlantic with Convoy HX 91, due to sail from Halifax on 25 November. But when the time came to leave, the majority of the *Stureholm*'s crew decided they had had enough of war, and refused to sail. Captain Olander, who as might be expected in view of the stress he had been under, was suffering from stomach ulcers, was powerless to act. He appealed to the local authorities for help, but while showing every sympathy for Olander's plight, they could do nothing to help him. It was politely pointed out that the men were neutrals on foreign soil, and if they did not wish to sail in the ship, they could not be forced to do so. When approached, the

British naval authorities in Halifax took a similar stance. Then, after a great deal of discussion and negotiating, the following message was sent to the Admiralty in London:

PTG 40/11/19/1055. FROM COAC HALIFAX. NUMBER OF STUREHOLM OFFICERS AND CREW REFUSED TO SAIL AFTER REACHING HALIFAX AND ARE BEING PAID OFF. HOPE TO COMPLETE CREW FROM OTHER HX 84 SURVIVORS AND SAIL STUREHOLM IN HX 91. NO DISCIPLINARY ACTION CONTEMPLATED AND NO AWARDS RECOMMENDED.

The naval authorities at Halifax had taken into account that since coming under British jurisdiction, the *Stureholm*'s crew had carried a number of vital cargoes across the Atlantic. They had also shown great courage in agreeing to go to the rescue of the *Jervis Bay* survivors when they were not obliged to do so. It was therefore decided that to force them to take their ship back out into the Atlantic bloodbath after all they had been through would be an abuse of their Swedish neutrality. Which makes the concluding remark 'NO AWARDS RECOMMENDED' seem somewhat churlish; for whatever their subsequent actions, these were very brave men.

It took longer than expected to organise a replacement crew for the *Stureholm*, with the result that she did not leave Halifax until 29 November, and then with Convoy HX 92. Captain Sven Olander remained in command, and he had with him just five of his original Swedish crew, namely First Mate Erling Hansen, Assistant Engineer Peder Stoveland, and the three engine-room mechanics Leif Johnsen, Olaf Opdal and Hans Marius Storbo. Volunteers had been called for from the other British survivors of HX 84, resulting in three ex-*San Demetrio* officers stepping forward. Extra Second Engineer Harold Duncan became the *Stureholm*'s chief engineer, while Fifth Engineer Thomas Mockford became Fourth Engineer, and Third Officer Sydney Wilson signed on in the same rank. Eight Canadian volunteers completed the crew.

HX 92's voyage did not begin well. Eleven ships, the vanguard of the convoy, including the *Stureholm*, sailed from Halifax on 29 November, the plan being to rendezvous off St John's, Newfoundland with ships coming from Sydney. Unfortunately, a mixture of fog, gales and possibly poor navigation resulted in a great deal of confusion. It was noon on 4 December before the two sections met up nearly 500 miles to the east of Newfoundland.

When finally formed up in nine columns abreast, Convoy HX 92 consisted of twenty-four merchantmen. They were an unusually cosmopolitan mix, with seven British, seven Swedish, four Norwegian, three Dutch, two Greek and one Belgian, all heavily loaded with steel and general. As had been the case with HX 84, their sole protection from the enemy lay with an armed merchant cruiser. She was HMS *Montclare*, commanded by 53-year-old Captain Herbert Spreckley, RN RD.

The *Montclare* was a 16,000-ton ex-Canadian Pacific passenger liner taken into service by the Admiralty and armed with the usual selection of outdated guns. High-sided, twin-funnelled, and with a maximum speed of 16 knots, she was really only a piece of window dressing, a compromise to reassure those manning the cargo carriers.

The convoy commodore, Rear Admiral John Fitzgerald, RN was in New Zealand Shipping Company's 10,890-ton *Rotorua*, which was carrying a refrigerated cargo and twenty-seven service personnel as passengers. This was Commodore Fitzgerald's first convoy.

For Captain Sven Olander and many of those on board the *Stureholm* the pattern was all too familiar. It was HX 84 all over again.

Foul weather dogged HX 92 right from the commencement of the voyage, becoming steadily worse as the ships progressed eastwards. Gale force winds, gusting to hurricane force 12 at times, made a mockery of station-keeping. The box-shaped merchantmen lumbered from crest to trough, straggling and romping helplessly. Slowly, the orderly ranks of the convoy drifted apart until each deep-loaded, under-powered ship was fighting her own personal battle with the wind and waves. HMS *Montclare*, slab-sided and riding high out of the water, suffered most, being constantly blown off course. Captain Spreckley increasingly found his ship out of sight and out of touch with the convoy she was meant to protect. Eventually, the *Montclare* ceased to function as an escort. Entries in her log for 8 December read:

> *0410 - Ship running at 70 revolutions on port and 30 revolutions on starboard engine; making 8½ knots. Heavy squall from 6 points abaft*

*beam and ship swung 53 degrees to port and remained on that course
for 10 minutes despite full speed on engines and full helm. Came back
onto course 2 cables from one of the convoy.*

0750 - Squall of force 12 hit ship and again she fell off her course.

*0920 - 0930 - Passed eight ships of convoy to SE of us. Did not see
Commodore's ship. Wind now 260 degrees force 12 and very heavy
sea, some ships may have hove to.*

*1000 - Attempted to alter course to 040 degrees, at 14 knots with helm
hard over the ship would not come past 350 degrees.*

*1035 - Depth charges went overboard and detonated, all depth charges
set to safe and primers withdrawn.*

By the morning of the 9th HMS *Montclare* had lost sight of the convoy,
and unless the weather moderated had little hope of re-establishing
contact. As they were now nearing the position where ships of Western
Approaches Command were due to take over the protection of the
convoy, Captain Spreckley decided he might just as well reverse course
and head back to Halifax.

The approach of the disorganised HX 92 to British waters had been
detected by German Intelligence, which had duly notified Admiral
Dönitz. At this time Dönitz had only five U-boats operating in the
North Atlantic. As for the twenty-seven Italian boats he had recently
taken under his wing, they had not proved to be a great deal of help. He
explained in an entry in his War Diary on 4 December:

*As no weather reports have been received from the Italian boats, I find
myself forced to detail one of our boats for this. It will have to be one
of the 5 in the attacking positions ready for the convoy announced by
Radio Intelligence. This is very undesirable, but I have no
alternative...This new, very modest attempt to cooperate with the
Italians had failed. Two of them were ordered to make the weather
reports. Neither of them produced messages which were any use.*

*This is unfortunately not the only disappointment. I did not expect
that the Italians would at once sink a lot of shipping...But I did at
least hope that they would contribute to a better reconnaissance of the
operations area. In actual fact during the whole time I have not
received one single enemy report from them on which I could take
action...*

Goering's Luftwaffe, heavily engaged in bombing raids on Britain's towns and cities, was dependent on the U-boats for regular weather reports from the North Atlantic. This was something Dönitz had promised to deliver when he was lobbying for more cooperation between the Luftwaffe and the U-boat arm. When the Italians let him down, he ordered the nearest available U-boat to fill the gap. This was U-96.

Newly commissioned in September, U-96 had sailed from Kiel on her maiden war patrol on the 14th under the command of 29-year-old Kapitänleutnant Heinrich Lehmann-Willenbrock. A regular Navy man who had served in cruisers between the wars, Lehmann-Willenbrock had transferred to U-boats early in 1939. His first command, U-5, had played a brief and undistinguished part in the Norwegian campaign, and he was yet to come to grips with the enemy. When Lehmann-Willenbrock commissioned U-96, a Type VIIC, he was ready to go to war, only to find himself assigned to weather reporting duties.

Of all the many functions a U-boat might be called upon to perform, weather reporting in the Atlantic was the most hated. It was a task usually assigned to a boat that had used up all her torpedoes, yet still had fuel to spare, and it entailed loitering in a specified position sending in weather reports twice a day. Not only was the work excruciatingly boring, for much of the year it was carried out in the most atrocious weather, the boat idling on the surface rolling drunkenly in the troughs, decks awash and spray raining down through the open conning tower hatch. And there was danger, too. Allied radio stations kept a continuous listening watch on the U-boat frequencies, and were sometimes able to fix the position of a boat by WT/DF. Then, the Sunderlands of Coastal Command came looking. Weather reporting in the North Atlantic was a miserable existence that no U-boat commander worthy of his rank would wish upon himself and his crew.

U-96 was rolling her gunwales under some 200 miles north-west of Cape Wrath dutifully recording the weather when the first ships of HX 92 came straggling in for the North Channel. They were led by the 10,890-ton *Rotorua*, commanded by Captain Edgar Kemp, and with the convoy commodore Rear Admiral John Fitzgerald and his staff on board. The 29-year-old *Rotorua* was nearing the end of a long and momentous voyage. Sailing from Liverpool in the spring of 1940, bound in convoy with a general cargo for Australia, she had been torpedoed soon after the convoy dispersed in 20 degrees West. It was feared she would have to be abandoned, but the damage was not serious, and she was able to reach Panama, where temporary repairs were carried out. The *Rotorua* then went on to Auckland, where she discharged her cargo and the repairs to her hull were made permanent. She then loaded a refrigerated cargo at various New Zealand ports. Now, after six months away, and having steamed 24,000 miles, she was on the home stretch.

When Captain Spreckley decided to leave the convoy and take the *Montclare* back to Halifax, he left with the assurance that a strong local escort force was on its way to lead HX 92 into the North Channel. Unfortunately, due to the persistently bad weather, the escort force, consisting of the destroyers *Chelsea*, *Veteran* and *Wolverine*, with the corvette *Camelia*, failed to find the convoy. When U-96 sighted HX 92 off the Outer Hebrides; it was completely unescorted.

The sight of two columns of loaded merchantmen crawling towards him at what was little more than walking pace, and with not a single enemy warship in sight, was the answer to the newly promoted Heinrich Lehmann-Willenbrock's dream. It only remained for him to use his torpedoes wisely. Hesitating briefly to scan the horizon once more, he brought U-96 to the surface and waited for the convoy to come to him.

Unsuspecting, and hampered by the poor visibility, Captain Kemp failed to see the U-boat on the surface, and steamed straight into Lehmann-Willenbrock's sights. The torpedo slammed into the *Rotorua*'s engine-room, and exploded with a deafening roar. Second Purser Bill Green recalled many years later:

We sank in 15 minutes with many lives lost. I went to look for my friend and when I got back all the lifeboats on the port side had sailed off. On the starboard side they were all storm-wrecked except one. We lowered this one and filled it with crew. The suction from the sinking ship was very hard to get away from and our hands were sore with rowing.

Four lifeboats left the *Rotorua* with 110 survivors on board. Twenty-two men were missing, including Captain Edgar Kemp and Rear Admiral John Fitzgerald. Once clear, the survivors lay back on their oars and watched the death throes of their ship. The *Rotorua* remained afloat for just a few more minutes, then lifted her bows high in the air, before sinking stern first, taking her precious cargo of food to the bottom with her.

U-96 approached the *Rotorua*'s lifeboats, questioned the survivors, and took two prisoners. But the U-boat was not about to escape retribution completely. As she cruised around waiting for her next victim, the 8,237-ton British tanker *Cardita*, loaded with gas oil for Glasgow, manned her 4-inch and opened fire. She landed six shells close alongside the submarine, causing her to dive in a hurry. It was superb gunnery from men who had had very little training in the art.

Deterred by this unexpected show of aggression by a seemingly harmless merchantman, Lehmann-Willenbrock did not surface again until after dark. At about 1800, he closed in on the Rotterdam-registered steamer *Towa*. The 5,419-ton *Towa*, commanded by Captain W. Smit, with nearly 8,000 tons of bulk grain in her holds and forty-eight lorries on deck, was a soft target, unarmed and slow-moving. Willenbrock's torpedo easily found its mark amidships.

The *Towa* came to an abrupt halt, but buoyed up by her grain cargo she stubbornly refused to sink. Lehmann-Willenbrock tried again with a second torpedo, and when this too failed to put the Dutchman down he resorted to using his deck gun. Even then, at close range, and with the *Towa* stopped and drifting, it took sixteen 88mm shells to deliver the *coup de grâce*. While his ship was under fire, Captain Smit ordered his crew to abandon ship. Three lifeboats were lowered, one of which capsized, throwing its occupants into the sea. Eighteen men lost their lives.

In answer to the frantic distress signals emanating from HX 92, the destroyers *Matabele*, *Escapade*, *Electra* and *Bulldog*, which had left Scapa Flow that morning to escort the battleship *Rodney* inward bound, were detached to go to the convoy's aid. Two other destroyers, *Veteran* and *Mashona*, were reported in the vicinity, but had been unable to find the convoy. HMS *Matabele* picked up eighteen survivors, including Captain Smit, from the *Towa*'s lifeboats.

The night wore on, and HX 92 was still without escort, but being now only 50 miles west of the Outer Hebrides, it was thought that the worst danger for the convoy had passed. Then U-96 struck again.

At four minutes to midnight, the faithful *Stureholm*, having survived so many dangers in the months just past, was 12 miles south of the lonely island of St Kilda when Lehmann-Willenbrock's torpedo blasted a huge hole in her stern. Dragged under by her cargo of steel, she sank like a stone in a pond. U-96 reported four lifeboats leaving the sinking ship; but as the Swedish ship had only two lifeboats, this report must be regarded with scepticism. No survivors from the *Stureholm* were ever found, so it is more likely that Captain Sven Olander and his crew of volunteers had no time to launch boats and went down with their ship. It was a thankless ending for those who had come through the trauma of HX 84, especially so for those who had put their lives on the line to go to the rescue of the *Jervis Bay*'s survivors. For the three men who had escaped the attack on the *San Demetrio* and the others who had stepped forward to help get the Swedish ship back across the Atlantic, it was poor recompense for their willing gesture.

The now ragged convoy was still without escort, and Lehmann-Willenbrock now made the most of his good fortune by sinking the 5,227-ton Belgian steamer *Macedonier*. The *Macedonier*, bound Billingham with phosphates, went down at 0330 on the 12th, taking four of her crew with her. Then it was time to call a halt to the shooting spree, for the destroyers *Veteran* and *Mashona*, along with several anti-submarine trawlers, had arrived on the scene. A thorough search was made for the U-boat, but by this time Lehmann-Willenbrock had taken U-96 out of harm's way over the horizon. It remained only for the naval ships to look around for survivors. Second Purser Bill Green of the *Rotorua* recalled what happened when his lifeboat pulled away from the sinking ship:

The weather was cold in the Atlantic in December. I don't think we would have survived 2 days.

However, after a day we were sighted by a Sunderland flying boat from the RAF reconnaissance patrol. We managed to send a flare up into the sky and after 2 or 3 she sighted us. She dipped her wings and photographed us and signalled that a trawler would eventually pick us up. The Sunderland then vanished into the distant sky.

The cold weather was getting the better of us and I felt frozen to death. You do not survive long in the Atlantic in the winter with no warm clothes on.

However, a trawler sighted us and picked us up. I was suffering from hypothermia and cold. After a few more days we were landed at Stornaway, Scotland. A week or more passed before we got home to Liverpool.

Nineteen survivors from the *Towa* were picked up by HMS *Matabele*, while thirty-seven men from the *Macedonier* were found by the Icelandic ship *Súlan* after being spotted by an aircraft.

In all, on her first Atlantic war patrol U-96 sank five ships totalling 42,264 tons, and damaged two others. For a newly commissioned boat commanded by a relatively inexperienced kapitänleutnant this compared very favourably with Kapitän-zur-See Theodor Krancke's big gun attack on HX 84. Admiral Dönitz was well pleased with Heinrich Lehmann-Willenbrock.

Finding sanctuary in Liverpool after her mid-Atlantic meeting with the *Admiral Scheer*, the *Rangitiki* was not long at rest after discharging her cargo. Captain Keith Barnett and his crew were then able to snatch only a few precious days' leave before they were back on board preparing the ship for her next voyage. Events were moving fast in North Africa; the Italian Army in the Western Desert had been routed, and there was now an urgent need for troops and equipment to consolidate the British victory. The *Rangitiki* was to go trooping.

Sailing from Liverpool on 19 December, the *Rangitiki* joined Convoy WS 5A, which was then assembling in the North Channel. When complete, the convoy consisted of mainly large and fast liners, including the Pacific Steam Navigation Company's 16,000-ton *Orbita*, the *Llandaff Castle* of Union Castle Line, the *Elizabethville* and *Leopoldville* of Compagnie Maritime Belge and Holland America's *Volendam*. The convoy commodore, Rear Admiral C.N. Reyne, RN, sailed in Shaw Savill's *Tamaroa*, a twin-screw 15-knotter taken up from the New Zealand run. WS 5A, carrying 40,000 troops and 150,000 tons of arms, equipment and vehicles, was said to be one of the most important 'Winston Specials' of the war. The majority of the ships were bound for Suez, via the Cape of Good Hope, while several were to enter the Mediterranean with supplies for Malta and Greece.

Escorting WS 5A was a formidable force, led by the heavy cruiser HMS *Berwick*, with the anti-aircraft cruisers *Bonaventure* and *Naiad*, the light cruiser *Dunedin*, the sloop *Wellington*, the Flower-class corvettes *Clematis* and *Cyclamen* and the two old, but effective aircraft carriers *Argus* and *Furious*. The carriers were playing a dual role; in addition to their Skua fighter-bombers, they had several squadrons of Hurricanes on board, which were to be flown off when abreast of Takoradi to go overland to the Middle East. *Bonaventure* and *Naiad*, both 32-knot light cruisers armed with eight 5.25-inch dual purpose guns, a 4-inch quick-firer and a formidable array of machine-guns, would escort the Malta-bound ships into the Mediterranean.

The heavy escort for the convoy was the result of a perceived threat posed by Krancke's *Admiral Scheer*, known to be at large somewhere in the Atlantic; the Admiralty being anxious to avoid a repeat of the fiasco of HX 84. Unknown to Whitehall at the time, the *Scheer* was, in fact, some 4,000 miles further south, and due to make a Christmas Day rendezvous with her supply ship *Nordmark*. Also unknown to the Admiralty, was the presence in the Atlantic of the German heavy cruiser *Admiral Hipper*. The *Hipper*, under the command of Kapitän-zur-See Wilhelm Meisel, had recently slipped unseen through the Denmark Strait, and was on her way south hoping to build on the limited successes of the *Scheer*.

While WS 5A was in the process of forming up, another more mundane convoy, OB 260, outward bound from Liverpool, had reached a position 750 miles west of Land's End, and was on the point of dispersing. Most of the twenty-nine merchantmen making up OB 260 were heading west across the Atlantic, the one exception being the Commodore's ship *Jumna*.

The 6,087-ton *Jumna*, owned by Nourse Line of London, and under the command of Captain Robert Burgess, was bound for Calcutta, via the Cape, with a general cargo. She also had on board, as passengers, forty-four Lascar seamen being repatriated to India following the loss of their ship, T & J Harrison's *Planter*, torpedoed by U-137 a month earlier. On her way to the Cape, the *Jumna* would call at Freetown to land the commodore and his staff. Coincidentally, OB 260's commodore was Rear Admiral H.B. Maltby, recently of the *Cornish City* and HX 84, back at sea again after a brief spell of leave.

Inevitably, the Atlantic weather dictated the course of events that followed. When the *Hipper* cleared the Denmark Strait, like her predecessor, she ran into a ferocious Atlantic storm that left her severely battered, with her starboard engine disabled. A second storm followed hard on the heels of the first, and for several days the German cruiser battled against heavy seas in poor visibility. She eventually ended up to the south of the Halifax-UK convoy track without having sighted a single ship. Kapitän Meisel, now concerned for his dwindling fuel supply, set course for Brest, intending to cross the Liverpool-Freetown convoy track with the hope of intercepting a large convoy which had been reported moving south.

Meanwhile, the convoy in question, WS 5A, had also found bad weather. After sunset on Christmas Eve, when 700 miles due west of Cape Finisterre, the British ships ran into a severe south-westerly gale that raged throughout the night. Battling against rough head seas, and hampered by blinding rain squalls, station-keeping became nigh impossible, and chaos reigned in the ranks of the convoy. When a grey dawn came on the morning of Christmas, the weather was showing signs of moderating, but there was precious little goodwill in the air. The wind had lost some of its strength, but the sky remained heavily overcast, the long Atlantic swell still persisted, and the sea was a restless chop. A mixture of drizzle and morning mist completed the picture of a thoroughly miserable Christmas Day.

There is a strong probability that the *Hipper* would have sailed past the convoy without sighting it, had it not been for the actions of one ship, ironically an ex-German vessel under the British flag.

The 14,000-ton *Empire Trooper*, ex-*Cap Norte* of the Hamburg South America Line, was captured off Iceland while trying to run the Royal Navy's blockade early in the war. Unfortunately, during the chase her German crew sabotaged her engines, as a result of which she had suffered chronic machinery problems ever after. During the night just past, there had been yet another engine breakdown, and the *Empire Trooper* had straggled some miles astern of the convoy. She was being escorted back into position early on the 25th by the corvette HMS *Clematis*, when the *Hipper* suddenly loomed up out of the mist. The little corvette, commanded by the intrepid Commander Yorke McLeod Cleeves, DSO, DSC, RNR, did not hesitate to give battle. With total disregard to the odds against him, Cleeves steered for the *Hipper* at full speed, his single 4-inch hurling shells at the enemy cruiser. His signal to the Admiralty, 'AM ENGAGING UNKNOWN ENEMY BATTLESHIP', was as audacious as the man himself. The corvette's shells made no impression on the *Hipper*'s armoured hull, but her brave action did alert the big ships of WS 5A's escort.

The 8-inch gun cruiser *Berwick*, followed by HMS *Dunedin* and the anti-aircraft cruiser *Bonaventure* came storming up to challenge the raider, and during the brief action that followed the *Hipper* returned shot for shot with her attackers. However, in the poor visibility prevailing she scored only one hit, knocking *Berwick*'s 'X' turret out of action and killing its crew of seven Marines. In return, the German cruiser received only minor damage, and suffered no casualties. But after considering the possibilities of a prolonged action Kapitän Meisel decided to retire from the fray. He wrote in his War Diary:

I have decided to break off the operation and to sail to Brest as fast as possible before measures are taken by the enemy, provoked by the attack on the convoy, take effect. If I continued at sea I would have to refuel tomorrow at the latest in order to remain in operation. This has been the task which was set me. I feel the moment has come where the limit of the efficiency of ship and crew is in sight.

Meisel's decision to disengage was a wise one. News of the attack reaching the Admiralty in London had resulted in a flurry of activity. HMS *Naiad*, which had left the convoy during the night to return north, was ordered to reverse course, while the battlecruiser *Repulse* and the heavy cruisers *Kenya* and *Nigeria* were despatched at full speed to join WS 5A. Units of the Home Fleet were sent to cover the Denmark Strait, and long range aircraft of Coastal Command began intensive patrols over the approaches to the Biscay ports. The *Admiral Hipper*, once the hunter, had become the hunted.

Fate, coincidence if you like, once more intervened in this drama of the high seas. Later that morning, driving through the rain at 30 knots, the *Hipper* sighted a lone merchant ship steaming south. It was the *Jumna*, late of Convoy OB 260, bound Freetown to land Rear Admiral Maltby and his staff, before continuing on to Calcutta. At first, Captain Burgess, believing he was well out of reach of the enemy, took the stranger to be a British warship, but some sixth sense warned him of danger. When the *Hipper* challenged by lamp, Burgess replied, but immediately turned his ship about and ran, at the same time instructing his radio officer to send out the RRR message indicating they were being attacked by an enemy warship.

As soon as the *Hipper* intercepted the *Jumna*'s call for help, Meisel opened fire on her with all guns he could bring to bear, looking for a quick kill. The destruction of the helpless merchantman took just a few minutes. Staggering under a hail of shells, the *Jumna* drifted to a halt, her bridge and midships accommodation in smoking ruins, her scuppers running red with blood. Captain Robert Burgess lay dead on his bridge, and at his side the broken body of Rear Admiral Maltby, who only seven weeks earlier had escaped the guns of the *Admiral Scheer*. It is almost certain that most of the Indian survivors of the *Planter*, who were accommodated on deck, also died then.

Although completely disabled and on fire from stem to stern, the *Jumna* stubbornly refused to sink, and Meisel had to resort to using two torpedoes at close range to send her to the bottom. That being done, he steamed away without attempting to pick up survivors. Meisel's excuse was that he expected the British cruisers he had engaged earlier in the day might come racing over the horizon.

In fact, Kapitän Meisel's fears were groundless. The *Jumna*'s distress had not been picked up by any ship or shore radio station, and it was not until she was several weeks overdue at Freetown that she was posted missing, believed sunk. No wreckage from the ship was ever found, and not one man of her total complement of 111 survived.

Chapter 14

THE RECKONING

Due largely to the stubborn resistance put up by the British cargo ship *Beaverford*, the *Admiral Scheer*'s attempt to wipe out Convoy HX 84 on 5 November had been thwarted for more than five hours. By the time the *Fresno City* had been despatched midnight was drawing near, and having used up a third of his ammunition, Kapitän Theodor Krancke decided it was dangerous to prolong his attack further. He left the Atlantic battlefield firmly convinced he had scored a major victory that would, once and for all, show the superiority of the surface raider over the U-boat. In a report wirelessed to Berlin, Krancke claimed to have sunk 86,000 tons of Allied shipping in one fell swoop.

In reality, Krancke's attack on the convoy had been nowhere near the rout he claimed. Discounting the *Jervis Bay*, he had sunk only five merchantmen totalling 33,363 tons and set one tanker on fire. However, it has to be admitted that the *Scheer* had achieved the main object of her operational orders, which was to 'create alarm and insecurity along the enemy's supply lines'. There can be no doubt that the sudden appearance of a German pocket battleship in the North Atlantic convoy lanes created near-panic in Whitehall. The Admiralty, by now frantic to avoid criticism for entrusting a valuable convoy to just one armed merchant cruiser, pulled out all the stops to apprehend and sink the *Scheer*. The 41,000-ton battle cruiser HMS *Hood*, the largest warship afloat at the time, accompanied by the battle cruiser *Repulse* and three cruisers of the 15th Cruiser Squadron, along with six destroyers, immediately left Scapa Flow for Biscay. At the same time, the 16-inch gun battleships *Nelson* and *Rodney* sailed for the Denmark Strait.

For a full week not one British merchant ship was allowed to venture out into the open Atlantic; while the Admiralty decreed that in future all large convoys must be escorted by a battleship or, at the very least, by several cruisers. It was the latter move that led to the *Admiral Hipper*'s ignominious defeat when she mounted her attack on the troop convoy WS 5A. The *Admiral Scheer*, meanwhile, had disappeared into the South Atlantic.

On her way south, the *Scheer* overtook the 7,448-ton Port Line steamer *Port Hobart*, bound for the Panama Canal and New Zealand to pick up a cargo of frozen meat. This was a remote part of the ocean, and Krancke was able to take a more leisurely approach. He first put warning shots across the British ship's bows from a distance of two miles, bringing her to a halt without resistance. An armed party was put aboard, and she was searched before being sunk with scuttling charges, her crew being first allowed to take to the boats. No bloodshed, no bad feeling. This was the way Theodor Kranke would have preferred all his sinkings to be, for he had no wish to butcher innocent seamen.

A rendezvous was made with the tanker *Eurofeld* and the supply ship *Nordmark* on 11 November to take on fuel, ammunition and stores. Krancke then headed towards the African coast, but it was not until 1 December that another British ship came his way. This was T & J Harrison's 6,242-ton *Tribesman*, bound from Liverpool to Calcutta with a general cargo. And here, 500 miles west of the Cape Verde Islands, Krancke met stiff resistance. The *Tribesman* refused to surrender, and she was sunk while running away. Fourteen of her crew, including Captain H.W.G. Philpott, lost their lives, but not before an SOS had been sent out.

Moving south, the *Scheer* was crossing the Equator 700 miles south-west of Freetown, when she chanced upon Houlder Brothers' coal-burning refrigerated ship *Duquesa*, homeward bound from the River Plate. The *Duquesa* was unarmed, and had a top speed of only 12 knots, but this did not deter her Master, Captain Bearpark from putting his stern to the *Scheer* and attempting to make a run for it. Krancke gave chase, but deliberately withheld his fire until the British ship had sent off her RRR message and received an acknowledgement. Only then did the Krancke bring the *Duquesa* to a halt with a few well-placed shells. A boarding party went aboard, and it was discovered that the refrigerated ship was a veritable storehouse afloat. In her holds she carried 14½ million eggs and 3,500 tons of best Argentinian beef, enough to feed the *Scheer* and her supply ships for months to come. The *Duquesa* was taken to a remote anchorage off the coast of Brazil, where for the next two months she fed much of the German raiding force in the South Atlantic.

She became known in the German ships as 'Food Supply Office Wilhelmshaven South'.

Krancke's object in allowing the *Duquesa* to transmit her RRR was to draw attention away from northern waters, where the *Hipper* had just emerged from the Denmark Strait. The ruse worked. The Admiralty immediately ordered the heavy cruisers *Dorsetshire* and *Neptune* out from Freetown for the position given by the *Duquesa*. At the same time the aircraft carrier *Hermes*, the armed merchant cruiser *Pretoria Castle* and the light cruiser *Dragon* were instructed to meet off St Helena, and from there conduct a search for the German raider. Not surprisingly, when the warships arrived the *Scheer* and her prize had long departed the scene.

On Christmas Day, while the *Hipper* was making her abortive attack on Convoy WS 5A, the *Scheer* was at a secret rendezvous 750 miles due west of St Helena with her supply ships *Nordmark* and *Eurofeld*, along with the commerce raider *Thor*, and her prize the Norwegian freighter *Storstad*. Eggs and beef in plenty were on the menu that day.

In the new year, on 18 January 1941 the *Scheer* captured the Dutch steamer *Barneveld* and sank the British tramp *Stanpark*, but now alarm bells were ringing loud in the South Atlantic, and Krancke decided it was time to move to fresh pastures. He steamed south, rounding the Cape of Good Hope, entering the Indian Ocean on 3 February.

The recognised shipping lane from the Cape to India and the Red Sea ran up the Mozambique Channel, which separates Madagascar from the mainland of Africa. This resulted in a steady stream of ships moving up and down the Channel all year round; outward from Europe with general cargo, and homeward with tea, jute and other produce from India, Ceylon and the Far East. Krancke took the *Scheer* to the northern end of the channel and waited for his victims to come to him.

The wait proved to be a long one, for it was 20 February before the first ship came under the guns of the raider. She was the 6,994-ton tanker *British Advocate*, loaded with 8,000 tons of fuel oil and petrol for Cape Town. The British tanker offered no resistance, and with a prize crew on board she was soon on her way to Occupied France with her precious cargo. Next day the small Greek freighter *Gregorious* and the Canadian-flag *Canadian Cruiser* steamed into Krancke's open arms. Two days later it was the turn of the Dutch collier *Rantau Pandjang*.

Unluckily for the *Scheer*, both the *Canadian Cruiser* and the *Rantau*

Pandjang sent out distress messages before being sunk. These were intercepted by the light cruiser HMS *Glasgow* which happened to be passing on her way to Singapore for repairs. The *Glasgow* launched her Walrus reconnaissance aircraft, which spotted the *Scheer* within hours. The alarm was raised, and soon the aircraft carrier *Hermes*, the heavy cruisers *Hawkins* and *Shropshire* and the light cruisers *Capetown and Emerald* had taken up the chase. They were later joined by the Australian cruiser *Canberra*. The hunt for the *Scheer* was on in earnest. But Kapitän Theodor Krancke, by long experience, was adept at avoiding his pursuers. Steaming at full speed to the south-east under the cover of darkness, he easily gave the British ships the slip. Nevertheless it had been a close run thing, and it was with some relief that next day Krancke received a signal from Berlin ordering the *Scheer* to return to Germany.

The British cruisers were still scouring the waters to the east of Madagascar when, on 3 March, the *Scheer* rounded the Cape of Good Hope and re-entered the Atlantic. After a rendezvous with the supply ship *Nordmark* on the night of 9/10 March, Krancke headed north, and once again the angels were on his side. At that time all British naval units in the Atlantic were fully occupied in chasing the German battleships *Scharnhorst* and *Gneisenau*, which were at large in the North Atlantic, and threatening merchant shipping.

Evading the light cruisers *Fiji* and *Nigeria*, on guard at its southern entrance, Krancke slipped unseen through the Denmark Strait on the 27th, and passing well to the north of Iceland, reached the Norwegian coast, anchoring off Bergen on 30 March. There the *Scheer* was joined by an escort of destroyers for the passage to Kiel, where she arrived safely on 1 April.

So ended the *Admiral Scheer*'s one and only cruise as a commerce raider. In five months away from Germany she had steamed over 46,000 miles, sunk fourteen enemy merchant ships, challenged and destroyed an armed merchant cruiser, and taken two loaded tankers as prizes. In all, she had accounted for 113,223 tons of Allied shipping, with another 27,844 tons damaged. Her arrival at Kiel was attended by an army of gold-braided admirals, the military bands played her alongside, and she was toasted as the 'most successful German capital commerce raider ever'.

Looking back over the years, the best that can be said about the *Admiral Scheer*'s days as a commerce raider is that she was successful, but not spectacular. It is well to remember that this was a 15,000-ton armoured ship carrying twenty big guns, and built at a cost of 90 million reichsmarks. She was manned by a crew of 1,150, and was equipped with radar and two spotter aircraft, the latter enabling her to see far over the horizon. Her eight MAN diesels developing 52,000 shaft horse power, gave her a service speed of 28½ knots, but only at the cost of seventy tons of fuel consumed per day. Compare this with Otto Kretschmer's 700-ton U-99, with a complement of only forty-four; which in the same period, November 1940 to April 1941, sank fifteen Allied ships totalling 140,430 tons. And that was just one U-boat. At the time Dönitz had over 250 boats in service.

The *Admiral Scheer* did not leave Kiel again until February 1942 when, under the command of Kapitän-zur-See Wilhelm Meendsen-Bohiken, she moved to Arctic waters accompanied by the heavy cruiser *Prinz Eugen* and five destroyers. On passage the *Prinz Eugen* was torpedoed and severely damaged by the British submarine *Trident*. The *Scheer* spent the next three months in Trondheim, before venturing to sea again with the intention of harassing British convoys running supplies to north Russia. She sank no ships, and her only success lay in the fact that she presented a constant threat to the convoys.

In November 1942 the *Scheer* returned to Germany and underwent a major overhaul in Wilhelmshaven, where she became a target for British bombers. Thereafter, she served as a cadet training ship; and as a floating gun platform in the eastern Baltic in the winter of 1945 in a vain attempt to stem the advance of the Russian armies.

The *Admiral Scheer*, her gun barrels worn smooth, ended her days back in Kiel at the Deutsche Werke, where she had begun her life. On the night of 9/10 April 1945, Kiel was attacked by a force of 300 Lancasters of the RAF, and the *Scheer* was hit by five 5-ton 'earthquake' bombs. She received major damage, and capsized at her berth. Fortunately for them, most of her crew were ashore at the time. After the war, the wrecked pocket battleship was stripped of any salvageable equipment, and what remained of her was buried when the dock was filled in. It was an ignominious end for a once-proud ship. Today, the grave of the mighty *Admiral Scheer* lies under a car park in Kiel harbour.

Of those ships that escaped the guns of the *Admiral Scheer* on that wild night in November 1940 when she set about Convoy HX 84, ten did not survive to see the end of the war.

Ellerman Papayanni's 3,082-ton *Andalusian* (No.21), bracketed at one time by the *Scheer*'s shells, and within a hairsbreadth of being destroyed, lasted another four months. Then, on the night of 17 March 1941, on passage with Convoy SL 68 from West Africa to Oban with 3,231 tons of cocoa, she fell victim to a torpedo fired by Jürgen Oesten in U-106. Captain Harry McHugh and his crew of forty-one were all saved, but their ship was lost.

The apparently indestructible tanker *San Demetrio*, patched up and back at sea under the command of Captain Conrad Vidot, met her end in the early spring of 1942. On the afternoon of 16 March, she was on her way unescorted from Baltimore to Halifax to join a convoy for the UK with 11,000 tons of alcohol and aviation spirit when what appeared to be a small fishing boat began following her. Suspicious, Captain Vidot made several large alterations of course, but all the time the stranger stuck doggedly to his wake. Then, as suddenly as she had appeared, the 'fisherman' disappeared from sight.

Vidot thought no more of it, until at around 1900, with darkness closing in, the *San Demetrio* was struck by two torpedoes, one of which went home in her engine-room destroying the main engine and killing most of those on watch below. The other torpedo struck forward, in the region of No.2 cargo tank, which immediately burst into flames. The fire spread quickly and the tanker began to sink. Two lifeboats were launched, and thirty-one men abandoned ship. They were rescued two days later by the American tanker *Beta* and landed at Norfolk, Virginia.

Meanwhile, the *San Demetrio* had reached the end of her final voyage. She sank 3,000 miles from home, in sight of Cape Charles, taking twenty-four of her crew with her. Her 'fisherman' shadow had, in fact, been U-404, on the surface and trimmed down so that only her conning tower was visible.

As a footnote to the eventual loss of the *San Demetrio*, it is relevant to mention the recurring bad luck, if you can call it that, her previous master Captain George Waite had suffered in the war. It began with the *San Alberto* in December 1939, when she was torpedoed off the south coast of Ireland. Less than a year later, Waite was forced to abandon the *San Demetrio* in the chaos of HX 84, although the ship did survive to sail another day. The third turn of the screw came in June 1943, when he was commanding the 8,078-ton *San Ernesto* in the Indian Ocean.

On passage from Sydney to Bahrain in ballast, the *San Ernesto* was torpedoed by the Japanese submarine I-37, and for the third time in his eventful sea-going career George Waite found himself giving the order to lower the lifeboats. One of the boats, containing nine men, drifted for 28 days under the hot sun, before coming ashore on the island of Fanhandu in the Maldives. Captain Waite and twenty-two others were picked up by the American freighter *Alcoa Pointer*.

As for the ship Waite abandoned, although burning fiercely, she remained afloat and, borne on the east-going current, drifted 2,000 miles across the Indian Ocean, finally running aground on the north-western tip of Sumatra. That the Japanese then dismantled her for scrap to use in their own war effort was another ironic twist to the end of the *San Ernesto*.

Lancashire Shipping Company's *Lancaster Castle* (No.24) ended her days on the cold and dangerous road to Russia. In March 1942 she had successfully run the gauntlet of German bombs and torpedoes in the Barents Sea to deliver a cargo of military stores to Murmansk, and was in that port loading magnacite ore for the return passage. At 1150 on the 24th, a flight of Ju 88s came roaring in at mast-top height. The attack was so sudden that there was no time to man the guns, and the *Lancaster Castle* was hit by several bombs, one of which landed in her engine-room. Her engines were completely shattered, ten firemen working below were killed, and two sailors caught on the open deck were injured. The *Lancaster Castle* remained at her berth until the night of the 29th, when she was towed out to an anchorage in the river. She lay there immobile for another thirteen days, before being moved to a more remote anchorage upstream.

Inevitably, the German aircraft attacked again, and this time the *Lancaster Castle* was smothered with bombs. Her gunners fought back, but she suffered five direct hits, which completely wrecked her hull. Fortunately, there were no more casualties, but within the hour the ship had settled on the bottom of the river with her decks awash. She would sail no more.

In that same month, April 1942, the tanker *Athelempress* (No.53), commanded by Captain Walter Jackson, was westbound in ballast for Port of Spain, Trinidad. She had left British waters with the Freetown bound convoy OS 25, detaching from the convoy when off the Cape Verde Islands on 19 April.

Having crossed the Atlantic unmolested, on the night of the 29th, the

Athelempress was 180 miles east of Barbados, and just over two days from her destination. It was a clear, moonlit night, with a calm sea, and being aware that U-boats were active in the Caribbean, Captain Jackson was zigzagging with extra lookouts posted.

For Jürgen Wattenberg in the conning tower of U-162, the tanker, silhouetted against the moon, presented the perfect target. At six minutes to midnight on the 29th he fired a spread of two torpedoes, both of which went home, one striking the *Athelempress* amidships, the other in her stern.

The stricken tanker drifted to a halt, taking on a heavy list to port, and it was quite obvious that she had come to the end of her days. Reluctantly, Captain Jackson gave the order to abandon ship. Forty-seven men got away in three boats, leaving three men unaccounted for. Wattenberg sank the *Athelempress* with gunfire. She disappeared beneath the waves at 0310 on 30 April.

Sister-ship to the *Athelempress*, the 8,992-ton *Atheltemplar* (No.92) met a similar fate four-and-a-half months later, but a long way from the benign warmth of the Caribbean. In the early hours of 14 September 1942, while carrying 9,400 tons of fuel oil from the Tyne to Archangel, she straggled from Convoy PQ 18 when south-west of Bear Island.

The isolated tanker became easy prey for Karl Brandenburg, who had been stalking the convoy in U-457. His torpedoes set her on fire, and she was abandoned by her crew. The minesweeper HMS *Harrier* attempted to sink the crippled ship by gunfire, but she stubbornly refused to go down. When last seen, the *Atheltemplar* was burning furiously, but still afloat. Later in the day, U-408 came along and obligingly put her out of her misery, sending her to the bottom with a few well-aimed shells. Captain Carl Ray and his crew of sixty were picked up by the rescue ship *Copeland*, but three men died of their injuries later.

The *Emile Francqui* (No.12) of Compagnie Maritime Belge sailed from Liverpool with Convoy ON 153 in December 1942 with a token cargo of 634 tons of stores consigned to St John's, New Brunswick. Four days out, the 43-ship convoy ran into very severe weather, with force 12 winds and 60ft waves. For the next forty-eight hours ON 153 made very little forward progress, most of the ships being reduced to a crawl as they fought to keep steerage way and avoid damage.

Despite the raging storm, a U-boat pack attacked shortly before dawn on the 16th, sinking one ship and damaging another. Later in the day, at about 1725, U-664 torpedoed the *Emile Francqui*, and she sank with the loss of forty-six lives. One of the escorts, the destroyer HMS *Firedrake* was also sunk.

The convoy commodore, Commodore Errol Manners, RNR, later remarked: 'By God's mercy this heavy weather undoubtedly saved more losses to the convoy.' This was no doubt true, but even so, a total of 249 men lost their lives that day.

The severe winter weather in the North Atlantic continued well into 1943. Convoy HX 224, fifty-eight ships strong, including the HX 84 survivor Bowring's motor tanker *Cordelia* (No.83), sailed from New York on 22 January 1943. Predictably, in mid-crossing, on the night of 30/31 January, the convoy ran into very heavy weather. Ships immediately began to straggle, and by nightfall eleven merchantmen were wallowing astern. The *Cordelia*, heavy with 12,000 tons of fuel oil from Curacao, was amongst them.

At 2154 on 3 February, the *Cordelia*, now sailing alone, was torpedoed by U-632 and sank at once. Only one man survived, and he was picked up by the U-boat and taken prisoner. It was unfortunate that this man had forgotten the wartime maxim 'Careless Talk Costs Lives'. In a conversation with Kapitänleutnant Hans Karpf he let slip that the slow convoy SC 118 was following on close behind HX 224. Kapf notified U-boat HQ at Lorient, and a pack of sixteen U-boats was formed to lie in wait for SC 118. In the battle that raged over the following three days eleven ships, including the convoy rescue ship *Toward*, were sunk and 621 men died.

The *Trefusis*, despite all the knocks she had suffered, continued to bring home the cargoes, until she came to the end of her road in March 1943. Homeward bound under the command of Captain R.T. Brown with 7,300 tons of iron ore from West Africa, she had sailed from Gibraltar with Convoy XK 2 on 28 February. At 1730 on 5 March, while 250 miles west-north-west of Cape Finisterre and steering north at 6½ knots, the convoy was attacked by U-130. Captain Brown later reported:

There was a moderate sea, with a SE wind, force 4. The weather was overcast, and visibility good. No one saw the track of the torpedo, which struck close to the engine room bulkhead in No.4 hold on the port side. The dull explosion shook the ship violently, and a huge column of water was thrown up. I did not see a flash with the explosion. The beams and hatches from No.4 hold were blown off, and the tarpaulin was blown up to the main aerial, where it remained hanging. The engine room immediately filled, the greaser on watch being lifted on to the top platform grating by the inrush of water. The starboard side of No.4 hatch coaming was split, and I believe there was a split down the ship's side in the vicinity of the engine room bulkhead on the starboard side. The after deck was awash, so I was not able to see if there were any splits or holes in it.

After throwing the confidential books overboard, I abandoned ship in the starboard lifeboat with some 12 of my crew. The port boat was smashed by the explosion. The ship also carried two jolly boats, but they were not lowered as the majority of the crew abandoned ship on four rafts, all of which were successfully launched. I had no difficulty in lowering the starboard lifeboat, which was fitted with skates, unfortunately it was slightly damaged as the sea washed it against the side of the ship, half filling it with water. We pulled clear of the ship in less than ten minutes after the torpedo struck. There was no time to send a wireless message or fire rockets.

The *Trefusis* went down stern first at approximately 1750, and as she went one of her PAC anti-aircraft rockets launched itself, bursting overhead in a brilliant display of white stars. It was as though the old ship, having survived everything the war had thus far thrown at her, was giving a two-fingered salute to the enemy.

Captain Brown and forty-three of his crew were picked up two hours later by the armed trawler *Loch Oskaig*. Three men were missing, believed killed in the engine-room when the torpedo struck.

By the summer of 1943, the *Cornish City*, HX 84's commodore ship, had moved into more congenial waters. She was in the Indian Ocean busy with the essential, but mundane business of carrying coal for the Admiralty from South Africa to the bunkering ports of Aden and Suez. 48-year-old Captain Henry Issac was now in command.

On the morning of 22 July, the *Cornish City* sailed from Durban, bound Aden with 9,600 tons of coal. Once clear of the breakwaters, she joined up with Convoy DN 53, comprising five merchantmen, escorted by two armed trawlers of the South African Navy. Captain Issac was aware that a number of U-boats had made the long voyage out from Biscay to round the Cape into the Indian Ocean, but he had been assured that none was in the immediate area.

The convoy – if it could be so called – dispersed at a prearranged position midway between Madagascar and the African mainland, and the *Cornish City* carried on to round the southern tip of the island, before turning north. The weather was fair, with good visibility, and the horizon remained encouragingly empty. Then, at about 0935 on the morning of the 29th, in this lonely spot 360 miles south-west of the island of Réunion, a torpedo slammed into the British ship's side in way of her engine-room. U-177, lying submerged at periscope depth, had been in the Indian Ocean since October 1942, during which time Korvettenkapitän Robert Gysae had added another 70,000 tons of shipping to his score. When the *Cornish City* came in sight, Gysae had already decided it was time to take the long road home around the Cape, but he had no hesitation in delaying his return long enough to claim yet another easy target.

Chief Officer K.E. Germaney later wrote:

I was on the port side of the lower bridge at the time of the explosion talking to the Master, and as it was obvious that the vessel was sinking rapidly, I hurried to the boat deck, where I found some of the crew had already lowered the starboard lifeboat; it was alongside, still attached to the ship by the painter. By this time the stern was awash, and a few seconds later I felt the ship shudder violently. Out of the corner of my eye I could see the Captain standing on the starboard side of the lower bridge; he shouted to me that the vessel was going, and as he did so the bows reared up, as if the ship's back was broken, whilst the boat deck remained level, and I just had time to put on my lifejacket and tie one string when the vessel sank beneath me. As I went under I caught sight of the starboard lifeboat, which was still attached to the ship by the painter, being dragged back on board with six men in it. When I broke surface the ship and the lifeboat had disappeared.

Fortunately for Chief Officer Germaney, he surfaced within yards of a liferaft, which already contained two survivors. He was hauled aboard, and later they were joined by another small raft to which four men were clinging. These seven men were all that remained of the *Cornish City*'s total complement of forty-three. Captain Henry Issac and thirty-six others had gone down with their ship, which had taken just two minutes to sink.

The rafts were sighted by an RAF Catalina later in the day, it is believed as a result of a radio message sent by Robert Gysae after he had cleared the area. The survivors were picked up by the destroyer HMAS *Nizam* just before dawn on the 31st, and landed on Mauritius. The humanitarian gesture made by Robert Gysae, even at this late stage of the war, indicates that the U-boat men were still seamen first and foremost, bound by the unwritten law of the sea to help fellow seamen in distress.

The other Belgian-flag ship sailing with HX 84, the 5,382-ton *Persier* (No.22), also owned by Compagnie Maritime Belge of Antwerp, escaped the guns of the *Admiral Scheer*, only to fall victim to the weather three months later. On 28 February 1941, she ran into a fierce storm off Iceland, and was driven ashore. She was refloated and towed to Reykjavik, but when beached she broke her back. At any other time the Belgian ship would probably have been abandoned, but then every ship still able to float was needed. The wreck was towed to the Tyne, where extensive repairs were carried out. The *Persier* returned to sea in February 1943.

The war in Europe had only three months to run when, on 10 February 1945, the *Persier* sailed from the Bristol Channel, bound Antwerp with 4,820 tons of stores for the advancing Allied armies. Captain Emile Mathieu was in command and acting as commodore for the 3-ship convoy BTC 65.

Rounding Land's End on the morning of the 11th, the convoy headed up Channel, and by late afternoon was passing 4 miles south of the Eddystone Light. There was a heavy sea running, backed up by a long swell rolling in from the Atlantic.

The winter darkness came early, enabling U-1017 to close the convoy unseen. At 1725 she fired a spread of three torpedoes, one of which exploded prematurely 200 yards off the *Persier*'s port beam. The second passed astern of her, but the third torpedo found its mark, blowing a large hole in the Belgian's port side forward.

The sea poured into the *Persier*'s breached hull, and she immediately began to settle by the bow. Captain Mathieu gave the order to abandon ship, but one boat was swamped by the rough seas, and another was smashed by the ship's propeller, which was still turning.

Of the *Persier*'s total complement of sixty-three – which for some unexplained reason included four stowaways – twenty men died, and eleven were injured. An attempt was made to tow the damaged ship to a sheltered anchorage, but she sank during the night.

EPILOGUE

Like Wagner's *Flying Dutchman*, the *Beaverford* will forever remain an enigma. We will never know what motivated this unpretentious Atlantic trader, manned by merchant seamen and sailing under the Red Ensign, to challenge the might of Germany's finest when the *Jervis Bay* had no fight left in her. Was it sheer bloody-mindedness – the merchant seaman with his back to the wall can be a formidable fighter – or was Captain Hugh Pettigrew prompted to act in compassion for those other ships under fire?

The *Beaverford*, 10,000 tons gross, twin-screw, 15 knots, was purpose-built for the demanding North Atlantic trade. Armed with a gun fore and aft, she was the only ship capable of taking the fight to the *Scheer* after Fogarty Fegen and his ship had gone. And this, to her eternal credit, she did with enthusiasm and consummate skill, thereby putting an end to Theodor Krancke's dream of laying waste to HX 84.

When the news reached London of the Atlantic battle, Acting Captain Edward Fogarty Fegen was posthumously awarded the Victoria Cross, while a number of his crew also received awards for bravery in action, including no fewer than seven Distinguished Service Medals. The story of the *Jervis Bay*'s last stand made headlines around the world. This was *Boy's Own Annual* stuff, and the British public, sickened by defeat after defeat, loved it. Over the intervening years countless books have been written, films made, and memorials to HMS *Jervis Bay* erected at home and overseas. The story of this heroic armed merchant cruiser is still recited with awe. The *Beaverford*, on the other hand, has no place in history. To this day, the Ministry of Defence refuses to acknowledge that she played any part in the defence of Convoy HX 84.

The only memorial ever commissioned to the *Beaverford* was a small bronze plaque in the assembly hall of Downhills Central School in North London. Downhills had adopted the *Beaverford* under the auspices of the Marine Society in the 1930s. When Downhills disappeared, swamped by the tsunami of comprehensives, the memorial plaque was lost. Many years later, it was found in a junk shop in Tottenham, anybody's for a few shillings. So were the *Beaverford* and the seventy-three men who died with her remembered.

No one would wish to belittle the glorious, if futile, sacrifice made by HMS *Jervis Bay* on that bitter November night in 1940. Fogarty Fegen did what he had to do, and as a result he lost his ship, his life, and the lives of 189 other men. No one should condemn him for that. It was war, and in war the Royal Navy must fight. However, it is fair to question why the men of the *Beaverford* received no recognition. It was Pettigrew and the last-ditch *franc-tireurs* of the *Beaverford* who saved HX 84 from complete annihilation; yet they were awarded no medals, no commendations even, only the cold comfort of a watery grave.

Nor was there any official recognition of the role played by the Swedish ship *Stureholm*. Captain Sven Olander and his crew put their lives on the line to save the sixty-five men of the *Jervis Bay* who were still in the water. They did get a brief mention in the programme for an annual gathering of the Royal Naval Association in 1959:

> *We pay tribute to Captain Sven Olander and the crew of the Stureholm, without whose gallantry in rescuing survivors it is unlikely that any member of the crew of the Jervis Bay would have lived.*

And that was that. Not a word from the Admiralty, the Ministry of Defence, or other official source. The *Stureholm* might never have existed.

One other question still remains unanswered in this tale of heroes and others. Did Commodore Maltby or Captain Fegen advise the Admiralty when Third Officer Fellingham of the *Trefusis* reported sighting an unidentified seaplane? And if they did so, why was no action taken to scatter the convoy there and then? With the recent sortie of the *Graf Spee* still fresh in mind, someone in Whitehall must have realised the significance of the appearance of a small seaplane in mid-Atlantic. Such an aircraft could only have come from an enemy surface raider. Forewarned, the convoy would have had ample time to show a clean pair of heels to the *Scheer*, instead of steaming straight into her arms.

It is worthy of note that in the Second World War the Canadian Pacific Steamship Company lost fourteen ships out of its original fleet of twenty-two. The company ended the war with the unenviable record of having the largest percentage loss of any British and Allied shipping company.

Appendix One

IN MEMORIAM

S.S. *BEAVERFORD*. Sunk North Atlantic, 5 November 1940

ANDERSON, Thomas, Fireman. Age 61

ARMSTRONG, Ernest M., Able Seaman. Age 29. Son of George & Maud Armstrong

ARNOTT, Evan Charles, Trimmer. Age 32

BADCOCK, James Clampitt, Storekeeper. Age 60

BARKER, Laurence Wilfred, Assistant Steward. Age 20. Son of Albert Ernest & Elizabeth Hepzibah Barker

BARROW, Charles John, Butcher. Age 48. Husband of Gladys M. Barrow of Cardiff

BAXTER, John George, Third Engineer Officer. Age 57

BERGIN, M., Trimmer. Age 50. Son of Edward & Johanna Bergin

BOWIE, Leslie Wilfred, Ordinary Seaman. Age 17. Son of Arthur & Catherine Bowie of Barking, Essex

BRACKLIN, Edward Durston, Greaser. Age 44

BRENNAN, John, Trimmer. Age 18. Son of William & Edna Brennan of Treforest, Pontypridd, Glamorgan

BROOKES, Warwick Thomas, Trimmer. Age 28. Son of Percy Warwick & Annie Brookes; husband of Mary Brookes of Weybridge, Surrey

CHAPMAN, Reginald M.M., Greaser. Age 42. Husband of E.F. Chapman of Roath, Cardiff

COLLINS, Daniel, Fireman. Age 31

CONNING, John, Fireman. Age 42

COOK, John, Baker. Age 21. Son of Mr & Mrs C.S. Cook

CROMARTY, George William, Fireman. Age 26. Son of George William & Dorothy Sarah Cromarty; husband of Maria Joanna Cromarty of Greenwich, London

CROOK, John Frederick, Trimmer. Age 54. Husband of Selina Crook of Whitechapel, London

CROOK, Stanley, Chief Cook. Age 37. Son of George Walter & Agnes Crook; husband of A. Crook of Brough, Yorkshire

CROWHURST, Eric Reginald, Steward's Boy. Age 16

DE CRUZ, Alfonso, Trimmer. Age 23. Husband of Ellen Kathleen De Cruz of Cardiff

DE SMET, Frank, Ordinary Seaman. Age 18

DOBBIE, Frederick, Ninth Engineer Officer. Age 19. Son of Frederick & Mary Anne Dobbie of Middlesbrough, Yorkshire

ELLIS, John, Sixth Engineer Officer. Age 32. Son of Frederick & Sophie Ellis; husband of Helen Ellis of Keith, Banffshire

EVANS, Evan John Parry, Boy. Age 18. Son of Josuah Parry & Anne Evans of Aberporth, Cardiganshire

EVANS, Edmund Ringrose, Assistant Steward. Age 52

FERRIS, Stanley Britton, Steward. Age 27. Son of Marion Britton & Emily Catherine Ferris of Harrow, Middlesex

FOREMAN, William Charles, Donkeyman. Age 36

FRASER, John Johnston, First Radio Officer. Age 40. Son of Robert & Helen Fraser; husband of Mary McKay Fraser of Logie-Coldstone, Aberdeenshire

FRASER, Robert, Ordinary Seaman. Age 17. Son of Alexander & Jane Fraser of Fochabers, Morayshire

GALLAGHER, Michael, Greaser. Age 40

GREEN, George, Trimmer. Age 20. Son of Edward William & Mary Arm Emma Green of Canning Town, Essex

GUSTAFSEN, Karl, Able Seaman. Age 55

HAMILTON, Christopher, Fireman. Age 49. (served as BARRETT) Husband of Annie Hamilton of Chelsea

HARRISON, Frederick George, Greaser. Age 34

HAVAMAA, Arthur, Carpenter. Age 37

HOWARD, Herbert Henry, Greaser. Age 53

HUGHES, Andrew, Greaser. Age 30

KAMMO, Karl, Able Seaman. Age 50. (Native of Estonia)

KEARY, Thomas, Fireman. Age 28

KING, Albert Edgar, Assistant Steward. Age 24. Son of Albert Edgar & E.L. King; husband of Nellie Gladys King of Folkestone

KING, John William, Greaser. Age 27

LAWRIE, John Kinloch, Eighth Engineer Officer. Age 24. Son of John & Elizabeth Clark Lawrie of Paisley, Renfrewshire

LOCKE, Peter, Third Officer. Age 25. Son of Joseph James & Isabel Gertrude Locke of Keston, Kent

MARSHALL, Samuel, Seventh Engineer Officer. Age 27. Son of Robert James & Ann Marshall of Slough, Buckinghamshire

MARTIN, John Frederick, Fireman. Age 40. Son of John Thomas & Catherine Helena Martin

MORRIS, Charles Stephen, Second Officer. Age 39. Son of George & Sarah Morris; husband of Irene Alexandria Morris of North Baddesley, Hampshire. (Master Mariner)

MOSS, Ernest Paul Albert, Ordinary Seaman. Age 17. Son of Charles Ernest & Ethel Moss of East Dulwich, London

MCKEON, Leonard, Fireman. Age 31

MCKNIGHT, N., Fireman. Age 47

O'BRIEN, Michael John, Able Seaman. Age 25. Husband of Elsie Florence O'Brien of Beacontree, Essex

O'NEIL, Patrick, Trimmer. Age 26

OATRIDGE, Chief Officer, Edwin John. Age 32. Son of Carthew & Louisa Oatridge of Backwell, Gloucester. (Master Mariner)

PETTIGREW, Hugh, Master. Age 60. Son of James & Margaret Pettigrew; husband of Mary Gardiner Pettigrew of Glasgow

PRATT, Eric Hazelhurst, Purser. Age 45

PRIOR, Gordon, Fourth Officer. Age 25. Son of Harriet Prior; husband of Cora K. Prior of Eggleston, Co. Durham

RATTISTE, Andres, Able Seaman. Age 45. (Native of Estonia)

REES, John Trevor, Cadet. Age 19. Son of Evan David & Eleanor Linda Rees of New Quay, Cardiganshire

ROBB, David Kinninmont, Fifth Engineer Officer. Age 30

SEARING, Edward, Greaser. Age 55. Son of Joseph & Cathrine Searing; husband of Mary Ann Searing of Stepney, London

SINCLAIR, John Morrison, Chief Engineer Officer

SMITH, Albert, Trimmer. Age 18. Son of Harry Herbert & Frances Elizabeth Smith of Whitchurch, Glamorgan

SYMONDS, Frank Brian, Cadet. Age 16. Son of Reginald Ernest & Daphne Symonds of New Barnet, Hertfordshire

TENNENT, George, Second Engineer Officer. Age 54. Son of Thomas & Christian Wylie Tennent; husband of Mary Lewars Tennent of King's Park, Glasgow

WASKE, Timothy, Boatswain. Age 48

WATTS, Norman Charles, Able Seaman. Age 22

WHITE, Ernest Frank, Fireman. Age 21. Son of Mr & Mrs Arthur Albert White of Dagenham, Essex

WHITING, Alfred, Able Seaman. Age 26. Husband of Mary S. Whiting of Rotherhithe

WILLIAMS, John, Fourth Engineer Officer. Age 38. Son of Thomas & Mary Jane Williams; husband of Elizabeth Williams of Liverpool

WOOLLEY, Richard Frank, Second Radio Officer. Age 25

WOOLVETT, John Norman, Greaser. Age 31. Son of John Norman & Helen Woolvett; husband of Melanie Johanna Woolvett of Greenwich, London

DEMS Gunners

IRVING, Richard, Acting Able Seaman

STEWART, Laughlin, Able Seaman

Appendix Two

SURVIVORS FROM *JERVIS BAY* PICKED UP BY THE SWEDISH MOTOR VESSEL *STUREHOLM*

APPLEYARD, Arthur Robert, Able Seaman, RFR. Boston, Lincolnshire.

ARMSTRONG, John Robert, Stoker, RCNR. Halifax, Nova Scotia.

BAIN, Donald, Seaman, RNR. Wick, Caithness. Awarded Distinguished Service Medal.

BARKER, John, Able Seaman, RNVR. Harlesden, Middlesex.

BARNETT, William, Assistant Steward, MN. Awarded Distinguished Service Medal.

BEAMAN, George, Stoker, RCNR. Halifax, Nova Scotia. Awarded Distinguished Service Medal.

BILLINGE, Frederick W.G., Able Seaman, RFR. Peckham, London.

BONNEY, Harry Lionel, Leading Seaman, RFR. Ealing, London.

BUTLER, Ronald Alfred Gardyne, Midshipman, RNR. Portsmouth, Hampshire. Awarded Distinguished Service Cross.

BYAM-CORSTIAENS, Guy Frederick, T/A Sub. Lieutenant (E), RNVR. Newport Pagnall, Buckinghamshire.

CASTLE, Charles, Petty Officer, RN. Dover, Kent.

CHRISTIE, Donald, Assistant Steward, MN.

COOPER, William James Albert, Able Seaman, RNVR. Edmonton, London. Awarded Distinguished Service Medal.

CROWSON, George, Stoker 1st Class, MN.

CURRIE, John Hewitt, 3rd Lieutenant (E), RNR. Totness, Cornwall.

DARNBROUGH, Walter L., Able Seaman, RCNVR. Toronto, Ontario.

DAVISON, Thomas, Able Seaman, RNR.

DOULL, George, Seaman, RNR. Wick, Caithness.

DOVE, Charles, Assistant Steward, MN.

DRAPER, Bernard, Able Seaman, RFR.

DRURY, Dennis, Stoker, MN. Awarded Distinguished Service Medal.

DUNBAR, David, Seaman, RNR. Lybster, Caithness.

DURRAND, John S., Seaman, RNR. Wick, Caithness.

DURRAND, Robert, Seaman, RNR. Wick, Caithness.

EGGLESTON, John Christopher, Able Seaman. Kingston-upon-Hull, East Yorkshire. Awarded Distinguished Service Medal.

ELLMES, Shedrack C., Stoker 1st Class, MN.

FUNGE, Christie, Stoker, RCN. Halifax, Nova Scotia.

GIBBS, Frederick, Leading Seaman, RFR. Hornchurch, Essex.

GREENE, Dalton, Engine Room Articifer, RCNVR. Ottawa, Ontario.
GRUBB, Victor S., Able Seaman, RNVR.
GUNN, Robert, Seaman, RNR. Wick, Caithness.
HANDLEY, Alfred, Able Seaman, RFR.
HANLON, John Thomas W., Leading Seaman, RFR. Shepherd's Bush, London.
LANE, Henry James, Able Seaman, RNVR. London.
LIS, Frank Sidney, Seaman, RNR.
MACQUEEN, William G., Storekeeper, MN. Lossiemouth, Morayshire.
MARGINSON, Kenneth, Engine Room Articifer, RCNVR. New Glasgow, Nova
   Scotia.
McCONNELL, John, Stoker 1st Class, MN.
MOONIE, Alec, Seaman, RNR. Wick, Caithness.
MORDAUNT, Charles, Assistant Steward, MN.
MORRILL, Thomas Arthur, Able Seaman, RFR.
MORROW, Everett, Scullion, RCNR. Saint John, New Brunswick.
MOSS, Harold Gordon, T/Lieutenant (E), RNR. Lambeth, London.
NICHOLLS, Horace J., Able Seaman, RFR.
OAG, William, Seaman, RNR. Thrumster, Caithness.
ORMSTON, Sidney Walker, Assistant Butcher, MN.
PATIENCE, Samuel S., Seaman, RNR. Inverness, Highlands.
PAYNE, Percy Charles, Assistant Steward, MN. Weymouth, Dorset.
REID, James, Seaman, RNR. Wick, Caithness.
ROBERTSON, Arthur John, T/Lieutenant (E), RNR.
RUSHALL, Francis B., Leading Seaman, RFR. Birmingham, West Midlands.
SARGEANT, John Gordon, T/Paymaster Lieutenant, RNR.
SHACKELTON, Richard, 2nd Radio Officer, RNR. Keighley, West Yorkshire.
SMITH, John Thomas, Stoker, RCNVR. Toronto, Ontario.
SPILLER, Charles H.J., Able Seaman, RFR.
SQUIRES, George Malcolm, Ordinary Seaman, RCNVR. St John's, Newfoundland.
SQUIRES, Robert A., Seaman, RNR. Kingston-upon-Hull, East Yorkshire.
STEVENS, Warren D., Stoker, RCNR. Lunenburg, Nova Scotia.
TAYLOR, Arthur William, Ordinary Seaman, RCNVR. St John's, Newfoundland.
TILLEY, Louis, Ordinary Seaman, RCNVR. St John's, Newfoundland.
URQUHART, Randolph William, 2nd Radio Officer, RNR. North Shields, Durham.
WALLIS, Walter R., Petty Officer, RNR. Kingston-upon-Hull, East Yorkshire.
WHITING, Hugh Douglas, Petty Officer Pensioner, RNR. Southend-on-Sea,
   Essex.
WOOD, James Harold, Leading Seaman, RNR. Southport, Lancashire. Awarded
   Conspicuous Gallantry Medal.
WOOD, Norman Edgar, T/Lieutenant, RNR. Awarded Distinguished Service
   Order.

DIED BEFORE RESCUE

HINSTRIDGE, Harold, 2nd Cook, MN.
PATTINSON, Hugh, Acting Sub Lieutenant (E), RNVR.
WEBSTER, Alexander, Seaman, RNR.

Bibliography

Ayre, David, *Air War at Sea*, Raphael Tuck
Bekker, Cajus, *The German Navy*, Hamlyn, 1974
Brown, Anthony Cave, *Bodyguard of Lies*, W.H. Allen, 1976
Buchheim, Lothar-Günther, *Das Boot*, Cassell, 1999
Buchheim, Lothar-Günther, *U-Boat War*, Collins, 1978
Churchill, Winston, *The Second World War, Vol II*, Cassell, 1950
Costello, John & Hughes, Terry, *The Battle of the Atlantic*, Collins, 1977
Course, Captain A.G., *The Deep Sea Tramp*, Hollis & Carter, 1960
Duskin, Gerald L. & Segman, Ralph, *If the Gods Are Good*, Crecy Publishing, 2005
Goodall, Felicity, *Voices from the Home Front*, David & Charles, 2004
Gretton, Sir Peter, *Convoy Escort Commander*, Cassell, 1964
Gunston, Bill, *World War II – German Aircraft*, Leisure Books, 1885
Haldane, R.A., *The Hidden War*, Robert Hale, 1978
Hanable, William S., *Case Studies in the use of Land-Based Aerial Forces in Maritime Operations 1939-1990*, Air Force History & Museums Programme, 1998
Holm, John, *No Place to Linger*, Holmwork Publishers, 1985
Jesse, F. Tennyson, *The Saga of the San Demetrio*, Alfred A. Knopf, 1943
Krancke, Theodor & Brennecke, H.J., *Pocket Battleship*, Universal-Tandem, 1973
Lamb, James B., *The Corvette Navy*, Macmillan of Canada
Lucas, James, *Last Days of the Reich*, Arms & Armour Press, 1986
Maclean, Alistair, *The Lonely Sea*, Collins, 1985
Martienssen, Anthony, *Hitler and his Admirals*, Secker & Warburg, 1948
McAughtry, Sam, *The Sinking of the Kenbane Head*, Blackstaff Press, 2004
Messimer, Dwight R., *Find and Destroy – Antisubmarine Warfare in WW1*, Naval Institute Press, 2001
Ministry of Information, *Merchantmen at War*, HMSO, 1945
Musk, George, *Canadian Pacific*, David & Charles, 1981
Padfield, Peter, *Dönitz: The Last Führer*, Cassell, 1984
Padfield, Peter, *The Great Naval Race*, Hart-Davis, MacGibbon, 1974
Pollock, George, *Jervis Bay*, William Kimber, 1961
Poolman, Kenneth, *Armed Merchant Cruisers*, Leo Cooper, 1985
Preston, Anthony, *Navies of World War II*, Bison Books, 1979
Richards, Denis, *History of Second World War – The Royal Air Force 1939-1945*
Slader, John, *The Fourth Service*, Robert Hale, 1994
Tarrant, V.E., *Jutland*, Arms & Armour Press, 1995
Terraine, John, *Business in Great Waters*, Leo Cooper, 1989

Thomas, David, *The Atlantic Star*, W. H. Allen, 1990
Williams, Andrew, *The Battle of the Atlantic*, BBC Worldwide Ltd., 2002
Woodman, Richard, *The Real Cruel Sea*, John Murray, 2004

MAGAZINES & NEWSPAPERS

Daily Telegraph
Halifax Mail-Star
London Evening Standard
Navy News
New York Times
Sea Breezes
Ships Monthly
Straits Times

WEBSITES

bbc.co.uk
bobhenneman.info
clydesite.co.uk
deutschland-class.dk
doverhistory.co.uk
fyffes.com
mercantilemarine.org
merchantnavyofficers.com
naval-history.net
navalwarfare.blogspot.com
radioofficers.com
royalnavalmuseum.org
saintjohn.nbcc.nb.ca
secondworldwar.org.uk
worldwar2.com
ww2today.com

OTHER SOURCES

Caithness Archives
Imperial War Museum
National Archives, Kew
Marine Society
Ministry of Defence
Royal Naval Museum

The author also wishes to thank Captain H.C. Fellingham for his invaluable help in the research for this book.

Index